THE FIGURE OF JOSEPH
IN POST-BIBLICAL
JEWISH LITERATURE

ARBEITEN ZUR GESCHICHTE DES ANTIKEN JUDENTUMS UND DES URCHRISTENTUMS

HERAUSGEGEBEN VON

Martin Hengel (Tübingen), Peter Schäfer (Berlin),
Pieter W. van der Horst (Utrecht), Martin Goodman (Oxford),
Daniël R. Schwartz (Jerusalem)

XVI

THE FIGURE OF JOSEPH
IN POST-BIBLICAL
JEWISH LITERATURE

BY

MAREN NIEHOFF

E.J. BRILL
LEIDEN • NEW YORK • KÖLN
1992

The paper in this book meets the guidelines for permanence and durability of the Committee on Production Guidelines for Book Longevity of the Council on Library Resources.

BS
580
.J6
N54
1992

Library of Congress Cataloging-in-Publication Data

Niehoff, M. (Maren)
   The figure of Joseph in post-Biblical Jewish literature / by M. Niehoff.
      p.   cm.—(Arbeiten zur Geschichte des antiken Judentums und des Urchristentums, ISSN 0169-734X; Bd. 16)
   Includes bibliographical references and index.
   1. Joseph (Son of Jacob) 2. Patriarchs (Bible)—Biography—History and criticism. 3. Bible, O.T.—Biography. 4. Bible.
O.T. Genesis XXXVII-L—Criticism, interpretation, etc., Jewish.
5. Philo, of Alexandria—Contributions in the biography of Joseph, son of Jacob. 6. Josephus, Flavius—Contributions in the biography of Joseph, son of Jacob. 7. Midrash rabbah. Genesis—Criticism, interpretation, etc. I. Title. II. Series.
BS580.J6N54   1992
222'.11092—dc20   91-35676
                                                                        CIP

ISSN   0169-734X
ISBN   90 04 09556 X

TABLE OF CONTENTS

ACKNOWLEDGEMENTS

This study is based upon my D.Phil. thesis, submitted to the University of Oxford in Trinity 1989. It is a great pleasure for me to thank Prof. G. Vermes for his supervision and in particular for inspiring me to take a broad, comparative approach to the subject. I am also grateful to Prof. M. Greenberg, Prof. D. Russell and Prof. E. Ullendorff who each carefully read drafts of parts of the original thesis.

CHAPTER ONE

INTRODUCTION

The present study of the figure of Joseph focusses on the hermeneutics of the Ancient interpretations of the biblical story. Assuming that every interpretation results from a creative encounter between the ultimately open text of Scripture, on the one hand, and the thought world of the exegete, on the other hand, I examine the particular way in which each exegete construes the biblical image of Joseph. It is the aim of this study to explore the new features and the diverse hermeneutic functions which are attributed to Joseph in these early interpretations.

Particular emphasis will be given to the comparison between Greek and Hebrew characterisations of Joseph. The relationship between these two cultural realms is known to be immensely complex. Especially in the wake of S. Liebermann's pioneering work,[1] it is impossible to reduce the issue to a simple dichotomy between Israel and the diaspora. On the other hand, one must not fall victim to "parallelomania" and regard all traditions as somehow the same.[2] A cautious approach is instead required which takes seriously each interpretation in its specific context.

---

[1] *Hellenism in Jewish Palestine*, New York 1950 and *Greek in Jewish Palestine*, New York 1965. See also: M. Hengel, *Judaism and Hellenism*, London 1974 (based on 2nd enlarged German ed; see also F. Millar's excellent review article in *JJS* 29/1978, pp. 1–21 and A.D. Momigliano's review of the German ed. in: *JThSt* 21/1970, pp. 149–53); L. Feldman, *How much Hellenism in Jewish Palestine?*, *HUCA* 57/1986, pp. 83–113; *Schürer* II, pp. 29–80; J. Levi's excellent yet too little known, עולמות נפגשים, Jerusalem 1969; J. Goldstein, *Jewish Acceptance and Rejection of Hellenism*, in: *Jewish and Christian Self-Definitions*, ed. E.P. Sanders, Philadelphia 1981; Z. Fraenkel, *Über den Einfluss der palestinensischen Exegese auf die alexandrinische Hermeneutik*, Leipzig 1951; H.A. Fischel (ed.) *Essays in Greco-Roman and related Talmudic Literature*, New York 1977 (he mainly discusses the possible Epicurean influence on rabbinic literature, which he, too optimistically, assumes to have been substantial); M. Hadas, *Hellenistic Culture Fusion and Diffusion*, New York 1959, pp. 72–82; C. Siegfried, *Der jüdische Hellenismus, Zeitschrift für wissenschaftliche Theologie*, Leipzig 1875, esp. pp. 485ff; R. Meyer, *Hellenistisches in der Rabbinischen Anthropologie*, Stuttgart 1937; G. Allon, תולדות היהודים בארץ ישראל בתקופת המשנה והתלמוד, Tel Aviv 1977, vol. II pp. 217–41.

[2] This point has been forcefully made by S. Sandmel, *Parallelomania*, *JBL* 81/

It is mainly with respect to its emphasis on comparative hermeneutics that this study differs from previous investigations of the
figure of Joseph in Ancient Jewish sources. Scholars have thus far
chosen either one group of documents or one specific aspect of the
Joseph story for closer scrutiny. As will become clear in the following, it is however of particular importance to assess the focal point
chosen by each interpreter in comparison with others.

The earliest encompassing investigation of the figure of Joseph in
Ancient Literature is that of M. Braun.[3] Examining the influence
of Hellenistic romance novels on the early Jewish re-writings of the
biblical story, he has conclusively shown the recurrence of certain
motifs from the Phaedra material. Regarding Josephus's *JA* he was
also able to isolate Stoic and Epicurean arguments in Joseph's
responses to Potiphar's wife.[4] In accordance with his interests M.
Braun dealt, however, mostly with this particular scene of the
Joseph story and predominantly with Potiphar's wife. He was also
more concerned with the phenomenon of Jewish adaptations of
Greek traditions than with the precise relationship between the
Vorlage and its various interpretations. Both of these aspects call for
further study.

In E.R. Goodenough's monumental work Philo's version of the
figure of Joseph takes a prominent place.[5] His approach being historical he attempts to identify its *Sitz im Leben* and draws valuable

---

1962, pp. 1–13; see also: R.S. Sarason, *The Study of Rabbinic Literature*, in: *Studies
in Aggadah, Targum and Jewish Liturgy in Memory of Joseph Heinemann*, Jerusalem 1981,
pp. 59–60; cf. works which tend to draw parallels in such uncritical fashion: A.A.
HaLevi, ערכי האגדה וההלכה לאור מקורות יווניים ולטיניים, Tel Aviv 1979; idem.
שערי האגדה, Tel Aviv 1982, idem, Tel Aviv 1973, פרשיות באגדה לאור מקורות יווניים
S. Belkin, המדרש הסמלי אצל פילון בהשוואה למדרשי חז״ל, in: *Jubilee Volume in honour of
H. Wolfson*, 1965; pp. 43ff; N. Cohen, בדיקה מחודשת: בכתבי פילון ,אגרפוס נומוס",
Da'at 15/, תשמ״ה esp. pp. 7–13; for a more careful approach see for example:
D. Flusser/S. Safrai, נדב ואביהוא במדרש וכדברי פילון ,מלאת, Tel Aviv 1984.
    [3] *Griechischer Roman und Hellenistische Geschichtsschreibung*, Frankfurt 1934; *idem*,
*Biblical Legend in Jewish Hellenistic Literature with special Reference to the Potiphar story in
the Testament of the Twelve Patriarchs*, in: *History and Romance in Graeco-Oriental Literature*,
Oxford 1938.
    [4] *ibid*, pp. 41–47, p. 63 and p. 74ff; *Legend, ibid*, pp. 90–93.
    [5] *The Politics of Philo Judaeus. Theory and Practice*, New Haven 1938, especially pp.
21–33 (p. 21: "It is my conviction that the entire allegory of Joseph is a clever piece
of *double entendre*, a fierce denunciation of the Roman character and oppression, done
in a way, and in a document which would give it fairly wide currency among the
Jews, but would seem quite innocuous if, as was unlikely, it fell into Roman hands")
and pp. 43–63; *idem, An Introduction to Philo Judaeus*, Yale 1940, especially chapters
II, IV and V; *idem, The Jurisprudence of the Jewish Courts in Egypt*, Yale 1929.

conclusions concerning Philo's political theory.[6] Nevertheless, his overall conjecture about the double-sidedness of Philo's works, parts of it allegedly directed to an internal, Jewish audience and other parts to the Romans, can hardly be substantiated and has rightly been criticised.[7] Philo's Joseph consequently needs to be reexamined in the light of the biblical context,[8] Philo's other works and the wider Hellenistic culture.

More recently, H.W. Hollander submitted the figure of Joseph in *XII* to close scrutiny.[9] His meticulous examination of the relevant passages constitutes, in a way, the much desired counterpart to M. Braun's earlier studies. His conclusions concerning the religious and moral values which Joseph represents in this source are moreover corroborated by a wealth of documentation. However, the early Christian framework, which he assumes for *XII* cannot, despite increased research,[10] be considered as certain.[11] Instead, the arguments for an earlier date and an essentially Jewish docu-

---

[6] For a detailed discussion of Goodenough, see R. Barraclough, *Philo's Politics: Roman Rule and Hellenistic Judaism*, in: *ANRW* II, 21,1, pp. 417–553, especially pp. 490–506.

[7] See especially A.H.M. Jones's review of the *Politics* in *JThSt* 40/1939, pp. 183ff; A. Momigliano's review of the *Introduction* in: *JRSt* 34/1944, pp. 163–65; and *Schürer* III, p. 817 n.21.

[8] See also V. Nikiprowetzky, *Le Commentaire de l'Ecriture chez Philon d'Alexandrie*, Leiden 1977, especially pp. 180–81, where he emphasizes the need to consider the Philonic exegesis as proper interpretation of Scripture and to study it in its appropriate biblical context.

[9] *Joseph as an Ethical Model in the Testaments of the Twelve Patriarchs*, Leiden 1981. For a general introduction, see: *Testaments of the Twelve Patriarchs*, *EJ* vol. 13, cols. 184–6.

[10] H.W. Hollander/M. DeJonge, *The Testaments of the Twelve Patriarchs, A Commentary*, Leiden 1985; M. DeJonge, *The Main Issues in the Study of the Testaments of the Twelve Patriarchs*, *NTSt* 26/1980, pp. 508–24.

[11] Most importantly, the emphasis on the lack of sources illuminating the precise nature of Early Christianity and its relation to contemporary Judaism, though correct in principle, is used too often as "evidence" for the document's Christian character. A general methodological statement is to be found in H.W. Hollander/M. DeJonge, *op. cit.*, pp. 82–85. For examples of this highly conjectural approach, see especially: p. 169 (where the expression "ungodliness of the high priest" is taken to refer to sins against Jesus), p. 170 (where the phrase "teaching the commandments contrary to the ordinances of God" is taken to mean: "disobeying Jesus Christ means disobeying God's ordinances"), p. 175–6 ("salvation of the world" is commented thus: "we would note also that the expressions used in this verse may suggest that this first annointed priest was a type of Jesus Christ"). See also: *Schürer* III, pp. 767–80. For a treatment of the figure of Joseph in Christian literature proper, see: A.W. Argyle, *Joseph the Patriarch in Patristic Teaching, The Expository Times*, 67/1955–56.

ment have still to be taken seriously.[12] Consequently, the Joseph
material in *XII* needs to be examined in a Jewish context and questions as to its influence must also be considered.

In his short study on Joseph,[13] E. Hilgert makes an important attempt to consider some Hellenistic interpretations of Joseph in the
light of the biblical evidence. He employs the very useful term
"polychrome thought world"[14] by which he accounts for the heterogeneous image of the figure in one and the same document. His
comparison of the exegetical material with the diverse biblical image
of Joseph, though not executed with sufficient caution,[15] sets a
methodological example.[16]

The most recent study of the figure of Joseph is that of J. Kugel,
who devotes half of his investigations into "the interpretative life of
biblical texts" to Joseph in the Midrash,[17] and in particular to
rabbninic interpretations of his affair with Potiphar's wife. Assuming that most, if not all Midrash can be traced back to some textual
oddity, for the explanation of which it emerged, the traces select motifs and detects their exegetical origin. Given this orientation of his
work, it is natural that he should have paid less attention to the hermeneutic function of the figure in each source.

Thus far, the comparative study of aggadic Midrash has concen-
trated on the history of specific motifs. These were isolated from
their respective literary context and their development in certain traditions was "followed through".[18] If the date of the latter could be

---

[12] For a historical documentation of the research, see: H.D. Slingerland, *The
Testament of the Twelve Patriarchs: A Critical History of Research*, Montana 1977. See
also: D. Flusser צוואות בני יעקב, *EB* vol. VI, cols. 689–92; D. Mendel's discussion
of the figure of Joseph in Jewish political thought of the intertestamental period assumes also an essentially Jewish document composed ca. 108–7 BCE (*The Land of
Israel as a Political Concept in Hasmonean Literature*, Tübingen 1987, pp. 89–108).

[13] *The Dual Image of Joseph in Hebrew and Early Jewish Literature, Biblical Research*
30/1985.

[14] *ibid*, p. 13.

[15] His explanation of the parallelism of positive and negative interpretations by
reference to positive and negative elements in the various biblical passages is too
simplistic and does not account for specifically Greek notions.

[16] Note also J. Heinemann's analysis of the midrashic interpretations of
Joseph material outside *Gen*, focussing on the motif of the bones of Joseph,
אגדות ותולדותיהן, Jerusalem 1974, pp. 49–56.

[17] *In Potiphar's House. The Interpretative Life of Biblical Texts*, Harper 1990, pp.
11–155.

[18] R. Bloch established this method theoretically, see especially her articles
Midrash and *A Methodological Note for the Study of Rabbinic Literature*, in: *Approaches to*

established with reasonable certainty, an exegetical history of that motif would emerge. It now seems appropriate to enrich this method by two considerations. First, the nature and the value of interpretation as a cultural activity requires special emphasis. For this purpose the questions raised in the field of Hermeneutics can profitably be applied also to Early Judaism. Second, the literary and narrative qualities of the aggadic material have to be fully appreciated. It is therefore crucial to increase our sensitivity to these aspects by using analytical tools developed in the field of literary criticism.

Among the biblical books, *Genesis* is one of the earliest to achieve the status of "Scripture"[19] and it is certainly an authoritative text to Philo,[20] Josephus and *GR*. As such it requires attention and interpretation. In the wake of H.G. Gadamer's work[21] both philosophers and literary critics have become increasingly conscious of the role of interpretation in culture and tradition. A general awareness has consequently developed to the complex nature of this process. Departing from earlier claims of absolute objectivity, it has become acceptable to think of reading as an undertaking in which the reader

---

Ancient Judaism: Theory and Practice, ed. W.S. Green, Montana 1978, pp. 29–76; *idem, Midrash*, Supplement to *DBV* 1955, cols. 1253–80; G. Vermes, *Bible and Midrash: Early Old Testament Exegesis*, in: *The Cambridge History of the Bible*, Cambridge 1970, vol. I pp. 199–231; *idem, Scripture and Tradition in Judaism. Haggadic Studies*; Leiden 1961; *idem, Post-Biblical Jewish Studies*, Leiden 1975.

[19] For a discussion of the intricate question of the canonisation of the Hebrew Bible, see especially: J. Barr, *Holy Scripture: canon, authority, criticism*, Oxford 1983; J. Barton, *Oracles of God*, Oxford 1986; J. Kugel, *Early Bible Interpretation*, Philadelphia 1986, chap. I, II and IV; Schürer II, pp. 314–21; D. Patte, *Early Jewish Hermeneutic in Palestine*, Scholars Press 1975, pp. 19–30; I. Grunwald, *From Apocalypticism to Gnosticism*, P. Lang 1988, pp. 23–32; H.W. Frei, *The Eclipse of Biblical Narrative*, Yale 1974, pp. 1–16; concerning the rabbinic views on this issue, see: S.Z. Leiman, *The Canonization of Hebrew Scripture: The Talmudic and Midrashic Evidence*, 1976.

[20] For a detailed discussion of Philo's concept of the biblical text and its possibly Greek connotation, see: Y. Amir, *Authority and Interpretation of Scripture in the Writings of Philo*, in: *Mikra*, ed. J. Mulder, Assen/Philadelphia 1988, pp. 421–54.

[21] *Wahrheit und Methode*, reprinted Tübingen 1986, see also the essays in vol. II. (This work has been translated and explained by J.L. Weinsheimer, *Gadamer's Hermeneutics: A Reading of Truth and Method*, New Haven/London 1985; see also D. Marshall's critical review in *PT* 8/1987, pp. 199–200). For a collection of passages from German hermeneutic philosophy translated into English, see: K. Müller-Vollmer (ed.), *The Hermeneutic Reader*, Oxford 1985; R.C. Holub's critical introduction *Reception Theory*, Methuen 1984; D. Shepherd, *The Authority of Meanings and the Meaning of Authority. Some Problems in the Theory of Reading*, PT 7/1986, pp. 129–45.

incorporates his own intellectual background and thus participates, to a certain degree, in the generation of meaning.[22] Some texts are naturally more ambiguous than others and so leave greater space for such creative activity on the part of the reader. But if a text is to be culturally significant, its invigoration and "completion" throughout the generations is an essential function. As F. Kermode put it:[23]

> From day to day we must cope with the paradox that the classic changes yet retains its identity. It would not be read, and so would not be a classic, if we could not in some way believe it to be capable of saying more than its author meant; even, if necessary, that to say more than he meant was what he meant to do.

Biblical narrative is known for its conciseness and its frequent opacity. These qualities seem directly to invite the reader's creative interest. The panorama of biblical events has furthermore come to

---

[22] The critics differ regarding the extent of the reader's role. On the one hand, E. Hirsch wishes to affirm his traditional role as rediscoverer of the authorial intention, see especially: *Validity and Interpretation*, Yale 1967, pp. 127–163; *idem, The Aims of Interpretation*, Chicago 1976. On the other hand, W. Iser went furthest to establish the reader's creative autonomy which he, however, still believes to be guided by the author's narrative devices, see especially: *Der Akt des Lesens*, München 1984 (1st ed. 1976), pp. 175–355; *idem, Der implizite Leser*, München 1979 (1st ed. 1972); partly available in Hebrew: אי-מנברות ותנובתו של הקורא בספורת: למבנה המשיכה של הטקסט הספרותי, *HaSifrut* 21/1975, pp. 1–16; see also M. Brinker's review article *Indeterminacy, Meaning and Two Phenomelogies of Reading: Iser and Ingarden*, PT 1/1980, pp. 203–212; for a collection of articles on the subject, see: *The Reader in the Text*, ed. S.R. Suleiman/I. Crosman, Princeton 1980; *Issues in Contemporary Critical Theory*, ed. P. Barry, Macmillan 1987, pp. 105–130; of lesser value: J.P. Tompkins (eds.), *Reader-Response-Criticism*, Baltimore 1980; see also: H. White, *The Rhetoric of Interpretation*, PT 9/1988, pp. 253–74; *idem, The Value of Narrativity in the Representation of Reality*, in: *On Narrative*, ed. W.J.T. Mitchell, Chicago 1980, pp. 1–24; W.B. Michealis, *Against Formalism: The Autonomous Text in Legal and Literary Interpretation*, PT 1/1979, pp. 23–34; D. Spearman, *The Novel and Society*, London 1966, pp. 227–38; R. Fowler, *Literature as Social Discourse*, London 1981; cf. also J.H. Miller, *The Geneva School*, Critical Quarterly 8/1966, pp. 305–21; S.N. Lawall, *Critics of Consciousness*, MA 1968; for an application of these hermeneutic theories to bible interpretation, see: D. Patte, *op. cit.*, pp. 1–18; R. Morgan with J. Barton, *Biblical Interpretation*, Oxford 1988; J. Barton, *Reading the Old Testament, Method in Biblical Study*, London 1984; consider reader-oriented criticism also in the context of other literary theories: *Modern Literary Theory*, ed. A. Jefferson/D. Robey, London 1988 (1st ed. 1982).

[23] *The Classic*, Harvard University Press 1983, p. 80; see also his discussions in: *How we read Novels*, Fourth G. James Memorial Lecture 1975; *Novel and Narrative*, Twenty-fourth W.P. Ker Memorial Lecture, printed Glasgow 1972; *Can we say ab-*

be regarded as an absolute reality which is to serve as a model for all subsequent generations. The stories and the characters from former times have thus become a kind of epistomological tool for understanding the ever changing realities of each epoch.

When analysing expositions of the biblical text, one therefore has to be particularly aware of the "hermeneutical cycle" which fostered each of them. Interpreting an interpretation means to unravel the complex interrelation between the authority of the text and the thought-world of the interpreter. Primarily, the exegete's choice of key-passages on which he will base his interpretation requires explanation. Subsequently, the exegesis of each biblical item needs to be analysed also in the context of the interpreter's general views. Proceeding in this fashion, it is possible to shed light on the way in which each reading—or should I say each "meaning"?—of the text is generated by the specific concerns of the exegete. Conversely, the function of the biblical figure of Joseph in different Jewish contexts will emerge.[24]

Furthermore, the Joseph story is a story. The earliest extant tale expresses the creative genius of the biblical narrator and is a *mimesis* of his reality. Its interpretations are transformations of a story which manipulate its narrative characteristics. It is therefore crucial to apply literary analysis not only to biblical stories, as has been done before,[25] but also to the interpretations of them.

In my analysis I shall assume certain literary concepts which have been dealt with in numerous works but most clearly formulated by S. Rimmon-Kenan.[26] Let me explain some of them for the sake of clarity.

---

solutely everything we like?, in: *Essays on Fiction*, London 1983, pp. 156–67 (1st printed 1977); *Institutional Control of Interpretation, ibid*, pp. 168–84 (1st printed 1979).

[24] See also H.R. Jauss's theoretical discussion of "the modes of reception" of literary characters in: *Levels of Identification of Hero and Audience, New Literary History*, 2/1974, pp. 283–318.

[25] For a theoretical discussion, see especially: M. Weiss, *Die Methode der "Total-Interpretation"*, *SVT* 22/1972, pp. 88–112 (more detailed in his book: המקרא וכדמותו, Jerusalem 1967), where he outlines the methodological departure from historical approaches, emphasises the essential function of language in literary art and examines hermeneutic issues of bible interpretation. See also: M. Perry/M. Sternberg, זהירות ספרות! לבעיות האינטרפרטאציה והפואטיקה של הסיפור המקראי, *Hasifrut* 2/1969–71, pp. 63–608; and J. Barr's more sceptical assessment in: *Reading the Bible as Literature, Bulletin of the John Rylands University Library of Manchester*, 56/1973, pp. 10–33. For the application literary methods to the analysis of the Joseph story, see below chapter II.

[26] *Narrative Fiction: Contemporary Poetics*, Methuen 1988 (1st English ed. 1983).

In a narrative things do not happen, rather a story is being relat-ed.[27] A narrative has furthermore two poles: events, on the one hand, and character, on the other.[28] These are interdependent in a complex fashion, or as H. James put it:[29]

> What is character but the determination of incident?
> What is incident but the illustration of character?

On the level of the actual text itself, one can distinguish three aspects: time, focalisation and characterisation. By comparison to other forms of art, literature is most dominated by the element of time. Every narrative is in fact constructed along a linear time axis.[30] It is important for the understanding of a narrative to re-main aware of the difference between narrative time, i.e., the time it takes to relate the story, and narrated time, i.e., time it takes for the events in the story to happen. Narrative time is individual to the author and primarily involves ordering the presentation of events. This may be done according to the underlying plot or may diverge from it.

The focalisation of a narrative indicates the perspective from which the story is told. Focalisation can be external, i.e. reflecting the narrator's (omniscient) perspective, or internal, i.e. representing the limited point-of-view of one character in the story. Both external and internal focalisation can be from within or without, depending on whether inward or outward manifestations are described. Thus, biblical narratives tend to have an internal focalisation from with-

---

For other theoretical works, see especially: W. Booth, *The Rhetoric of Fiction*, Chica-go 1961; S. Chatman, *Story and Discourse*, New York 1978; E.M. Forster's lively and very insightful *Aspects of the Novel*, Harmondsworth 1963 (see especially his treat-ment of character, where he makes the influential distinction between "round" and "flat"); H. James, *The Art of the Novel*, New York 1962; F. Kermode, *The Genesis of Secrecy*, Harvard University Press 1979; E. Laemmert, *Bauformen des Erzählens*, Stuttgart 1955; F.K. Stanzel, *Theorie des Erzählens*, Göttingen 1979.

[27] See also: E. Auerbach, *Mimesis*, Princeton 1974 (1st ed. 1946); and also F. Kermode's discussion of the tension between literary fiction and reality in: *The Sense of an Ending. Studies in the Theory of Fiction*, Oxford 1967, pp. 127–52.

[28] See also S. Rimmon-Kenan's discussion of "the death of character in fic-tion", *op. cit.*, pp. 29–34.

[29] *op. cit.*, p. 80; see also: U. Margolis, *The Doer and the Deed. Action as the Basis for Characterisation in Narrative*, PT 7/1986, pp. 205–25.

[30] See also G. Zoran, לקראת תיאוריה של המרחב בסיפור, Hasifrut 30–31/1981, pp. 20–34, where he discusses in detail how spacial notions are transferred into the time-oriented scheme of literature.

out, as for example in the famous case of the Sacrifice of Isaac (*Gen* 22). Most events are here related from Abraham's point of view but the reader learns nothing about his inner reactions to the events.[31]

By characterisation I understand the sum of the textual indications pointing to the character of a fictional person. This category, though the least researched,[32] is the most complex dimension of narrative because it operates on a literal level but incorporates conceptions about real humans and often also personal experience. The most comprehensive study of characterisation to date is Y. Ewen's.[33] He initially distinguishes between a character's complexity and his development which, he insists, are complementary but not identical: the more complex a person is, the greater is the likelihood, but not necessity, of his changing and developing.[34] Among the means of characterisation Ewen differentiates between explicit definitions[35] and more indirect manifestations. The latter category is further subdivided into: *a* external appearance, *b* deeds, *c* speech,[36] *d* relationships to other fictional characters or significant parallelism of figures.[37]

In the fields of Bible, independent Midrashic stories[38] and Clas-

---

[31] For a more detailed discussion, see: S. Rimmon-Kenan, *op. cit.*, pp. 71–85; for a critical discussion of her terms, see also: S. Chatman, *Characters and Narrators. Filter, Center, Slant and Interest Forms, PT* 7/1986, pp. 189–204.

[32] J. Frow, *Spectacle, Binding: On Character, PT* 7/1986, pp. 227–250, rightly draws attention to this *desiteratum*, but his own proposals to apply cinematographic categories to literary analysis are less convincing.

[33] הדמות בסיפורת, Tel Aviv 3rd ed. 1986; see also his shorter treatment in: התיאוריה של הדמות בסיפורת: מעמדה, תפקידה ביצירה ודרכי בניתה בסיפורת, *Hasifrut* 1/1971, pp. 1–29; S. Rimmon-Kenan, *op. cit.*, pp. 59–70, is on this issue greatly indebted to Ewen. For other, less clear treatments, see: W.J. Harvey, *Character and The Novel*, London 1965; J. Garvey, *Characterization in Narrative, PT* 2/78, pp. 63–78; R. Wilson, *The Bright Chimera: Character as a literary Term, Critical Inquiry* 5/1979, pp. 725–50.

[34] *op. cit.*, pp. 34–42.

[35] *ibid*, pp. 49–56.

[36] See also Ewen's discussion in: הדיבור הסמוי, *Hasifrut* 1/1968–9, pp. 140–52; and see also: G. Scheintuch, לקראת ניתוח אלקוציוני שלהשיחה בסיפור המקרא, *Hasifrut* 30–31/1981, pp. 70–75 (she offers a highly interesting analysis of the narrator's influential presence in biblical speech acts which are usually regarded as "neutral").

[37] *ibid*, pp. 56–99. Note that Y. Ewen also discussed in detail indications of the "life of the soul" (*ibid*, pp. 136–194). But this modern pre-occupation with psychology and inner life is not paralleled by the Ancients and is therefore not relevant to our study.

[38] O. Meir's D.Phil. thesis, הדמויות הפועלות בסיפורי התלמוד והמדרש, Jerusalem תשל"ז; *idem*, הסיפור הדרשני, Tel Aviv 1987, pp. 52–62.

sical Literature,[39] the concept of fictional character and its literary expression have recently become a topic of research. Scholars have become aware of the potential reward but also of the problems in applying such "modern" questions to the ancient texts. Consequently, discussions concerning the degree of personhood have been prominent; and questions have been raised with regard to the "depth" or complexity of the figures. Perhaps the most important issue has been the function of character in these types of fiction: to what extent is the category of character subordinated to action, ideology or ethics? Is it meant to entertain or to teach about human nature? This research in adjacent fields must now be continued in the area of post-biblical Judaism, and particularly the interpretation of biblical stories.[40]

Obviously, the various interpretations of the Joseph material do not lend themselves equally to the above outlined approach. The earliest exegetical evidence, from late biblical and early post-biblical sources, consists in each case only of a few sentences. These scattered references do not take into account the whole story but isolate one or two significant aspects of it. They can thus not be analysed from the point of view of narratology. Since they are nevertheless important indications of hermeneutic developments, I shall treat them in some detail in my second chapter in continuation of the Joseph story in *Gen*.

Furthermore, the three earliest complete interpretations of the Joseph story are not suited in the same way to a literary approach. Only one source, namely Philo's bios, is explicitly regarded by its author as a distinct work on the Joseph story. While Josephus's ac-

---

[39] Ch. Gill's excellent article, *The Question of Character and Personality in Greek Tragedy*, PT 7/1986, pp. 251–73; idem, *The Ethos/Pathos Distinction in Rhetorical and Literary Criticism*, CQ 34/1984, pp. 149–66; A. Momigliano, *M. Mauss and the Quest for the Person in Greek biography and autobiography*, in: *The Category of Person*, ed. M. Carrithers a.o., Cambridge 1985, pp. 83–93; R. Hirzel, *Die Person. Begriff und Name derselben im Altertum*, Sitzungsberichte der Königlich Bayrischen Akademie der Wissenschaften 1914; A.M. Dale, *Ethos and Dianoia*, in: *Collected Papers*, Cambridge 1969; T.B.L. Webster, *Some Psychological Terms in Greek Tragedy*, Journal of Hellenic Studies 77/1957, pp. 149–54. Numerous studies have been undertaken in connection with Aristotle's *Poetics* (especially chap. VI); see also St. Halliwell's recent treatment in: *Aristotle's Poetics*, London 1986, pp. 138–67; idem, *The Poetics of Aristotle*, London 1987, pp. 88–98; and H. House *Aristotle's Poetics*, London 1958, pp. 68–81.

[40] An initial step in this direction has been made by O. Meir, סיפור מחלת חזקיהו באגרת חז"ל, Hasifrut 30–31/1981, pp. 109–30.

count, though part of his general history, is still a continuous paraphrase, *GR* is but an accumulation of diverse exegetical pieces of uncertain date and authorship. With a view to this issue I shall now examine the nature and the provenance of each of the three sources.

The earliest of these expositions is that of Philo. He can confidently be addressed as the narrator of his Joseph story. We even have some information concerning his *persona* which might shed light on the process of his hermeneutics: he produced an almost overwhelming amount of tractates on various Jewish and Greek topics. It can be disputed to what extent these were truly philosophical or original.[41] But it is beyond doubt that he struck the right chord among his contemporary, 1st century Alexandrians.[42] For the Jews he examplified how to combine a definite Jewish identity with Greek *Lettres*;[43] and to the nascent Church he left a crucial intellectual heritage.

Of aristocratic origin, he could enjoy a *Vita contemplativa* and this also seems to have been his greatest devotion in life. Other occupations which are marginally mentioned include political involvement on behalf of the local Jewish community and a pilgrimage to Jerusalem.[44]

---

[41] Using a "hypothetico-deductive method", H.A. Wolfson tried most to prove Philo's originality and philosophical coherence; see especially: *Philo: Foundations in Religious Philosophy in Judaism, Christianity and Islam*, Harvard 1949, particularly vol. I where he discusses Jewish Hellenism and Philo's exegetical methods. Generally, his contribution to Philonic scholarship is now regarded sceptically. For different assessments, see: E.R. Goodenough, *Wolfson's Philo, JBL* 67/1948, pp. 87–109; A. Mendelson, *A Reappraisal of Wolfson's Method, SP* 3/1974/5, pp. 11–26. A good general account is to be found in H. Chadwick, *Philo*, in: *The Cambridge History of Later Greek and Early Medieval Philosophy*, Cambridge 1967, pp. 137–57.

[42] For a general background, see: B. Porten, *The Jews in Egypt*, in: *The Cambridge History of Judaism*, Cambridge 1984, pp. 372–401. The evidence on Philo's precise *Curriculum Vitae* is sparse and mostly derived from indications in his works. The only chronologically fixed date is therefore his embassy to Gaius in AD 39–40. For a detailed discussion, see: *Schürer* III, pp. 814–16, and below chap. III.

[43] The nature of Philo's intellectual synthesis and his loyalty to Judaism have been the subject of prolonged scholarly dispute. See especially: I. Heinemann, *Philon's Griechische und Jüdische Bildung*, Breslau 1929; S. Sandmel, *Philo of Alexandria*, Oxford 1979; E. Brehier, *Les idées philosophiques et religieuses de Philon d'Alexandrie*, Paris 1907; A. Mendelson, *Secular Education in Philo of Alexandria*, 1982; G. Delling, *Perspektiven der Erforschung des Hellenistischen Judentums, HUCA* 45/1974, pp. 144ff; D. Satran, *Hellenism*, in: *Contemporary Religious Thought*, ed. A.A. Cohen/P.M. Flohr, New York 1987, pp. 333ff; H. Tyen, *Die Probleme der Neueren Philon-Forschung, Theologische Rundschau* 23/1955, p. 234. See also: I. Cohen-Yashar, מקומו של פילון במחשבת ישראל, Sinai 84/1974.

[44] This will be discussed more in chap. III.

Like most of his *Expositions* of Scripture, he probably wrote his bios
on Joseph in the twilight of his life.[45] Since his Hebrew was at best
meagre, it must be assumed that he mostly relied on *LXX* as a *Vorlage*
for his paraphrase.[46] He himself considered this work as part of a
series of *Lives* on the patriarchs, some of which are still extant.

Josephus deals with the Joseph story in his *magnum opus* on Jewish
history which he finished AD 93–94.[47] It is here part of his continuous narrative about the events of Ancient Israel. In contrast to
Philo, Josephus was a man of action who was for a significant period
involved in political and military affairs.

During his lifetime he witnessed momentous events which neces-
sitated a substantial re-organisation of the Jewish people and which
changed its relationship to other nations. Josephus's role in these
transformations was highly controversial already at the time. His
function in the initial stages of the Revolt against Rome consequently remained the most sensitive point in his personal apologetics.

Questions as to Josephus's exact version of the biblical text and
his possible reliance on Philo have not yet been conclusively settled.[48] Only a careful analysis of detailed examples can shed further
light on these intricate issues.

---

[45] For a discussion on the chronology of Philo's work, see especially: L. Cohn,
Einteilung und Chronologie der Schriften Philos, Philologus, Sup.Bd. 7/1899, pp.
389–436; L. Massebieau/E. Bréhier, *Essai sur la Chronologie de la vie et des oeuvres de
Philon, RHR* 53/1906, pp. 25–64, pp. 164–85 and pp. 267–89. For a survey, see
especially: R.G. Hamerton-Kelly, *Sources and Traditions in Philo Judaeus: Prolegomena
to an Analysis of his Writings, SP* 1/1972, pp. 3–26.

[46] This view is now commonly accepted (see e.g. Y. Amir, *Philo and the Bible,
Studia Philonica* 2/1973). For other views, see: H.A. Wolfson, *op. cit.*, p. 89 ("Still,
while there is no positive evidence of his knowledge of Hebrew, the burden of
proof is upon those who would deny that he possessed such knowledge"); R.
Marcus, *A textual-exegetical note on Philo's Bible, JBL* 69/1950; J. Cohen-Yashar,
‏האם ידע פילון האלכסנדרוני עברית?‏, Tarbiz 34/1965, pp. 337–45; Ch. D. Mantel,
‏האם ידע פילון עברית?‏, Tarbiz 32/1963, pp. 98–99.

[47] For a good survey of Josephus's work, see: *Schürer* I, pp. 43–63; A. Schalit,
Josephus, EJ vol. 10, cols. 251–65; H.W. Attridge, *Josephus and his works*, in: *Jewish
Writings of the Second Temple Period*, ed. M. Stone, Assen/Philadelphia 1984, pp.
185–232 (especially pp. 210–11); *idem, The Interpretation of Biblical History in the Antiquitates Judaicae of Flavius Josephus*, Scholars Press 1976, pp. 29–71 on "the character and programmatic aims of the Antiquities"; S. Rappaport, *Agada und Exegese
bei Flavius Josephus*, Frankfurt 1930, "Einleitung"; T. Rajak, *Josephus: The Historian
and His Society*, London 1983, especially pp. 11–64 and pp. 174–84; and also P.
Bilde's survey of current trends in scholarship on Josephus, *Flavius Josephus between
Jerusalem and Rome*, 1988.

[48] For an annotated bibliography on the issue, see: L.H. Feldman, *Josephus and*

Is it possible to speak of a narrator in the case of *GR*? It is a well-known fact that rabbinic Midrash is a highly associative kind of exegesis which bursts the narrative framework and often serves educational purposes.[49] To be meaningful, the term narrator must therefore be used here in a broader sense. It does not refer to one historically identifiable author who reshaped the character of Joseph in his own personal way. It designates instead the mind responsible for the present form of *GR*'s exegesis on the biblical figure. In many cases the narrator will thus be identical with the redactor of the Midrash. But frequently he will also present his views in a more direct way.[50]

It is for several reasons meaningful to speak of a narrator in *GR*. The term primarily highlights that there was a certain purpose in the collection and the arrangement of the midrashic material. Rather than focussing on the questionable historical reliability of the traditions and their attribution to specific rabbis,[51] we should inquire

---

Modern Scholarship 1937–80, New York/Berlin, pp. 130–39.

[49] The most encompassing study to date is still: I. Heinemann's, דרכי האגדה, Jerusalem תשי״ד, *idem*, מדרש, *EB* vol. IV, cols. 695–701; *idem*, להתפתחות המונחים המקצועיים לפירוש המקרא, Leshonenu 14/תש״י; pp. 89–182. For other treatments, see: J. Heinemann, *op. cit.*, especially pp. 7–15; Y. Frankel, שאלות הרמנוטיות בחקר סיפור האגדה, *Tarbiz* 47/תשל״ח, pp. 139–72; O. Meir, *Story, op. cit.*, pp. 11–62; E.Z. Melammed, מפרשי המקרא, Jerusalem תשל״ח, pp. 1–129; Z. Levi, הרמנויטיקה, Tel Aviv 1986, pp. 17–35 (on rabbinic hermeneutics he maintains the problematic emphasis on a clear distinction between Peshat and Derash as objective and subjective); M.D. Herr, *Midrash, EJ* vol. 11, cols. 1507–14; L. Jacob, *Hermeneutics, EJ* vol. 8, cols. 366–72; A.G. Wright, *The Literary Genre Midrash*, New York 1967, pp. 17–31 and pp. 49–75; G.G. Porton, *Understanding Rabbinic Midrash*, Hoboken 1985, pp. 1–18; G.H. Hartman/S. Budick, *Midrash and Literature*, Yale 1986; R.S. Sarason, *op. cit.*, pp. 55–73; J. Neusner, *Midrash in Context: Exegesis in formative Judaism*, Philadelphia 1983; *idem, Judaism and Scripture*, Chicago 1986, *idem, What is Midrash?*, Philadelphia 1983; A. Holz's discussion of questions raised by M. Kaddushin's research in: עולם המחשבה של חז״ל, Tel Aviv 1978; J. Goldin, *From Text to Interpretation and from Experience to Interpreted Text*, in: *Studies in Midrash and Related Literature*, New York 1988, pp. 271–82; Cf. also: M. Kadushin, *The Rabbinic Mind*, New York 1952, D. Boyarin, *Old Wine in New Bottles: Intertextuality and Midrash, PT* 8/1987, pp. 539–56; *idem, Intertextuality and the Reading of Midrash*, Indiana University Press, 1990.

[50] For examples and more detailed discussion, see: O. Meir, *Story, op.cit.*, pp. 161–63.

[51] For a detailed discussion of the historiographical problems regarding rabbinic intellectual history, see especially: E.E. Urbach, חז״ל-פרקי אמונות ודעות, Jerusalem 1969; for methodological considerations, see especially pp. 1–14; P. Schäfer, *Studien zur Geschichte und Theologie des rabbinischen Judentums*, Leiden 1978; cf. also J. Neusner's research, e.g.: *Development of a Legend, Studies in the Tradition concerning Yohanan ben Zakkai*, Leiden 1970.

why the material was presented in that fashion. Questions as to how the reader's understanding of the figure of Joseph in *GR* is influenced by the narrator's devices need to be treated seriously.

The use of the term narrator moreover enables us to examine how the story and the character of Joseph are reflected in the earliest, fifth century compilation of midrash on *Gen*.[52] It will thus be possible to evaluate the choice of key-passages, the manipulation of narrative perspectives and the presentation of the figure within the larger context. Despite the variety of interpretations there nevertheless emerges a set of Joseph-images which is distinct to *GR* and differs from that of other midrashic compilations. As we know today from the case of free association in psychoanalytic discourse, heterogeneity and abruptness do not necessarily indicate lack of coherence, but rather highlight the complexity of any oral or written exposition.[53]

Thus, the sources to be examined in this thesis are the biblical Joseph story in *Gen* and its early complete expositions by Philo, Josephus and *GR*. These not only range over a considerable period of time but also cover different cultural environments. Most notably, they derive both from the Hebrew and the Greek speaking world.[54]

---

[52] For an introduction, see: Ch. Albeck's "Einleitung" to his edition, *Bereschit Rabba*, Jerusalem 1965, vol. III pp. 1–151; and also: L. Strack/G. Stemberger, *Einleitung in Talmud und Midrasch*, München 1982, pp. 257–63.

[53] See also: D.P. Spense, *Narrative Truth and Historical Truth, Meaning and Interpretation in Psychoanalysis*, New York 1982, pp. 137–214; R. Schafer, Narration in the Psychoanalytic Dialogue, in: *On Narrative* ed. W.J.T. Mitchell, University of Chicago Press 1980, pp. 25–49.

[54] *The Testaments of the Twelve Patriarchs* will, despite its considerable length, not be treated separately. My reasons for this are the following: firstly, this source focusses on the Blessing of Jacob as related in *Gen* 49, and does not even purport to treat the whole Joseph story. Its emphasis on particular points can thus offer only a vague indication as to how the figure was grasped as a whole. Secondly, the figure of Joseph in this document has, as I mentioned earlier, been treated recently and in considerable detail. Although my conception of the nature and the provenance of the *Testaments* differs significantly from that of Hollander, many of the details of his investigations are nevertheless valuable. Given the extant form of this source, an analysis of its relevant passages would furthermore necessitate a prior presentation of a detailed text-critical apparatus, which is clearly beyond the scope of the present study. I nevertheless do suggest, on the basis of my earlier investigations of the *Testaments*, how numerous of its traditions influenced later Midrash.

CHAPTER TWO

THE BIBLICAL JOSEPH

The biblical Joseph story is well-known and its contents do not require reiteration.[1] I intend instead to highlight some of its narrative characteristics in this chapter. In the first section the focus will be on two aspects of the story in *Gen*, namely its narrative rhythm and its focal points. In the second section I shall outline the narrative rhythm of the three major interpretations and compare each to that of the *Vorlage*. Then the biblical characterisation of the figure will be analysed, paying special attention to its exegetical potential. In the final section of this chapter the earliest pieces of exegesis on the Joseph material will be introduced.

For many of the insights on the biblical story I am indebted to a particularly rich history of research, starting from medieval[2] French[3]

---

[1] For good summary treatments of the biblical figure, see: *Joseph*, *EB* vol. III, cols. 16–613; *Joseph*, *IDB* vol. II, pp. 981–86.

[2] For a general introduction see: *Bible, Exegesis and Study: Medieval Rabbinic Commentaries*, in *EJ* IV: 889–899; פרשנות המקרא, *EB* vol. VIII, cols. 641–737; N. Sarna, *Hebrew and Bible Studies in Medieval Spain*, in: R. Barnett, *The Sephardi Heritage* I, N.Y. 1971, pp. 323–366 (especially on the contribution of the Hebrew grammarians); M.Z. Segal, פרשנות המקרא, Jerusalem 1980; concerning the place of Jewish exegesis in medieval bible studies see: B. Smalley, *The Study of the Bible in the Middle Ages*, Oxford 1952, especially pp. XI–XXII and pp. 103–4, 150–52 and 363ff; E.J. Rosenthal, *Anti-Christian Polemic in Medieval Bible Commentaries*, *JJS* 11/1960, pp. 115–35; idem, סובלנות ודתית בפרשנות המקרא של ימי הבינים, in: מחקרים ומקורות, Jerusalem 1967, pp. 203–13; L. Jacobs, *Jewish Bible Exegesis*, N.Y. 1973, provides a useful collection of select pieces in translation with introductory remarks.

[3] For an introduction to Rashi see: E. Shereshevsky, *Rashi: The Man and His World*, N.Y. 1982, especially pp. 36–57 and pp. 73–119 (S. Kamin's critical review in *JJS* 36/1985, pp. 130–132); B.J. Gelles, *Peshat and Derash in the Exegesis of Rashi*, Leiden 1981 (S. Kamin's review in *JJS* 36/1985, pp. 126–30); S. Kamin, רש"י, פשוטו של מקרא ומדרשו של מקרא, Jerusalem 1986 (A. Touito's qualified appraisal in *Tarbiz* 66/1987, pp. 433–447), regarding Joseph especially p. 163, pp. 170–71 and pp. 142–43; E.Z. Melammed, *op.cit.*, vol. I, pp. 353–449; on the "synthetic" interpreters D. Kimhi and Nahmanides, who were geographically detached from Spain see: F.E. Talmage, *David Kimhi: The Man and His Commentaries*, Harvard University Press 1975, especially pp. 58–83; I. Baer, *A History of the Jews in Christian Spain*, Philadelphia 1966, especially pp. 102–5, 143–59, 245–50; G. Scholem, *Ursprung und Anfänge der Kabbala*, Berlin 1962, especially pp. 325–30, pp. 360–5 and pp. 376–80; I. Twersky, *Introduction*, in: *Rabbi Moses Nah-*

and Spanish[4] exegetes[5] up to modern text-critical[6] and literary[7] approaches. As far as I am aware, however, a comprehensive study of the Joseph story as a narrative has not yet been undertaken.[8]

It is appropriate at this point to recall the overall structure of *Gen* 37 – 50. As is well known, the narrative is concerned with two themes: the family history and Joseph's political career in a foreign country. Although these narrative components are set in Canaan

---

manides (Ramban), Explorations in his religious and literary Virtuosity, Harvard University Press 1983, pp. 1 – 11, B. Septimus, *Open Rebuke and Concealed Love, ibid*, pp. 11 – 35, M. Idel, *We Have no Kabbalah on this, ibid*, pp. 51 – 75; A. Funkenstein *Nahmanides' Symbolical Reading of History*, in: *Studies in Jewish Mysticism*, ed. J. Dan and F. Talmage, Cambridge 1982, pp. 129 – 51.

[4] For an introduction on Ibn Ezra see: M. Friedländer, *Essays on the Writings of A. Ibn Ezra*, vol. IV, London 1877; E.Z. Melammed, *op. cit.*, pp. 519 – 714.

[5] Some modern interpreters incorporate numerous insights of these medieval exegetes into their commentaries, see especially B. Jacobs, *Genesis: Das erste Buch der Tora*, Schocken Verlag 1934; N. Leibovitz, עיונים בבראשית, Jerusalem; J. Horovitz's more apologetic approach in: *Die Josephserzählung*, Frankfurt 1921.

[6] For most up-to-date and well documented yet not always precise work see: C. Westermann, *Genesis 37 – 50*, Neukirchener Verlag 1982; summary of the history of research by L. Ruppert, *Die Josephserzählung der Genesis*, München 1965, pp. 15 – 29. For classical text-critical studies, see: A. Künen, *An Historico-Critical Inquiry into the Origin and Composition of the Hexateuch*, London 1886; J. Wellhausen, *Die Composition des Hexateuchs und der Historischen Bücher des Alten Testaments*, Berlin 1889, pp. 53 – 63; H. Gunkel, *Die Komposition der Josephsgeschichte, ZDMG* 76/1922; *idem, Genesis, übersetzt und erklärt*, Göttingen 1910; G. v. Rad, *Genesis, A Commentary*, 2nd English ed., London 1963, pp. 342 – 423; more recently D.B. Redford, *A Study of the Biblical Story of Joseph*, Leiden 1970, *STV* XX; and W. McKane, *Studies in the Patriarchal Narratives*, Edinburgh 1979, pp. 1 – 17, pp. 72 – 4, pp. 101 – 3, pp. 146 – 50; cf. also: M.G. May, *The Evolution of the Joseph Story, AJSLL*, 47/1931.

[7] D. Robertson, *Literature, bible as, IDB* Suppl., pp. 547 – 51; *idem, The Old Testament and the Literary Critic*, Philadelphia 1977, for theoretical considerations, especially: pp. 1 – 15; S. Bar-Efrat, העיצוב האמנותי של הסיפור במקרא, 2nd and revised version Jerusalem 1984 (1st edition 1979); R. Alter, *The Art of Biblical Narrative*, London 1981; *idem, Joseph and his Brothers, Commentary* 7/1980, pp. 59 – 69; J. Licht, *Story Telling in the Bible*, Jerusalem 1978 (concerning Joseph, especially pp. 138 – 42); A. Berlin, *Poetics and Interpretation of Biblical Narrative*, Sheffield 1983 (J. Rosenberg's review in *Prooftexts* 5/1985); M. Sternberg, *The Poetics of Biblical Narrative*, Indiana University Press 1985 (L. Poland's review in *JR* 68/1988, especially pp. 429ff); S.A. Geller, *Some Pitfalls in the Literary Approach to Biblical Narrative, JQR* 74/1984; W. Richter, *Exegese als Literaturwissenschaft*, Göttingen 1971.

[8] M. Savage's article, *Literary Criticism and Biblical Studies, A Rhetorical Analysis of the Joseph Narrative*, in: *Scripture in Context*, ed. C.D. Evans and others, Pittsburgh 1980, pp. 79 – 100, promises to do precisely that. Her discussion, however, amounts to no more than a reiteration of previous interpretations in modernist terminology; J.S. Ackerman, *Joseph, Juda and Jacob*, in: *Literary Interpretations of Biblical Narratives*, Abingdon 1982, ed. J.S. Ackerman, pp. 85 – 113 approaches a modern paraphrase; A.C. Welch, *The Story of Joseph*, Edinburgh 1913, amounts to a preacherman's popular reading of the story for the purpose of ethical teachings.

and Egypt respectively, they are artfully interwoven and brought together towards the end of the story.[9] The starting point is a family conflict which results in the selling of Joseph to Egypt; and it is the latter's career there which culminates the final family reunion.

Narrative Rhythm and the Central Points of the Story

The biblical Joseph story is a "scenic"[10] narrative which is dominated by a quick succession of events and a contraction of much narrated time into little narrative time.[11] Yet the narrative rhythm does not remain the same throughout the story; and the relation between narrated and narrative time changes significantly. By measuring these oscillations we can identify the focal points of the story. Whenever the rhythm decelerates, i.e., when the narrated time approaches the narrative time, we can isolate a focal point, and vice versa for accelerating rhythm.[12]

In the Joseph narrative, we find few precise indications of narrated time, but those present tend to indicate significant contractions. For example in *Gen* 39:10, only six words describe the continuous attempts at seduction by Potiphar's wife. According to the narrator himself, these extend over a long period of time ("day after day") and the narrative pace of this passage is consequently rather fast. This is further corroborated by a comparison of this passage with the previous description of the woman's first advance, on which the narrator rests significantly longer (*Gen* 39:7).

Also Joseph's imprisonment is evidently condensed in the narrative. In *Gen* 40:4 his initial time in jail is summarized in eleven words. Subsequently, four words indicate that two whole years

---

[9] In accordance with biblical practice the narrator arranges the complicated interplay of the different elements almost without leaving any trace in the narrative itself; see also S. Bar-Efrat, *op. cit.*, pp. 44–72, where he gives excellent examples of how linguistic minutiae can nevertheless betray the narrator's presence. See also: S. Talmon, *The Presentation of Synchroneity and Simultaneity in Biblical Narratives, Scripta Hierosolymitana* 27/1978, pp. 9–26.

[10] The distinction between "scenic" and "panoramic" was first introduced by P. Lubbock, *The Craft of Fiction*, London 1921, especially pp. 69, 72 and 110–23; see also E. Laemmert, *op.cit.*, pp. 92–4.

[11] See also: S. Rimmon-Kenan, *op.cit.*, pp. 42–43; E Laemmert, *op.cit.*, pp. 24–42 and pp. 73–94; S. Bar Efrat, *op.cit.*, pp. 151–98, has applied the distinction between narrated and narrative time to some biblical stories (especially in *Sam*) and contributed new and highly interesting insights to our understanding of them.

[12] Narrative time is measured by the number of words used to describe a particular event, thought, etc.

elapsed between the preceding events and what follows (*Gen* 41:1).[13] The biblical narrator passes in the same way over the "three-day" confinement of Joseph's brothers (four words in *Gen* 42:17). These episodes receive little detailed attention and must be considered as the low points of the story.

We may gather more indirect, yet no less meaningful evidence for quick narrative passages from other textual indications. In this respect it is significant that the biblical narrator tends to condense the family's travels. He describes for example the brothers' journey to Shechem with only seven words (*Gen* 37:12). That of Joseph's from Hebron to Shechem is outlined in five words (*Gen* 37:14) and from Shechem to his brothers at Dotan in six (*Gen* 37:17). The transfer of Joseph's coat to his father is similarly related in merely seven words (*Gen* 37:32). In all these and other such passages[14] no narrative time is devoted to geographical descriptions or to the protagonists' thoughts on their way.

Equally, Joseph's success in Potiphar's house is told rapidly. The reader learns from only seven words that he was prosperous, a state which presumably developed and lasted for a considerable amount of time (*Gen* 39:2). The relative speed of this scene is further stressed by the subsequent deceleration at Potiphar's recognition of Divine providence behind Joseph's success (*Gen* 39:3): twelve words are used to relate this comparatively much shorter episode.[15]

Likewise, the biblical narrator does not focus on the circumstances of Joseph's imprisonment. He describes Potiphar's measures (*Gen* 39:20) in only seventeen words, while he had used the same amount to relate how the latter heard the news and was enraged (*Gen* 39:19).

---

[13] See also *Gen* 40:6, where one word indicates that a night had passed in prison and *Gen* 40:20, where seven words point out that three days elapsed between Joseph's prognosis and Pharaoh's birthday.

[14] See also *Gen* 42:3 where seven words relate the brothers' journey to Egypt; *Gen* 42:26, where the biblical narrator relates in seven words that the brothers packed and left Egypt; and *Gen* 42:29. where he informs the reader in another six words of the completion of the brothers' journey and their arrival in Canaan. Similarly regarding the second journey: in *Gen* 43:15 six words for their descent and arrival before Joseph; *Gen* 44:4 four words for their departure. Only Jacob's journey to Egypt is described more slowly since genealogical details are added (*Gen* 46:1–28, three hundred-and-five words).

[15] This relation is paralleled in *Gen* 39:4–5. Whereas fourteen words are used to specify Joseph's responsibility in Potiphar's house, twenty-six describe God's blessings of this.

Little attention is also paid to the magicians' unsuccessful attempts at interpreting Pharaoh's dreams. Nine words describe how they were called and five more are used for Pharaoh's report to them (*Gen* 41:8). By comparison, the description of Joseph's call is much fuller. In five words Pharaoh's request is related, but nine more are used to depict the details of Joseph's preparation and only then is the king's address communicated (*Gen* 41:14–15).[16]

Joseph's activities as Egypt's governor receive different notice depending on whether they treat the years of plenty or of hunger. In *Gen* 41:45 the reader learns in five words that Joseph "went out into Egypt" and this is repeated in eight words a verse later. In *Gen* 41:48 the narrator pauses and suggests in ten words that Joseph collected the corn and in another ten that he supplied all the cities. Despite these details, the description is relatively fast, since it is meant to cover the seven years of plenty in Egypt (*Gen* 41:47). By comparison, the narrative decelerates at the seven years of hunger. Twenty-seven words are used to highlight the change for the worse and to mark the fulfilment of Joseph's prognosis. In nine further words the Egyptian's plight is related. Then the biblical narrator uses seven words to describe Pharaoh's turning them to Joseph and an extra four words to stress his transfer of all authority to him. In an additional eight words Joseph's selling of the corn is mentioned; and finally the strength of the famine is accentuated again (ten words in *Gen* 41:56). In chapter 47 of *Gen* the narrator dwells again on Joseph's administrative activities. In the concluding phrase he makes a very rare direct statement which reflects his own position: "So Joseph made it a statute concerning the land and *it stands to this day*" (*Gen* 47:26).[17] The authorial comment here discloses an awareness of the lasting importance of Joseph and perhaps also a degree of proud identification with this national figure. The relative deceleration of the narrative speed is moreover to be understood from the story's overall composition. The focussing of the reader's attention on this point also prepares for the subsequent family encounter.

By contrast, the biblical narrative reaches its focal points in the numerous direct speeches, where the narrated time naturally equals

---

[16] The reader's attention has previously already been focussed on Joseph by the chief butler's report about him (*Gen* 41:9–13).

[17] For a similar expression, see e.g. *Gen* 19:37 (the name of Moab up to this day).

the narrative time. This is evidently the case when dreams are told (*Gen* 37:5–10; 40:8–11 and 16–17; 41:1–24), when Jacob orders Joseph to enquire about his brothers (*Gen* 37:14), when Judah/Reuben admonish them (*Gen* 37:21–22 and 26–27; *Gen* 42:22), when Potiphar's wife denounces Joseph (*Gen* 39:13–18) and when Joseph discloses his identity (*Gen* 45:3–8). Particularly dramatic are the two main dialogues, i.e., when Joseph first confronts Potiphar's wife (*Gen* 39:7–9) and the encounter between Joseph and Judah (*Gen* 44:15–34).

Other climaxes may be established by reference to significant decelerations of the narrative speed in comparison with adjacent passages. This is the case, for example, in the opening passage of chapter 37. The few introductory remarks concerning Jacob's history in Canaan cover an extensive, but not clearly defined amount of time (ten words in *Gen* 37:1–2a). The reader's attention is then centered on a more specific point, namely Joseph's occupation at the age of seventeen. For the description of this limited period a parallel amount of ten words is used. Subsequently, the narrative is further slowed down by additional information of the fellow guardians (also ten words, *Gen* 37:2). The passage culminates in Joseph's ill report about his brothers. The biblical narrator uses seven words to relate this event, which is far more specific and limited than any of the preceding information.

The same technique of increasing deceleration is to be found in the subsequent verse (*Gen* 37:3). In six words Jacob's general attitude towards Joseph is introduced; and it is amplified by a five-word explanation. The resulting action, specific and limited in time, is then described with another four words. Thus, the decreasing narrative speed indicates that Joseph's report and Jacob's gift are the focal points of the opening scenes.

A similar process of concentration is to be found in *Gen* 39:11–12. Ten words relate that Joseph returned to an empty house. More narrative time is then devoted to the subsequent quick succession of events: two words for the woman's approach, three for her repeated request. Joseph's reaction deserves even further attention and the reader learns in three words that he left his coat and in another three how he fled. It is also significant that the narrator dwells on Joseph's retreat and uses two different verbs for this action. In this fashion the narrative is evidently arrested and the central point emphasised.

In *Gen* 42:6–7, too, a narrative climax is reached. Ten words are initially used to summarize Joseph's activities as governor during the drought. Then more limited actions are related, namely his brother's arrival (three words) and their prostration (four words). The focal point of this passage emerges subsequently when the narrative time exceeds the narrated time. In four words the reader is told that Joseph saw his brothers and another word indicates that he recognized them.[18] After this climax the narrative speed increases immediately and fewer words are used to communicate complex conversations.[19]

The above investigation has shown that the narrative speed of the biblical Joseph story varies considerably in its different parts. Central points can be located in the slow passages of the dialogues and some other scenes. The above examples furthermore demonstrate to what extent the figure of Joseph dominates the narrative. Whether as the subject or the object of the action, he usually is the focus of the scenes. He is central in the story's climaxes.

Before examining the biblical characterisation of the figure, I shall complete the analysis of narrative time by a study of this aspect in the three interpretations.

The narrative Rhythm of the Interpretations

It is vital for a proper evaluation of the early exegetes to appreciate whether they adopted the original setting of the Joseph story or whether they changed its focus. Since the narrative is relatively long and diverse there are numerous ways to select the material or to devote large amounts of narrative time to particular aspects of it. Consequently, each exegete may be characterized by his attitude towards the original narrative rhythm.

The graph below depicts the relation of each interpretation to the original narrative rhythm. Its horizontal axis indicates the verses and chapters of the biblical text;[20] and its vertical axis shows the relation of the ratio of words each interpreter used to the number of

---

[18] A similar, yet less intense climax is reached in *Gen* 43:29, when Joseph sees and recognizes his brother Benjamin; see also *Gen* 45:1 where it is related that Joseph could no longer control his emotions.

[19] *Gen* 42:7 two words for Joseph's estrangement, three for his harsh address to the brothers, etc.

[20] Each verse is represented by one millimeter or one square on the graph paper which I originally used for the drawing.

words of the respective item in the *Vorlage*. Consequently, increasingly high numbers on the vertical axis[21] reflect an increasing number of words to represent a biblical unit.[22] The interpretation equals quantitatively the original if the value on the graph is one.

For greater perspicuity the results are presented in form of a histogram, where the values between low points (i.e. zero-representation) are sketched as averages covering several units.[23]

This graph produces highly interesting results. The most immediate conclusion is that all interpreters decelerate the fast pace of the biblical narrative by adding material to the original. But this general tendency is implemented by each interpreter in his own way and these differ at the various points of the narrative. In this way the distinct interests of each interpreter emerge and it is clear that no structure of one paraphrase is identical to the other. A closer examination of the graph will yield further insights into structural characteristics of the interpretations.

The earliest of the interpreters in question, Philo, is characterized by an overall strong interest in the opening chapters and the later passages which relate Joseph's career in Egypt. On these points he enhances the biblical climaxes by inserting additional material. On the other hand, he neglects long episodes in the latter parts of the biblical narrative, omitting such items as the blessings of Jacob[24]

---

[21] Please note that for reasons of practical necessity I have chosen to represent the extraordinarily high numbers in "abbreviated" form (indicated in each case by a slash in the column). Similarly, the range between zero and five are represented in greater detail than the following numbers. This has lead to a calculated "distortion" of the picture.

[22] I have chosen these units according to criteria of syntax and content. They do, however, not extend the limit of one verse. For valuable general remarks on this verbal level of structure in biblical narrative, see: S. Bar-Efrat, *Some Observations on the Analysis of Structure in Biblical Narrative*, *VT* 30/1980, pp. 154–73, especially pp. 157–58.

[23] The approximate nature of this graph should not be neglected. It naturally cannot take into account the possible use of Hebrew versus Greek bible (or Targum?) at different points in Philo's or Josephus's interpretations. But since the Septuagintal translation of *Gen* is highly literal (See: E. Tov, *The Septuagint*, in: *Mikra*, ed. M.J. Mulder, Assen/Philadelphia 1988, pp. 161–88; especially pp. 169–73) deviation of this sort would not change the outline of the graph. Another aspect which cannot be reflected in the graph is the order of the items. There is no indication whether the rendering of a biblical unit is to be found in a parallel sequence to the original. Changes of this sort can substantially manipulate the narrative and will be analysed in the chapters on each interpreter.

[24] Including the details of Jacob's blessing of Joseph's sons Ephraim and Menasse, related in *Gen* 48.

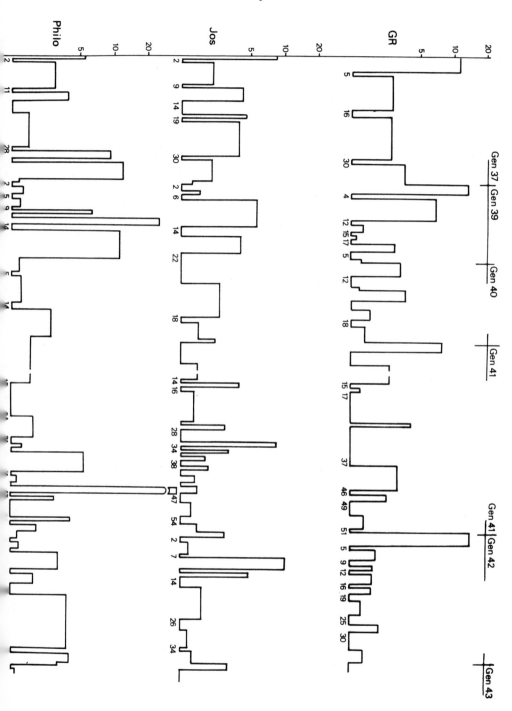

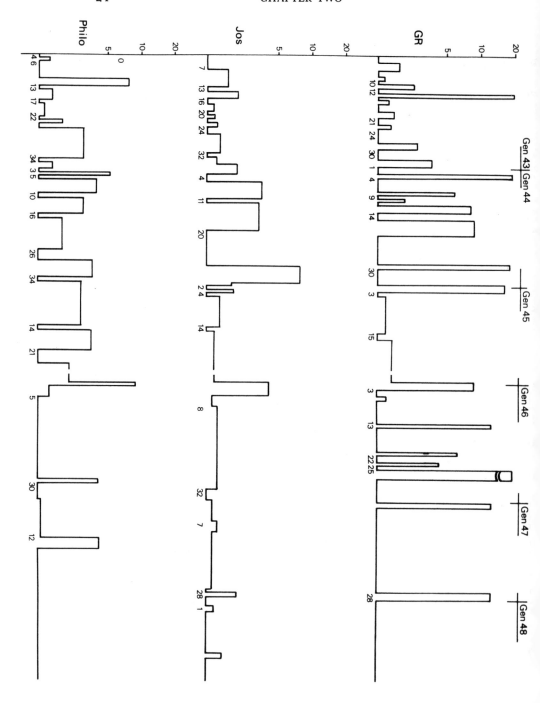

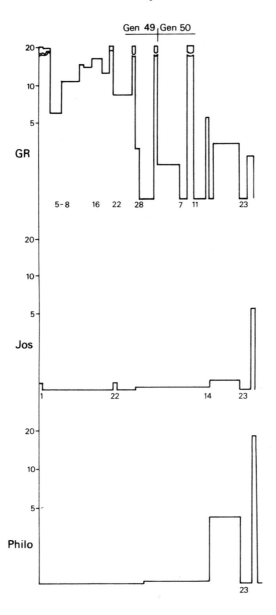

and details of the family's arrival in Egypt. It is furthermore remarkable that he does not mention, for example, Joseph's ill report about
his brothers (*Gen* 37:2) or Jacob's gift to him (*Gen* 37:3). We may furthermore gather from the graph that Philo chooses particular points
in the earlier parts of the narrative where he stops to insert vast
amounts of material. These do not usually correspond to the focal
points of the *Vorlage* but signify the end of contextual components or
phases. On the whole, Philo emerges as the author of the ''slowest''
version of the Joseph story. We shall see how he achieves this in
chapter III.

Josephus parallels Philo's interest in the opening chapters and his
neglect of significant items in *Gen* 37:2 – 3. He also expands the passages on Joseph's career, particularly those dealing with dream interpretation. Like Philo he decelerates the narrative at the point of
the brothers' encounter in Egypt. Yet in proportion to his overall interpretation, Josephus gives this episode far more emphasis than
both the biblical narrator and Philo. Josephus furthermore increases
the narrative speed towards the end and passes over numerous items
in the closing chapters. On the whole, he emerges as the interpreter
who remains closest to the structure of the *Vorlage*. We shall have to
examine more carefully whether this relative similarity in form is
also corroborated by faithfulness in contents.

The structure of the midrashic interpretation is most variegated.[25] Whereas a steady interest is shown at the beginning, the contributions become increasingly more discontinued but longer in
each case. *GR* shares the other exegetes' focus on Joseph's encounter
with Potiphar's wife and embellishes it accordingly. But by contrast
to them, the first focal point in the biblical narrative, i.e., Joseph's
ill report, is also highlighted. In further contrast to Philo's and
Josephus's narrative intuition. *GR* does not deal at length with the
climax of the brothers' encounter. Instead of decelerating the speed,
it passes quickly over this episode. It is moreover characteristic of the
Midrash that it highlights narrative points which relate to the nation's fate, such as the family's voyage to Egypt (*Gen* 42:1 – 60) and
the various blessings. Also the few references to the Divine are dwelt

---

[25] See also Y. Frankel's study on: הזמן ועיצובו בסיפורי האגדה, in: *Studies in Aggadah, Targum and Jewish Liturgy, op cit.*, pp. 133–52, where he analyses four independent, midrashic stories and shows the various relations of narrated and narrative time in them.

upon at exceptional length. The figure of Joseph in *GR* needs therefore to be evaluated within the framework of this theological orientation.

The Characterisation of Joseph

Biblical characters are presented in a different way than the modern reader used to novels would expect.[26] In fact, few direct descriptions of personality, individual looks or detailed expositions of inner life are to be found.[27] On the other hand, indirect means of characterisation are used with great sophistication; and usually every detail of the text is intended to contribute to the portrait. It is in this context that I shall examine the means by which the biblical figure of Joseph is characterised.

After a brief prelude,[28] Joseph is immediately introduced in *Gen* 37:2. The reader initially learns about his age and his occupation. He is then informed that the protagonist is a youth[29] with his brothers who are, it is emphasized, the sons of the maids. In this way the biblical narrator places Joseph within the prolonged rivalries of Jacob's wives. He thus alludes to further tensions among the offspring.[30]

---

[26] Compare especially: Th. Mann, *Joseph und seine Brüder*, Fischer Verlag.

[27] See also: J. Zakovitz, סיפור במקרא, מימד נוסף להערכתהבסיפור הדמויותבסיפור במקראי, *Tarbiz* 54/1985, pp. 65–76; S. Bar-Efrat, *op. cit.*, pp. 75–88; R. Alter, *op. cit.*, pp. 114–30, idem, סצנותדפוס במקרא וחשיבותה של הקונוונציה, *HaSifrut* 27/1978, pp. 7–14; A. Berlin, *op. cit.*, p. 23 and pp. 33–34; R. Scholes/R. Kellog, *The Nature of Narrative*, Oxford 1966, pp. 160–206, focusing on the tension between action and inner life, the authors approach the subject from a more historical perspective. This intention is, however, not executed with a sensitive and sympathetic understanding of "primitive narrative" (p. 166) and non-Christian literature of antiquity (pp. 181–85) which lack, according to them, the inner life and the psychological development of character (which are valued most, p. 171); Cf. also: B. Hochman, *Character in Literature*, Cornell University Press 1985.

[28] Cf. G. Josipovici, *Joseph and Biblical Revelation*, *Salmagundi* 66/1985, p. 123, who overly stresses the fact that the Joseph story is embedded in the family history.

[29] The usage of the term נער in II*Kg* 5:20 might also suggest a different nuance of meaning, i.e., that Joseph stood in an ancillary position to his brothers. Ibn Ezra, מקראות גדולות, *ad. loc.*, interprets similarly that Joseph was young and thus served them; A. Weiser (1976, I אבן עזרא פירושי התורה, U. Simon's critical review, *Kiriat Sefer* 51/תשל"ו, pp. 646–58) paraphrases Ibn Ezra's exegesis and locates its inspiration in *Ex* 33:11. Cf. also M. Steif, *Zur Bedeutung von* נער *in der Bibel*, *MGWJ* N.F. 37/1929, pp. 315–18, mistakenly regards it as a "Vorzugstellung".

[30] J. Wellhausen, *op. cit.*, was the first of the modern text-critical scholars to consider this information altogether superfluous. But this conclusion evidently overlooks the function of the item in the narrative structure.

The above characterisation is marked by an external focalisation from without. The narrator describes the situation from his standpoint and refrains from disclosing anything personal about the figure. In the subsequent passage, however, the reader receives his first impression of Joseph as an individual. Here, the description of the character approaches a focalisation from within.[31]

The biblical narrator draws the figure primarily by reference to his behaviour, namely that Joseph brought an ill report[32] about the brothers to his father. The details of these accusations are not elaborated.[33] The reader furthermore does not learn whether they were justified or whether they circulated independently.[34] The narrator's intention is nevertheless clearly expressed in the epithet רעה: he presents Joseph as a person whose prime objective it is to embarrass his brothers.[35] The accuracy of the accusations used for this purpose is only of secondary importance to both Joseph and the narrator.

The first piece of individual characterisation thus reflects negatively on Joseph.[36] The brothers are presumably unaware of what

---

[31] See also: A. Berlin, *op. cit.*, p. 48, she unfortunately does not deal with this important passage but holds that the first three verses "open with Jacob in focus".

[32] Y. Ewen, *op. cit.*, pp. 68–80, distinguishes between customary and extraordinary actions which each contribute to the outline of the character. In the case of *Gen* 37:2 it is impossible to determine the frequency of Joseph's action. It remains nevertheless clear that, whether or not it was a one-time-event, the biblical narrator considered it "characteristic" of Joseph. For a discussion of the linguistic aspects of the term, see: R. Gordis, *The Text and the Meaning of Hosea 14:3, VT* 5/1955, p. 21.

[33] See for example also: G. v. Rad, *op. cit.*, p. 345. Medieval exegetes dealt in different ways with this problem. Thus, Rashi (*ad. loc.*) explains the passage with midrashic material; Ibn Ezra (*ad. loc.*) quotes Rashi's interpretation and typically rejects it with reference to the *Vorlage*; and according to D. Kimhi's original conjecture (ed. קמלהר, Jerusalem 1970, *ad. loc.*), Joseph claimed that his brothers hated him and thus solicited his father's sympathy and help.

[34] For a history of exegesis on this issue, consider also the following: The Ramban stresses that Joseph slandered merely the maids' sons but provoked also the others' dislike by Jacob's favoritism (ed. שעועל, Jerusalem תשי״ט). This argument renders the independent circulation of these reports more likely. In modernity, also B. Jacob, *op. cit.*, p. 695, and C. Westermann, *op. cit.*, p. 21, assume this to be the case.

[35] Whereas the medieval interpreters tend to highlight Joseph's vicious intention, J. Horovitz, *op. cit.*, p. 35, suggests unconvincingly that he hoped to assist his father in their education; see also: L. Ruppert, *op. cit.*, p. 31, who points to the significant ambiguity in the text.

[36] The importance of this fact has already been pointed out by A. Berlin, *op. cit.*, p. 48, and M. Sternberg, *op. cit.*, p. 98–99. For a general discussion, see: J. Licht, *op. cit.*, pp. 9–23, who defines this realism of characterisation as one of the typical aspects of biblical narrative; E. Auerbach, *op. cit.*, pp. 14–23, where he con-

he has done.[37] But the reader's image of Joseph is shaped by it and he consequently anticipates complications in the family relations. This premonition is further strengthened in the following scene (*Gen* 37:3), in which Joseph is merely the object of the action.[38] The view of him from Jacob's[39] perspective (love,[40] coat[41]) accentuates the protagonist's increasing isolation.[42]

The following scene provides the story's central theme[43] in the form of Joseph's two dreams[44] and his family's reactions to them (*Gen* 37:5 – 11). The reader is informed of Joseph's possible destiny[45]

---

trasts the aspect of realism in patriarchal stories to Homeric mythology. Cf. also: *The Dictionary of the Bible II*, N.Y. 1911, p. 770, mistakenly postulates an idealisation of the biblical figure.

[37] By contrast, A. Kuenen, *op. cit.*, p. 328, conjectures that the brothers' knowledge of Joseph's defamations stimulated their hatred towards him.

[38] Consider in this context also that the reason for Jacob's love is, according to the bible, not a specific trait of Joseph but the circumstance of his late birth. The expression בן זקונים has stimulated numerous speculations and few exegetes were able, like Ibn Ezra (*ad. loc.*) to take it at face value. The Ramban, for example, pointed to the insignificant age gap between the sons; and he conjectured that the term indicates Joseph's service to Jacob in the latter's old age (*ad. loc.*).

[39] For a summary of the research on the inconsistent biblical use of "Jacob" and "Israel", see: C. Westermann, *op. cit.*, pp. 127 – 29.

[40] For the biblical description of Jacob's loving relation with Rachel and the resulting special position of Joseph, see: *Gen* 29 – 30 and 35:24.

[41] For a good discussion of the term כתונת פסים see: E.A. Speiser, *Genesis, The Anchor Bible*, Vol. I, N.Y. 1964, pp. 289 – 90. The extravagance of this gift may further be gathered from II*Sam* 13:18 where such a coat is mentioned as the garb of the royal princesses.

[42] See also: M. Weiss, *Einiges über die Bauformen des Erzählens in der Bibel*, VT 13/1963, p. 467, who discusses the narrative function of Jacob's behaviour. For criticism of the paternal favouritism, see among others: D. Kimhi (*ad. loc.*) and C. Westermann, *Studien zur Vätergeschichte, Verheissungen an die Väter*, Göttingen 1976, p. 38.

[43] Traditional text-critical scholarship nevertheless regards this passage as a separate layer, see for example: H. Gunkel, *op. cit.*, p. 400ff. By contrast, G.v.Rad, *op. cit.*, pp. 346 – 47, tends to regard this and the previous scene as a coherent picture which reflects a complex life-situation.

[44] E.L. Ehrlich, Die Träume im Alten Testament, *BZAW* Berlin 1953, p. 58, defines this pair of dreams as symbolical in the sense that their images represent humans. M. Dobschani, החלומות בסיפור יוסף, *Beit Mikra* 21/1964, pp. 557 – 65. For the general biblical background, see: חלום, *EB* vol. III, cols. 143 – 52; I. Mendelsohn, *Dream, IDB* vol. I, pp. 868 – 69; E.R. Dodds, *The Greeks and the Irrational*, United California Press 1951, pp. 102 – 35; J. Trachtenbrg, *Jewish Magic and Superstition*, New York 1987, pp. 203 – 48.

[45] By contrast both to the patriarchs' direct revelations and to some dreams (such as Abimelech's, *Gen* 20:6) the divine background of Joseph's dreams is only indirectly assumed, see also: B. Jacob, *op. cit.*, p. 698; E.L. Ehrlich, *op. cit.*, p. 61; and Westermann, *op. cit.*, p. 28. Consistent with his dominant interest in theology

and of his brothers' objections.[46] In this way he becomes curious,
like Jacob,[47] as to whether these aspirations of Joseph will be fulfilled.

In addition to being the point of interest, Joseph is presented here
as an acting subject. Although his reasons for announcing the
dreams are not specified, his behaviour discloses significant character traits.[48] The biblical narrator in fact highlights Joseph's self-
assurance through his speech.[49] Instead of directly reporting his visions,[50] Joseph is presented as addressing his brothers with an extra
command: "Listen now!". These words indicate an alarming
degree of insensitivity to their previous open hostility. On the basis
of this evidence Joseph must be judged frivolous,[51] if not ill-mean-
ing.[52]

In the remaining part of *Gen* 37 only limited indications of
Joseph's character are to be found. This is partly the case because
most scenes are clearly focalised on his brothers.[53] In addition, the
evidence of him as acting subject needs to be evaluated carefully in
terms of its relevance to establish the figure's distinct traits.

In *Gen* 37:13 the reader learns that Joseph readily accepts his
father's request to enquire about his brothers. This willingness is
perhaps remarkable in view of the family tensions.[54] The narrator

---

L. Ruppert, *op. cit.*, overvalued divine providence also at this point.

[46] Consider also: C. Westermann, *op.cit.*, p. 12 and p. 29. Based on a striking
insensitivity to the biblical context, he claims that the brothers' response refers to
political theories on the best governent.

[47] On the narrative function of Jacob's reaction, see also A. Berlin, *op. cit.*, p.
49, and E.L. Ehrlich, *op. cit.*, p. 62. On the complex shades of meaning of the verb
נער see: A.A. Mac-Intosh, *A Consideration of Hebrew ga'ar*, *VT* 19/1969), especially
p. 474.

[48] Cf. also: A. Berlin, *op. cit.*, p. 48–49, who concentrates perhaps too exclusively on the family's reaction and thus disregards this dimension of Joseph.

[49] For a treatment of speech as a means of characterisation in fiction, see: Y.
Ewen, *op. cit.*, pp. 80–89; and especially S. Bar-Efrat, *op. cit.*, pp. 89–99, who
points out that not all categories of literary analysis on this subject are applicable
to the biblical narrative; foremost among them is the individual, socially or ethni-
cally coloured style of speech.

[50] As for example the cup-bearer does in *Gen* 40:9–11.

[51] Similarly, B. Jacob, *op. cit.*, p. 699, and C. Westermann, *op. cit.*, p. 29–30,
who argued that Joseph himself was overwhelmed by his youthful enthusiasm.

[52] In this vein D. Kimhi (*ad.loc.*) for example interpreted that Joseph wished
again to hurt his brothers.

[53] See also: A. Berlin, *op. cit.*, pp. 49–50.

[54] This point has been emphasised by such exegetes as Rashi (*ad.loc.*); he draws
on *GR* 1016.

stresses this aspect by the expression "here I am" which is otherwise used of man's response to a Divine command (e.g. *Gen* 22). This episode provides the first clearly positive, though not extraordinary, evidence about the protagonist. It ushers in the subsequent developments by inviting the reader's sympathy towards Joseph.

In the following verses (*Gen* 37:14–17) the reader accompanies Joseph in his search for his brothers.[55] The narrator presents him as somewhat helpless and dependent on foreign assistance. In view of the whole story it is, however, doubtful to what extent this scene is characteristic of Joseph. In most other instances he appears anything but "lost". It seems that the function of this interlude is rather to create a clear separation between the events at home and those outside in a hostile environment.[56]

During the episode of the brothers' plot[57] and the selling of Joseph,[58] the reader learns remarkably little about the protagonist. The narrator in fact refrains completely from describing Joseph's emotional reactions at this point.[59] Het presumably considers Joseph's outburst as a too natural behaviour to deserve mention for its own sake.

---

[55] The starting point of Joseph's journey, "from the valley of Hebron", is problematic; for a discussion of this term and its incompatibility with other biblical evidence, see also: A. Kuenen, *op. cit.*, p. 231, and H. Gunkel, *op. cit.*, p. 406, who both regard the term as a later addition to the text, belonging to a layer in which Hebron is especially emphasized.

[56] This incident also highlights Divine providence, as in the case of Hagar after she has been expelled by Sarah and wanders about in the desert (*Gen* 16 and 21).

[57] On the moral aspects of the plot see: K. Koch, *Der Spruch 'Sein Blut bleibe auf seinem Haupt' und die israelitische Auffassung vom vergossenen Blut*, VT 12/1962, pp. 396–416, especially p. 389 and p. 407; R. Burgmeister, *Das Streben nach Gewinn: des Volkes A'von*, ZAW 81/1969, pp. 93–97. For various suggestions to understand the textual problems revolving around Reuben's/Judah's admonitions, see: L. Ruppert, *op. cit.*, p. 37ff; A. Berlin, *op. cit.*, pp. 119–21; J. Horovitz, *op. cit.*, pp. 26–27; D.B. Redford, *op. cit.*, pp. 132–42, mistakenly idealizes Reuben as the "good brother" on which Judah's speech was alledgedly modelled; C. Westerman, *op. cit.*, pp. 34–35, advances far-fetched political "explanations". For a discussion of whether the brothers themselves delivered the coat to Jacob, see also: L. Ruppert, *op. cit.*, p. 39.

[58] For a classical examination of the identity of the Midianites/Ismaelites see: H. Gunkel, *op. cit.*, pp. 408–10; on the identity of Potiphar, see also: פוטיפר, *EB* vol. VI, cols. 440–41; J. Wellhausen, *op. cit.*, p. 54; B. Jacob, *op. cit.*, p. 709; on the identity of the sellers see also: Z. Werblowsky, *Stealing the Word*, VT 6/1956, especially pp. 105–06.

[59] Significantly, in *Gen* 42:21 the brothers, overcome by guilt, confess to having

Finally, the question may be raised whether the fact that Joseph approaches his brothers with his coat on (*Gen* 37:23) is intended as an indication of his personality. It might in fact testify to his provocative spirit. Such conjectures, however, ignore the context. Since the whole episode is related from the brothers' point of view, the narrator is likely to have used the motive of the coat as an explanation of *their* emotions and behaviour.

Chapter thirty-nine of *Genesis* tends to be more directly focalised on Joseph.[60] Yet its opening contributes remarkably little to the picture of his individual character. It in fact emerges that the two important pieces of information, namely his success in Potiphar's house (vs 2 – 6) and his beauty (vs 6) serve other narrative functions.

Joseph's properity[61] is thus a welcome opportunity to mention Divine providence in political and professional life.[62] Instead of describing Joseph's personality as reflected in his career,[63] the narrator provides a witness to God in His actions on earth. One important conclusion may nevertheless be drawn with regard to the protagonist. He is considered sufficiently important by the narrator to be presented as a type who deserves God's explicit protection.

Also Joseph's beauty remains an unspecified topos;[64] and serves to promote the action of the story.[65] Together with the ambiguous

---

been aware of Joseph's desperate implorations from the pit. See also: M. Weiss, *Weiteres über die Bauformen des Erzählens in der Bibel, Biblica* 46/1965, pp. 102 – 03, who points out how strongly the biblical style in *Gen* 37 contradicts modern expectations; Y. Ewen, *op. cit.*, p. 184, on the narrative function of retrospections.

[60] See also: A. Berlin, *op. cit.*, p. 76.

[61] For a lexicographical discussion of the root 'zlh', see: H. Tawil, *Hebrew hzlh/zlh, Akkadian eseru/susuru: a lexicographical note, JBL* 95/1976, especially p. 407.

[62] This is a rather popular motive, see for example: *Gen* 26:24 – 28; 30:27 or also I*Sam* 18:12. Compare D. Kimhi, *ad. loc.*, who stresses in his interpretation that thanks to his talents Joseph was successful in whatever he did; in modernity also G.v.Rad, *op. cit.*, pp. 358 – 59, argues that the reference of God is ''only of mediate significance here'' and that the narrator is concerned ''to draw a sharply defined picture of Joseph''.

[63] Compare, for example, the description of Jacob's cleverness in Laban's household, *Gen* 30:29 – 40.

[64] As mentioned above, this is typical of biblical narrative; note that Joseph's beauty is inherited and that his mother is described in the same terms in *Gen* 29:17. See also J. Kugel, *op. cit.*, p. 78, in view of later Midrashic interpretations, he emphasizes the dynamic nature of the verb ויהי, suggesting that Joseph in fact consciously *became* handsome.

[65] Inspired by midrashic exegesis, numerous medieval interpreters were sensitive to this causative connection which they, however, understood in moral and

reference to the bread,[66] this feature provides a basis for the subsequent events. It is for this reason that the narrator inserts it somewhat abruptly at this point.

Joseph's encounter with Potiphar's wife (*Gen* 39:7–20) is divided into two distinct episodes. The narrator highlights Joseph's personality in both of these challenges. But whereas he characterizes him in the first through his speech, he describes him in the second by reference to his action.

In vs 8–9 the reasons for Joseph's refusal to sleep with the woman are specified. In his immediate response, he insists on his responsibility towards his master who, so he reminds her, has been particularly benevolent towards him. It is conceivable that the narrator attributed this argument to Joseph first for reasons of the narrative context. The protagonist is presented in a situation where he is attempting to change the mind of Potiphar's wife. He therefore has to advance arguments which are most likely to convince her.[67] Under these circumstances a reference to her husband is more likely to be effective than the subsequently advanced religious argument. If this is the case, the biblical Joseph is depicted as exceptionally sharp. On the other hand, there is no reason to assume that these universalistic-moral considerations did not naturally come to Joseph's mind first.[68] In fact, the hasty way in which Joseph enumerates the

---

theological terms, see for example: Rashi, D. Kimhi and Ramban (*ad. loc*).

[66] For a good summary of the arguments in support of an erotic allusion in *Gen* 39:6, see L. Ruppert, *op. cit.*, pp. 46–47; J. Kugel, *op. cit.*, p. 74; E.A. Speiser, *op. cit.*, p. 303, who suggests that the reference is "possibly an allusion to Egyptian dietary taboos"; and C. Westermann, *op. cit.*, p. 60, who holds that the bread stands *pars pro toto* for private affairs in general. This conflict of opinions is to be found already in medieval exegesis, where Ibn Ezra argued against Rashi that the verse simply refers to the different dietary customs of the two peoples (*ad. loc.*).

[67] Cf. J. Kugel, *op. cit.*, p. 99. He regards the detailed enumeration of Joseph's reasons as an indication of some hesitation on the part of Joseph and paraphrases his speech: "Well, perhaps ... after all, I am not accountable to anyone else in the house, and besides, Potiphar did tell me that everything was given over to me ... though he did, come to think of it, exclude you, since you are after all his wife, but besides to do such a thing would be a terrible sin against God". It seems, however, that Joseph's elaborate style is in keeping with his attempt at convincing Potiphar's wife. It is moreover likely that the narrator, at least partly, expresses in this direct way his own ideals.

[68] It is certainly not the narrator's intention to contrast Israelite moral standards with Egyptian culture, as H. Gunkel assumed (*op. cit.*, p. 423). See also the Ramban (*ad. loc.*): explaining the repeated term "his master's wife", he

proofs of Potiphar's confidence betray a spontaneous excitement
and genuine nervousness. We may furthermore trust that the biblical narrator would have indicated if Joseph were not naturally expressing his devotion to his master.[69] It is also important not to
overestimate the sequence of the arguments. The biblical narrator
evidently had to present one after the other, but he presumably per-
ceived of them also as two aspects of the same concept. In his view,
the severity of the ethical transgression consisted also in its being an
offence against God.

Subsequently, Joseph submits to the woman his objections on religious grounds.[70] This is the first time that the biblical narrator in-
timates a consciousness of God on the part of the protagonist. At this
stage the reader meets a person who has significantly matured since
his youth when he treated his family recklessly. Joseph has now become an exemplary figure with regard to religious morals.[71]

The second episode is provoked by Joseph's entering the house
and rapidly terminated by his escape from there (*Gen* 39:11 – 12).
Whereas he can only be praised for his unblemished reaction to the
approach of Potiphar's wife,[72] his initial behaviour is less transparent. This uncertainty derives from the unusual phrase כהיום הזה
and from an ambiguity in the narrative perspective.

The expression כהיום הזה has been understood either as a regular[73] or a special day.[74] In the former case, the expression would

---

sugggests the social gap between the two as a central issue of the confrontation and
thus accentuates Joseph's incorruptability.

[69] Compare for example his sophisticated description of the machinations of
Potiphar's wife (*Gen* 39:13 – 19).

[70] For a background on this issue in the bible, see: O.J. Baab, *Adultery*, *IDB* I
1962, p. 51; idem, *Marriage*, *IDB* III 1962, pp. 279–87.

[71] This is further established by the emphasis on Joseph's continuous resistance
in the subsequent verse. For a discussion of G.v.Rad's theory of wisdom motives
in this scene (*Josephgeschichte und ältere Chokma*, *SVT* 1/1953, pp. 120–127), see:
L. Ruppert, *op. cit.*, pp. 57–58. Cf. R. Scholes/R. Kellog, *op. cit.*, p. 176, who argue mistakenly that the invocation of religious motives and supernatural forces is
an unsophisticated substitute for psychology in "primitive literature".

[72] The narrator stresses Joseph's determination by the use of two verbs for his
quick exit. For a discussion of repetition as a stylistic technique, see: J. Muilenberg,
A Study in Hebrew Rhetoric: Repetition and Style, *STV* 1/1953, pp. 97–111.

[73] Thus, E.A. Speiser, *op. cit.*, p. 301, translates: "on one such day, when
...". For the most recent analysis, see: C. Westermann, *op. cit.*, pp. 54–55; thus
interpreted also medieval exegetes such as Ibn Ezra and D. Kimhi (*ad. loc.*).

[74] E. Kautzsch, *Gesenius' Hebrew Grammar* (edited and enlarged), 18th English
edition, Oxford 1985, p. 408; thus also Rashi (*ad. loc.*).

merely serve as a general introduction. In the latter, it suggests extraordinary circumstances, possibly pertaining also to Potiphar's wife, of which Joseph might have known. In the first instance the narrative perspective is undoubtedly authorial, whereas in the second it might also reflect Joseph's point of view.

After the narrator has related that Joseph returned to do his work[75] he adds that the house was in fact empty. The conjunction "ו" which is used here can function as a simple connective or also as an *explanativum*.[76] As a result, the narrative perspective of the verse is ambiguous. It is thus possible to take the adjunct as an authorial description of the situation which Joseph faced upon arrival. On the other hand, if the supplement is understood as an interpretation of the preceding action, it reflects Joseph's point of view and thus his objective. It is moreover significant that the tense changes in this verse from a narrative past ("ויבא") to the present ("ואין"), suggesting that the narrator might actually be quoting Joseph's thoughts.[77]

For the above reasons the reader can, on the basis of *Gen* 39:11, visualise the figure of Joseph in distinctly different ways. The imagination is, however, limited by the overall context. One must not overlook that the biblical narrator emphasizes Joseph's innocence both before and after this passage. A kind reading of some textual ambiguities seems therefore appropriate.

The next positive evidence of Joseph's character[78] is provided in *Gen* 40 and illuminates his *Weltanschauung*. The figure is depicted in relation to both the human world and the Divine realm. The narrator furthermore adumbrates the possible tension between these two dimensions.

---

[75] In the Tora the term מלאכה is unanimously used for work in the literal sense, in the halachic passages frequently with reference to Shabbat observance and the temple, see: A. Ewen-Shoshan, קונקורדנציה חדשה, Jerusalem 1980, vol. II, pp. 659–60; Ibn Ezra thus follows the narrator's intention by pointing to Joseph's administrative work and in expressing reservations about midrashic expansions, such as used by Rashi (*ad. loc.*).

[76] See: E. Kautzsch, *op. cit.*, p. 483; L. Koehler/W. Baumgartner, *Lexicon in Veteris Testamenti Libros*, Leiden 1985, pp. 244–45.

[77] On forms of quoting literary characters' thoughts, see especially: D. Cohn, *Transparent Minds, Narrative Modes for Presenting Consciousness in Fiction*, Princeton 1978, pp. 58–98.

[78] Joseph's point of view on the defamations of Potiphar's wife and on his own imprisonment is not even alluded to by the narrator. On the technique and narrative value of the woman's repeated speech, see especially: M. Sternberg, *op. cit.*, pp.

Joseph is primarily presented as a type who, consistent with later wisdom literature, is able to solve riddles in the form of dreams.[79] In *Gen* 40:8 he explicitly attributes this ability to Divine inspiration and insists that "interpretations belong to God". Joseph's consciousness of God's omnipresence is further developed in *Gen* 45:5–8 where he makes a more comprehensive statement which provides the overall theme of the narrative.[80] It emerges from this concurrence of the story's theme and Joseph's personal convictions that the narrator in fact uses this figure to express his own ideas. However, this intellectual aspect is not overemphasized and the narrator places it well within the context of the character's social talents.

Joseph's sensitivity to human and political realities, which he put to ill use in his youth, is now shown in fuller maturity. The narrator describes in *Gen* 40:6–7 how Joseph is so attentive to his fellow prisoners that their faces immediately betrayed to him a certain anxiety. The narrator also here relates sympathetically how Joseph enquires about the reasons for their state of mind.

In *Gen* 40:14–15 the reader learns that Joseph asks the butler to return him a favour and to promote his case he is in a better position. This behaviour testifies again to Joseph's developed sense for wordly affairs. On this occasion, however, the narrator takes a more critical distance to this trait. Thus, he highlights in *Gen* 40:23 that the butler did not fulfil Joseph's expectations. By way of repetition he further adumbrates that Joseph had been too involved in the human realm.[81]

מבנה החזרה בסיפור המקרא: אסטראטגיות של עודפות אינפורמאציונית, idem ;423–27
Hasifrut 25/1977, pp. 109–50; and also: B. Jacob, *op. cit.*, pp. 730–31; H. Gunkel, *op. cit.*, p. 425; J. Licht, *op. cit.*, p. 87 and p. 104, mistakenly emphasises the lack of "formal precision in these repetitions" which, according to him, create a "wild" effect. For a discussion of Potiphar's reaction and surprisingly lenient punishment, see also: A. Kuenen, *op. cit.*, p. 234; H. Gunkel, *op. cit.*, p. 426; L. Ruppert, *op. cit.*, p. 55; who suggest that he doubted the trustworthyness of his wife's accusations.

[79] See e.g. *Dan* 2–6 and *The Story of Ahikar*; for the general background also: S. Niditch/R. Doran, *The Success Story of the Wise Courtier; A Formal Approach*, JBL 96/1977, pp. 179–93, where the relevant texts are compared, especially pp. 185–87; W. Schmitt, *Die Hintergründe der neuesten Pentateuchkritik und der literarische Befund der Josephsgeschichte in Genesis 37–50*, ZAW 97/1985, especially p. 174ff. For a discussion of the expression "each according to the interpretation of his dream", see: E.L. Ehrlich, *op. cit.*, pp. 66–71; I. Rabinowits, "Pesher/Pittaron". Its Biblical Meaning and its Significance in the Qumran Literature, *R.Q.* 8/1973, pp. 219–32.

[80] For a discussion of this motive in general, see: I.L. Seeligmann, *Menschliches Heldentum und göttliche Hilfe*, Theologische Zeitschrift 19/1963, pp. 385–411.

[81] Ibn Ezra shows a fine awareness of this point; and Rashi further expands the

These characteristics of Joseph's personality come into full light
in the subsequent chapters of *Genesis*. Under more dramatic
circumstances[82] he succeeds in interpreting the dreams[83] of
Pharaoh himself (*Gen* 41:15–36)[84] and again attributes this ability
to God (*Gen* 41:26). At this stage, Joseph has further opportunity to
demonstrate his administrative genius for which he is quickly re-
warded. Both the insignia of Egyptian royalty (vss 42–45)[85] and
the designation ''a wise and clever man'' (vs 33)[86] attest Joseph's
political competence.

The last important facet of Joseph's character is fashioned by his
attitude towards his brothers in Egypt. His posture towards them is
apparent already in their first encounter at the corn market (*Gen*
42:6–9).

The narrator introduces this scene by a conspicuous reference to
Joseph's superiority in status. He then briefly stops to consider
Joseph's viewpoint and relates that he saw and recognized his
brothers. This insight into the protagonist's mind is necessary for
the reader to appreciate the subsequent, authorial description of his
outward behaviour. Without further explanations Joseph is reported to have made himself a stranger[87] and to have spoken harshly to

---

delicate allusion in the text to a general exhortation (*ad. loc.*).

[82] For the possibly historical background of the magicians' performance, see: J.
Vergote, *Joseph en Égypte*, Louvain 1959, pp. 80–94.

[83] Consistent with his theological interests, L. Ruppert, *op. cit.*, p. 79, mistakenly stresses the prophetic significance of this interpretation.

[84] For a fine analysis of the relation between the narrator's and Pharaoh's account of his dreams, see: M. Sternberg, *op. cit.*, pp. 394–400; and J. Licht, *op. cit.*,
pp. 75–76. Cf. H. Gunkel, *op. cit.*, p. 436, who was unaware of the significance
of this ''duality'' and concluded mistakenly that it ''only'' served for emphasis. On
the number seven, see: A.S. Kapelrud, *The Number Seven in Ugaritic Texts*, VT
18/1968, pp. 494–99.

[85] For the local coloration of these items, see: J. Vergote, *op. cit.*, pp. 116–34;
and also G.v.Rad, *op. cit.*, pp. 373–74. For a discussion of the expression אברך,
see: *EB* vol. I, cols. 67–8; C. Westermann, *op. cit.*, pp. 98–99.

[86] Note that in later accounts of biblical rulers these are royal attributes, e.g.
I*Kg* 3:12. For a general, albeit too theological discussion of the terms סופר, יועץ, שר
in their biblical wisdom context, see: W. McKane, *Prophets and Wise Men, Studies
in Biblical Theology*, 44/1965, pp. 13–23; G.W. Coats, *The Joseph Story and Ancient
Wisdom*, CBQ 35/1973; E.W. Heaton, *The Joseph Saga, The Expository Times* 59/
1974–48, pp. 134–36.

[87] E.A. Speiser, *op. cit.*, p. 321, translates the term ויתנכר more idiomatically as
''kept his identity from them'', but subsequently acknowledges the more literal
meaning.

them. The fact that while Joseph does recognize them, they fail to
identify him, adds to the suspense of the plot.

The first hint at Joseph's motivation in these dealings is provided
in vs 9. Here, the narrator mentions that Joseph remembers the
dreams of his youth before he continues to interrogate his brothers.[88] But also this indication appears to raise more questions than
it solves since it is possible to consider Joseph's dreams fulfilled by
his brothers' prostration at that moment.[89] It nevertheless seems
that the narrator does not attribute feelings of revenge to Joseph.
Otherwise he would have made him remember his brothers' earlier
brutality against him.

This ambiguity continues to permeate Joseph's attitude towards
his brothers. On the one hand, he imprisons them for three days and
binds Simon "before their eyes" (*Gen* 42:17 – 20), for no reasons obvious to the reader. But on the other hand, Joseph is said to care for
them and to be touched by the sight of them (*Gen* 42:42). These
different strands culminate in the recognition scene in *Gen* 45:1 – 3.
At this stage, the narrator presents Joseph in a very favourable light.
He is described as a delicate and sensitive person who shows consideration for his brothers' feelings. He himself is so excited by the
prospect of re-uniting with his family that his speech comes as an
abrupt surprise to the brothers and overwhelms them. And this ami-
able image is the final and remaining impression which the reader
receives of Joseph's character.[90]

Sparks of Late Biblical and Early Post-Biblical Exegesis

The exegesis of the Joseph story begins in biblical times. Most of
these early references give us a brief summary interpretation of
Joseph and do not relate in detail to the whole story. They are im-

---

[88] As R. Alter, *op. cit.*, pp. 157–76, pointed out, this flash-back in itself is a
rare and remarkable element in biblical characterisation. See also: J. Licht, *op. cit.*,
pp. 80–86, who stresses the dramatic effect of this scene and points to the (subsequent) unconventional emphasis of the emotions; N. Toker, אומנות הגילוי והכיסוי
בסיפורי יוסף ואחיו, Beit Mikra 24/1965, pp. 129–49.

[89] For modern interpretations, see: M. Sternberg, *op. cit.*, pp. 286–88; R.
Alter, *Joseph, op. cit.*, p. 63; B. Jacob, *op. cit.*, pp. 762–66; G. v. Rad, *op. cit.*, pp.
377–78 and pp. 392–94; L. Ruppert, *op. cit.*, pp. 90–91; C. Westermann, *op. cit.*,
p. 113. Medieval exegetes were, on the whole, less intrigued by this issue; but cf.
Ramban (*ad. loc.*) who suggested that Joseph intended to fulfil his dreams by bringing down Benjamin, too.

[90] For the report of Joseph's death and his burial, see: *Gen* 50, *Ex* 13:19 and *Jos*
24:32.

portant indications of intellectual developments which enable us to evaluate better the significance of the later treatments of the complete narrative. In this section I shall discuss some of these fragments of Joseph material, focussing on the Blessing of Moses, *Ps* 105, I*Chron*, the book of *Jubilees*, the *Liber Antiquitatum Biblicarum* Artapanus' account. *Ben Sira*, Matthatias's speech in I*Macc*, and Stephen's speech in *Acts*. Both chronologically and geographically, these notices cover the span between the biblical account, on the one hand, and Philo and *GR* on the other. They are expressed in various languages and they represent different cultural spheres. Due to the limited scope of this work, I shall not be able to introduce in any detail the documents from which the different passages on Joseph are taken. Instead, I shall focus on each writers particular interest in the figure of Joseph and establish what is in each case regarded as his essential feature.

Moses' blessing of Joseph (*Dtn* 33:13 – 17) is obviously modelled on that of Jacob in *Gen* 49:22ff.[91] It expands the former mainly in two respects: it highlights Joseph's fruitfulness and his strength, while generally de-emphasising Judah. At the same time it is his land and his offspring which is the centre of attention.[92] This mention of Joseph is close to the frequent prophetic reference to him as a tribe or as a symbol for the Northern kingdom.[93]

In the Chronicler's paraphrase of Israelite history[94] the subject of Joseph's relation to the other brothers is further developed. It is conjectured in I*Chron* 5:2 that on account of his transgression Reuben's birthright had been transferred to Joseph.[95] The narrator thus

---

[91] See also: S.R. Driver, *A Critical and Exegetical Commentary on Deuteronomy*, 3rd ed. Edinburgh 1902, pp. 385 – 89; A.B. Ehrlich, *Randglossen zur Hebräischen Bibel*, Hildesheim, vol. II, p. 349.

[92] See also: Rashi's commentary *ad. loc.*.

[93] E.g.: *Ez* 37:15 – 23 and see also: R. Smend, *Ezechiel*, Leipzig 1880, pp. 290 – 92 and W. Zimmerli, *Ezekiel*, Neukirchener Verlag 1965, pp. 903 – 13; *Amos* 6:6 and see also: S.R. Driver, *The Books of Joel and Amos*, Cambridge 1915, p. 199 and W.R. Rainey Harper, *Amos and Hosea*, Edinburgh 1910, p. 149; *Obadja* 18 and see also: J.A. Bewer *Obadja*, Edinburgh 1912, p. 30 and H.W. Wolff, *Dekapropheten*, Neukirchener Verlag 1977, vol. III pp. 40 – 46; see also *Num* 13:11 and *Jos* 17:14 – 18 where the division of the land is described in historical terms. Note that in some Psalms the tribe of Joseph/Northern kingdom is viewed in distinctly negative terms, see especially *Ps* 78:67 and the commentaries by F. Delitzsch, *Die Psalmen*, Leipzig 1883, pp. 566 – 67; H.J. Kraus, *Psalmen*, Neukirchener Verlag 1966, vol. I pp. 535 – 48.

[94] For a general background, see: דברי הימים, *EB* vol. II, cols. 596 – 606.

[95] This is presumably the more original version since it is the one translated in

makes explicit some pentateuchal allusions[96] and enhances Joseph's position among Israel.[97] It emerges that those early interpreters who show an interest in the status of Joseph among the tribes, tend to raise his position and to glorify the importance of his offspring.

A completely different concern prompts the interpretation of Joseph in the historiography of *Ps* 105 from approximately the 3rd century BCE.[98] Joseph is here the first patriarch whose history is related in some detail. Consistent with the Psalmist's dominant concerns,[99] Joseph's life is seen in the context of Israel's exile in Egypt. In vs 17–22 the following picture is presented:

> When He summoned a famine on the land and broke every staff of bread, He had sent a man ahead of them,
> Joseph who was sold as a slave, his feet were hurt with fetters, his neck was put in a collar of iron,
> until His promise was fulfilled[100] the word of the Lord tested him (צרפתהו;[101] the king sent and released him, the ruler of the people set him free, he made him lord of his house and ruler of all his possessions to instruct[102] his princes at his pleasure and to teach his elders wisdom.

In this review the Psalmist stresses the underlying theme of the

---

LXX (I*Chron* 5:1 τῷ υἱῷ αὐτοῦ ιωσηφ); the Massoretic text preserves the form לבני יוסף; for a discussion of these textual problems, see: E.L. Curtis, *The Books of Chronicles*, Edinburgh 1910, p. 119; E. Kautzsch, *Die Heilige Schrift des Alten Testaments*, 4th ed. Tübingen 1923, vol. II p. 573.

[96] E.g.: *Gen* 35 and 49:4; perhaps also *Dtn* 21.

[97] See also Rashi's commentary *ad. loc.*, where he equates the birthright with kingship and justifies on these grounds Juda's predominance among the brothers; on the other hand, D. Kimhi, *ad. loc.*, explains that the background to Joseph's reception of the birthright was in fact Jacob's special love for him.

[98] For a general background, see: תהלים, ספר, *EB* vol. VIII, cols. 437–62 and on the subject of historiography in thirteen of the Psalms, see especially cols. 456–59; also J. Hempel, *Psalms, book of*, *IDB* vol. III, pp. 942–58.

[99] See also: S.A. Löwenstamm, מסורת יציאת מצרים והשתלשלותה, Tel Aviv 1965.

[100] Vs 19 reads: עד עת בא דברו. It is discussed among scholars whether the emphasis is here on Joseph's own visions or on God's promise; F. Delitzsch, *op. cit.*, p. 694 assumes the former while M. Dahood, *Psalms*, The Anchor Bible New York 1970, vol. III pp. 56–58, and H.J. Kraus, *op. cit.*, p. 721, conjecture the latter. A similar conflict of opinion is to be found already in medieval exegesis: while Rashi, *ad. loc.*, asserts Divine providence which leads Israel into exile in Egypt, Ibn Ezra, *ad. loc.*, takes דברו as a reference to Joseph's dream interpretation to Pharaoh.

[101] Cf. also H. Graetz, *Kritischer Kommentar zu den Psalmen*, Breslau 1883, vol. II p. 564, where he tries to argue that the meaning here cannot be "geläutert".

[102] See note in the apparatus, *Biblia Hebraica Stuttgartensia*, Stuttgart 1967/77, *ad. loc.*; for further discussion, see: M. Dahood, *op. cit.*, p. 58.

Joseph story in *Gen*[103] as its central message. In addition to understanding the story in terms of Divine providence, he identifies the stages of Joseph's life as trials by God.[104] For this purpose he especially mentions his suffering at the hands of his brothers and in prison.[105] He furthermore enhances Joseph's hardship by providing concrete details of his pain. Thus, whereas the narrator of *Gen* merely relates that Joseph is sold, the Psalmist adds that he is sold into slavery; and while Joseph is "simply" imprisoned according to *Gen*, the Psalmist knows that he was kept in fetters and neck-chains. These embellishments increase Joseph's misery and points enthusiastically to God's trustworthy salvation.

Another characteristic feature of this early interpretation of the Joseph story is its focus on those aspects which relate to Egypt. The protagonist's rise to power is highlighted and his activities at court are described. Joseph's alleged wisdom is particularly noted in this context. Since the terms חכם and זקניו are mentioned in close connection it is not impossible that Joseph's wisdom is exegetically derived from *Gen* 37:3.[106] In any case, the Psalmist significantly expands the royal setting of Joseph's intellectual prosperity. He is in fact presented here as a wise courtier *à la* Solomon.

Among the non-canonical works, the *Book of Jubilees* is of special significance because of its early date (2nd c. BCE) and its heterogeneous character.[107] In this narrative the Joseph material is

---

[103] In *Gen* 45:5 Joseph, after having disclosed his identity, says to his brothers: "Now do not be distressed or angry with yourselves, because you sold me (מכרתם אתי), for God sent me before you to preserve life (למחיה שלחני אלהים לפנ יכם); this theme is expressed in similar terms also in *Gen* 50:20.

[104] Note that in late biblical texts the verb צרף is frequently used in connection with בחן, see e.g.: *Ps* 17:3 and 66:10; *Is* 48:10; *Jer* 9:6; *Zech* 13:9; see also *Dan* 11:35. For a background, see: J. Licht, הניסיון במקרא וביהדות של הבית השני, Jerusalem 1973, pp. 9–29 (analysis of biblical passages where the term נסה occurs) and pp. 40–47.

[105] Note that the advances of Potiphar's wife are not mentioned! It is, however, not surprising that Rashi, *ad. loc.*, applies later interpretations to this passage and mentions the woman in the context of these trials.

[106] Regarding the interpretation of "בן זיקונים" as "wise", see below.

[107] For a background on this document, see especially: Schürer, vol. III pp. 308–18; A. Dillmann, *Das Buch der Jubiläen, Jahrbücher der biblischen Wissenschaft*, Göttingen 3/1951, pp. 72–96; L. Finkelstein, *The Book of Jubilees and Rabbinic Halakha*, *HTR* 16/1923, pp. 39–61; R.H. Charles, *The Book of Jubilees*, London 1902, p. XLVIIIff; J.C. VanderKam, *Textual and Historical Studies in the Book of Jubilees*, Scholars Press 1977, p. 116ff; R. Travers Herford, *Talmud and Apocrypha*, London 1933, p. 229ff.

presented selectively and not in the form of a continuous story. Its most noticeable features are a new chronological framework, its treatment of Joseph and his brothers and its description of the encounter between Joseph and Potiphar's wife.

In accordance with his calendrical interests,[108] the narrator of *Jub* inserts precise dates to Joseph's life.[109] These do not appear to have been exegetically derived from the biblical text[110] and are not preserved in similar tables in later midrashic works.[111] In addition to these idiosyncratic dates, *Jub* associates Jacob's mourning over the loss of Joseph with the institution of the Day of Atonement (*Jub* 34:18 – 19):[112]

> Therefore, it is ordained for the children of Israel that they should be distressed on the tenth of the seventh of the month, on the day when that which made him cry about Joseph reached Jacob his father, so that they atone for themselves thereupon with a young kid on the tenth of the seventh of the month once a year on account of their sins for they had grieved the affection of their father for Joseph his son. And it was ordained on that day that they should be grieved thereon for their sins and for all their transgressions and for all their mistakes so that they cleanse themselves on that day once a year''.

It is common for the narrator of *Jub* to explain the holidays as commemorations of events in the patriarchal history.[113] The impe-

---

[108] For a background, see also: H. Cazelles, *Sur les origines du Calendrier des Jubilées*, Biblica 43/1962; A. Jaubert, *Le Calendrier des Jubilées et la Secte de Qumran. Ses Origines Bibliques*, *VT* 3/1953; A. Baumgarten, הלוח של ספר היובלים והמקרא, Tarbiz 32/1962–63, pp. 317–28.

[109] According to *Jub* 39:14 Joseph spent two years in prison; in *Jub* 46:3 further dates are provided: he was a servant for ten years, spent three (!) in prison and was for eighty ruler over Egypt; together with the seventeen years of his youth in Canaan these amount to the biblical age of a hundredandten, when the patriarch is said to have died.

[110] Cf. for example the chronological conjectures in *ExR* 7:1; there Joseph is said to have stayed in prison for ten years so as to be punished for his treatment of each of the brothers whom he had defamed.

[111] Such as *Seder Olam Rabbah*, ed. B. Ratner, Wilna 1897, p. 11; where the years of imprisonment are said to be twelve. B. Ratner (*ibid.* n29) makes an unconvincing attempt to reconcile this number with the account in *Jub*.

[112] This passage is preceded by a detailed description of Jacob's pain and mourning, see especially *Jub* 34:13. Note that the following translations are my own and I wish to thank Prof. E. Ullendorff for giving me tuition in Ge'ez during the academic year 1986–87.

[113] Thus, the Feast of Weeks is said to commemorate God's covenant with Noah (*Jub* 6:17); and the Feast of Tabernacles allegedly represents Abraham's rejoicing over Isaac's birth (*Jub* 16:29). For a background, see especially: J.B. Segal,

tus for the specific frame for Joseph[114] may be the following: the Day of Atonement is at that time considered a minor holiday and thus appropriate, it would seem, for an association with Joseph. The atmosphere in the biblical scene furthermore resembles that later described in *mYoma* 4:2 and, finally, an analogy may be drawn between the scape-goat and the one slaughtered instead of Joseph.

This interpretation of *Jub* is adumbrated in *tBer* 4:18 and *GR* 1020 where it is emphasized that the brothers' selling of Joseph cannot be atoned for until their death. Except for these, post-biblical interpreters do not seem to have been concerned with this aspect and *Jub* remains an isolated case of exegesis.

Concerning Joseph and his brothers, both the quantity and the nature of the insertions suggest that it is of considerable interest to the narrator. He highlights their unity in Egypt and especially mentions Jacob's joy other this.[115] Otherwise he presents Joseph in a favourable light when describing their relations. Thus, when relating Joseph's approach to his brothers' pasturing site, he stresses their cruelty by inserting the expression: "they inflicted pain upon him" (*Jub* 34:11 paraphrasing *Gen* 37:18). In *Jub* the question of Joseph's motivations in the initial meeting with his brothers is also addressed for the first time. The narrator explains his behaviour thus (*Jub* 42:25):

The Hebrew Festivals and the Calendar, *JSS* 6/1961, p. 92ff; R.H. Charles, *op. cit.*, p. XLIX; Dillmann, *op. cit.*, pp. 84–85; A. Baumgarten, *op. cit.*, p. 320; J.C. VanderKam, *op. cit.*, p. 244.

[114] Many scholars have previously pointed to the "unparalleled" nature of *Jub*'s inference; see especially: Ch. Albeck, *Das Buch der Jubilaeen und die Halacha*, *47er Jahresbericht für die Wissenschaft des Judentums*, Berlin 1930, p. 18–19, who studied particularly its relation to *mTan*; B. Beer, *Das Buch der Jubilaeen und sein Verhältnis zu den Midraschim*, Leipzig 1856, p. 51; M. Testuz, *Les idées religieuses du livre des Jubilées*, Geneve/Paris 1960, p. 150; vol. V, p. 1382, who interprets the Day of Atonement in view of his assumption of *Jub*'s Samaritan origin, (these conjectures have, however, long been refuted, see especially: W. Singer, *Das Jubiläenbuch oder die Leptogenesis*, Stuhlweissenburg 1898, pp. 6–7); S. Zeitlin, *The Legend of the ten Martyrs and its apocalyptic Origins*, *JQR* 36/1945–46, pp. 1–16; idem, *The Book of Jubilees and the Pentateuch*, *JQR* 48/1957–58, pp. 218–35, who argues, on unconvincing grounds, for an early testimony in *Jub* of the concept of Original Sin; *Jubilees, book of*, *IDB* vol. I, p. 314.

[115] *Jub* 45:5 reads: "They were eating bread before their father, Joseph and his brothers, and they drank wine and Jacob rejoiced with great joy because he saw Joseph eating together with his brothers and drinking before him and he blessed the Creator of all things, who had protected him and had preserved for him twelve sons".

> And Joseph thought of a plan by which he might learn their thoughts, whether thoughts of peace prevailed among them and he said ....[116]

The narrator is obviously aware of Joseph's harshness which is biblically not accounted for. In his paraphrase he provides a rational motive and thereby transforms Joseph into the "peace maker" of his family! In early Jewish exegesis an interest in Joseph's behaviour at this point remains rare. As we saw in the graph at the beginning of this chapter it is mainly the Hellenistic interpreters who later raise this issue.

Jub is also our earliest witness to an exegetical interest in Joseph's encounter with Potiphar's wife. The reasons for this perseverance are carefully analysed and the whole scene is embellished in terms typical of the work (*Jub* 39:6):

> He did not surrender his soul and he remembered the Lord and the words which Jacob his father used to read from among the words of Abraham that no-one should fornicate with a woman who has a husband, that for him the death sentence has been ordained in the heavens before the Lord the Most High and the sin will be recorded against him in the eternal books for ever before the Lord.

In this passage further insight is provided into the biblical Joseph's inner life at this crucial moment (*Gen* 39:10). In addition to Joseph's explicit arguments, the reader thus learns also of the spiritual reasons for his behaviour. It is argued here that the memory of his family's ethical instruction prevents him from committing the sin. This picture of Joseph's loyalty is then further embellished by religious imagery, such as the reference to the heavenly tablets.[117]

The nature of the sin is also clearly defined. It consists of fornication with a married woman.[118] The reference to the death penalty for this transgression is elsewhere specified as burning (*Jub* 20:4).

---

[116] In *Jub* 34:14 Joseph is described in similarly benevolent terms before the final family reunion: "And Joseph saw that the heart of all of them was in accord with one another for good and he could not hold himself back and he told them that he was Joseph".

[117] See also *Jub* 4:5, 5:13 etc.; R.H. Charles, *op. cit.*, p. 24 n10; *idem, The Apocrypha ad Pseudepigrapha*, Oxford 1913, vol. II p. 316 n3; R. Travers Herford, *op. cit.*, p. 230. Note that the image of the heavenly tablets is a rather wide-spread topos in contemporary apocalytic literature, see especially *En* 96:4 and 97:7.

[118] Cf. M. Testuz, *op. cit.*, p. 113, who attempts to show that Joseph really avoided contact with a non-Jewish woman. This interpretation cannot be substantiated by the text and must have resulted from M. Testuz' own preoccupation with questions of purity and inter-marriage.

This punishment is more severe than the respective decrees in the *Mishnah* and *Tosefta*.[119] Therefore, R.H. Charles[120] and Ch. Albeck[121] suggested that this form of execution in *Jub* is derived from *Gen* 38:24, where burning is demanded for Tamar. In view of P. Segal's recent studies of priestly halacha,[122] however, the above passage emerges as a possible case where *Jub* applies the stricter priestly code to the whole of Israel.[123]

In *Jub* the idealized figure of Joseph who is shown to behave in accordance with all the religious and ethical precepts, receives a final laudatory note in the description of his administration in Egypt. (*Jub* 40:8–9):

> And Joseph ruled over all the land of Egypt and all the notables of Pharaoh and all his attendants and all those who did the king's business esteemed him highly, for he walked in uprightness, and he had no pride nor arrogance nor partiality and there was no bribery, for in uprightness did he judge all the people of the land. And the land of Egypt was at peace before Pharaoh thanks to Joseph, for the Lord was with him and gave him favour and mercy for all his family before those who knew him and those who heard about him, and the kingdom of Pharaoh was well ordered and there was no Satan and no evil.

The narrator replaces here the biblical portrait of Joseph's severe rule over the Egyptians by the harmonious picture of a highly popular ruler who is acclaimed by everybody on account of his uprightness. A. Büchler therefore argues that this scene reflects the narra-

---

[119] The injunction of death penalty for fornication is based on *Lev* 20:10 and *Dtn* 22:21. In biblical law both the man and the woman are to be executed, but the form of execution is not specified. The *Mishnah* and *Tosefta* enjoin different forms of death in accordance with the status of the woman: a married woman is to be strangled and a betrothed one is to be stoned (*mSan* 11:1–6; *tSan* 7:2 and 10:9–10). Although there are conflicting views which of these two is more severe, both are considered by everybody harsher than burning, the form of execution enjoined for a priest's daughter (*mSan* 7:2 and 9:1; *tSan* 12:1–5).

[120] *Op. cit.*, p. 129 n4 and p.231 n25–26.

[121] *Op. cit.*, p. 19ff.

[122] *The Divine Death Penalty in the Hatra Inscriptions and the Mishnah*, *JJS* 40/1989, pp. 46–52, especially p. 50–51 n27; and his doctoral thesis חיוב בדיני שמיים, חיובי מיתות בית דין וחיובי מיתה לשמיים.

[123] Note that also the figure of Potiphar's wife receives particular notice in *Jub*. Expanding on the brief remarks in *Gen* 39:5–8, the narrator describes how "she embraced him and she seized him and she closed the doors of the house and seized him" (*Jub* 39:9). In this way, the strength of her desire is illustrated and emphasised. Yet in comparison with other early treatments of her (e.g.: *TJos* 3:1) these embellishments remain scarce and simple.

tor's Hellenistic environment and shows that he wishes to impress his Greek readers.[124] It is, however, to be considered that the most important items, namely uprightness, modesty and the absence of evil and Satan, are typical features of *Jub*'s religious views[125] and certainly not identifiably Greek. It is therefore possible that the narrator of *Jub* combined an interest in Joseph's good relations with the Egyptians, a theme later developed by the Hellenistic exegetes, with his own genuine concepts.

From the above analysis of Joseph in *Jub* we may draw the following conclusions: the narrator deals with the major aspects of the biblical story and draws an idealised picture of the protagonist. Focussing on Joseph's relations with his brothers, Potiphar's wife and with the Egyptians, he presents him as a proto-type of his particular religious and ethical ideals.

In Pseudo-Philo's *Liber Antiquitatum Biblicarum* (*LAB*), a work of presumably Palestian-Hebrew origin dating to the first century C.E.,[126] the figure of Joseph receives but short notice. The narrator presents a very concise summary of the whole story, thus selecting and refocusing only a few highlights. His account is nevertheless of great interest because it preserves somewhat unusual views of Joseph.[127]

> Now Jacob and his twelve sons dwelt in the land of Canaan. And they hated (oderant) their brother Joseph whom they handed over (tradiderunt) into Egypt, to Potiphar, the chief cook of Pharoah, and he stayed with him for fourteen years. And it happened after the king of Egypt saw a dream and they told him about Joseph and he interpreted the dreams to him. And it happened after he had interpreted the dreams to him, that Pharaoh made him ruler over all the land of Egypt. At

---

[124] *Traces des Idées et des Coutumes Hellénistiques dans le Livre des Jubilées*, *REJ* 1930/82, especially pp. 329ff.

[125] Cf. *Jub* 20:9; 21:24 and 10:11; 23:29, 50:5.

[126] For a discussion of the background and the original language of the document, see especially: L. Cohn, An Apocryphal Work ascribed to Philo of Alexandria, *JQR* 10/1989, pp. 277–332; D.J. Harrington, The Original Language of Pseudo-Philo's Liber Antiquitatum Biblicarum, *HThR* 63/1970, pp. 503–14; *idem*, The Biblical text of Pseudo-Philo's "Liber Antiquitatum Biblicarum", CBQ 33/1971, pp. 1–17; G. Kisch, Pseudo-Philo's Liber Antiquitatum Biblicarum, Postlegomena to the New Edition, *HUCA* 23,2/1950, pp. 81–93; M.R. James, Notes on Apocrypha, *JThSt* 16/1915, pp. 403–05; *Schürer* III, 1 pp. 325–331.

[127] *LAB* 8:9–10. My translation is based on D.J. Harringon's critical edition of the Latin text, *Pseudo-Philo Les Antiquités Bibliques, Introduction et Texte Critique*, Paris 1976, vol. 1, pp. 102–04.

that time there was a famine on the whole earth just as Joseph had esti-
mated and his brothers came down to buy food in Egypt, since only
in Egypt was there food. And Joseph recognised his brothers, but he
was not known to them. And he did not bear any grudge against them
(non malignatus est cum eis) and sent and called for his father from
the land of Canaan and he came down to him.

Creating a new narrative framework, *LAB* introduces the Joseph
story by pointed reference to Jacob's twelve sons. Thus contracting
the first two verses of *Gen* 37, the somewhat awkward biblical phrase
"these are the generations of Jacob, Joseph . . ." is transformed into
a more convenient opening. The narrator further deminishes the
biblical emphasis on the special relationship between Joseph and his
father by not mentioning either Jacob's particular love for him nor
Joseph's peculiar behaviour towards his brothers. As a result, the
sons' hatred of him remains rather unexplained and therefore appears more severe.

The subsequent parts of the Joseph story are abbreviated to such
an extent that they are almost rendered incomprehensible without
prior knowledge of the biblical account. The narrator thus mentions
in passing how Joseph was "handed over into Egypt", here perhaps
reflecting some manuscript tradition of the Old Latin version of *Gen*
37:36,[128] and how he stayed with Potiphar for fourteen years.[129]
Further omitting references both to the affair with Potiphar's wife
and Joseph's dream interpretation in prison, the narrator immediately relates Joseph's encounter with Pharaoh and his great success
as his administrator.

In view of this extremely concise style it is particularly remarkable
that the narrator does in fact dwell on the latter parts of the Joseph
story.[130] He does not only refer to Joseph's interpretation of
Pharaoh's dreams but furthermore emphasizes that the occurrence
of the famine is in exact accordance with his earlier predictions.
Most notable is the extended and clearly apologetic treatment of
Joseph's encounter with his brothers in Egypt. Replacing the biblical description of Joseph as stern and harsh towards them (*Gen*

---

[128] *Vetus Latina Die Reste der altlateinischen Bibel nach Petrus Sabatier, neu gesammelt
und herausgegeben von der Erzabtei Beuron*, Verlag Herder Freiburg 1951–54, vol. 2,
ad.loc., Ms E "Madinei autem tradiderunt Joseph in Aegyptum".

[129] Regarding the presentation here of Potiphar as the "chief cook", see C.
Perrot and M.P. Bogaert, Pseudo-Philo, *op. cit.*, vol. 2 p. 100.

[130] See also C. Perrot and M.P. Bogaert, *op. cit.*, p. 100.

42:7 – 8), *LAB* highlights that he "did not bear any grudge against them" and instead showed his friendliness by immediately inviting their father down to Egypt. This point is further made by a later comparison between Joseph and Moses at his descent from Mount Sinai. Concerning the latter it is said: "This (the people's non-recognition of their leader) happened in a similar way as in Egypt when Joseph recognized his brothers but they did not recognize him".[131]

Though generally corresponding to the outline of Joseph's encounter with his brothers in *Jub*, the narrator's focus on this point clearly goes far beyond earlier treatments. It is therefore likely to respond to an increasing criticism of the figure regarding this aspect.

In the remaining part of this section I shall examine references to Joseph in documents composed in or translated into Greek. They tend to be of later date, ranging from Artapanus' treatment to Stephen's speech in *Acts*. The question of how they compare to the previously analysed Palestinian interpretations will be of particular interest.

Artapanus is known for his imaginative writing[132] and this can clearly be seen in his treatment of Joseph. His vision of the patriarch is based only vaguely on the biblical account and highlights the following aspects:[133]

> Artapanus says in his *Book on the Jews* that Joseph was a descendent of Abraham and son of Jacob; and because he surpassed his brothers in understanding and wisdom they plotted against him. But he became aware of their conspiracy and besought the neighbouring Arabs to convey him across to Egypt . . . And when he had come to Egypt and been commended to the king, he was made administrator of the whole country. And whereas the Egyptians previously occupied the land in an irregular way because the country was not divided, and the weaker were unjustly treated by the stronger, he was the first to divide the land and mark it out with boundaries and much that lay waste he rendered

---

[131] LAB 12:1. See also: O. Eissfeldt, Zur Kompositionstechnik des Pseudo-Philonischen Liber Antiquitarum Biblicatum, *NTT* 56/1955, pp. 53 – 71 and especially p. 55.

[132] For a background on this Jewish-Egyptian "historian" and the probable date of his activity (some time after 250 BC), see especially: *Schürer* III pp. 521 – 525; A. Schalit, *Artapanus, EJ* vol. I, pp. 146 – 77; M. Braun, *History, op. cit.*, pp. 26 – 31 and pp. 99 – 102.

[133] My translation is based on E.H. Gifford's edition of Eusebius' *Prep. Ev.*, Oxford 1909, pp. 539 – 40.

fit for tillage and allotted certain of the arable land to the priests. He
was also the inventor of measures and for these things he was greatly
loved by the Egyptians.

The changes which Artapanus introduces to the figure of Joseph
are striking. His interest in this biblical story is strongly coloured by
his concerns as an Egyptian. His description of the brothers' relations has thus only an introductory function. But it is the earliest extant exegesis on this part of the story and therefore deserves our attention.

According to Artapanus, Joseph is completely innocent of the tensions in the family. While he excels in the most desirable virtues of
wisdom, he is said to become the victim of their jealousy. The narrator succeeds in this way to reshape the biblical account substantially.
His exaggerations go even further when he claims that Joseph himself arranged his transfer to Egypt. It may be conjectured that this
innovation is important to Artapanus because it provides him with
an even more heroic founder of Hebrew civilisation in Egypt.

The narrator's most urgent concern is obviously Joseph's stay in
Egypt and in particular his achievements as a secular administrator.[134] He provides numerous additional details of his activities and
stresses especially the improvement which Joseph brought to the
country. In this way, Joseph becomes the founder of Egypt's social
and economic structure. Artapanus also takes the trouble to mention
Joseph's popularity among the indigenous population. Taken together these facets of Artapanus's figure establish Joseph as an important νομοθέτης, second only to Moses.[135]

In *Ben Sira*'s famous ''Praise of the Fathers''[136] mention is also
made of Joseph (*Sir* 49:15):

> Was there ever a man born like Joseph?
> And his bones are taken care of.

---

[134] Note that his encounter with Potiphar's wife is not mentioned at all.

[135] For Artapanus's treatment of Moses, see: *Prep.Ev.* IX, 27.

[136] For a background on this document, see especially: *Schürer* III pp. 198–213;
B.L. Mack, *Wisdom in the Hebrew Epic. Ben Sira's Hymn in the Praise of the Fathers*,
Chicago 1985, see especially his thematic treatment of the characterizations in Ben
Sira, pp. 11–36; T. Middendorp, *Die Stellung Jesu Ben Siras zwischen Judentum und
Hellenismus*, Leiden 1973 (with an over-emphasis on the Greek elements); O. Rick-
enbacher, *Die Weisheitsperikopen bei Ben Sira*, Freiburg 1973; J. Haspecker, *Gottes-
furcht bei Jesus Sirach*, Rome 1967, especially pp. 3–105.

In this stichos Joseph's uniqueness is established on the basis of his bones being carried back to the Holy Land. This is presumably highlighted also in view of Enoch's transfer to heaven.[137] It is remarkable that only references to Joseph from *Ex* deserve mention here and that no other item of the main story is alluded to.[138]

In the Greek version, however, an additional line is inserted which sheds different light on Joseph. He is presented here as "the leader of his brothers and the support of the people".[139] The first item in this addition phrases in unusually political terms what presumably amounts to the attribution of the first-birth rights to Joseph. The second aspect of the Greek figure of Joseph remains more opaque since it cannot be established with certainty whether the Egyptian or the Hebrew people is referred to. Thus the biblical emphasis is either maintained or Joseph's role in the salvation of his own nation is highlighted.[140] Since this notice concerning Joseph is added to the "Praise of the Fathers" it is, however, likely that it enhances the patriarch's importance to Israel. It remains in any case noteworthy that only the Greek version of *Ben Sira* calls to mind Joseph's economic beneficence.

Joseph is further mentioned in another piece of sapiental literature, namely the *Wisdom of Solomon* (10:13 – 14):[141]

> When a righteous man was sold, she (wisdom) did not desert him but delivered him from sin (ἐξ ἁμαρτίας ἐρρύσατο) ... and when he was in prison she did not leave him until she brought him the sceptre of a kingdom.

In this passage Joseph is placed among the forefathers who are shown to have been protected by Wisdom's providential guidance. The treatment which he receives here is quite standard for this historical review in *Wis* 10. The narrator in fact tends to classify all

---

[137] See also Box/Osterly, *Sirach*, in: R.H. Charles, *Pseudepigrapha*, *op. cit.*, p. 506; R. Smend, *Die Weisheit des Jesus Sirach*, Berlin 1906, p. 475.

[138] On the motive of "Joseph's bones" and its Acaditions, see especially J. Kugel, *op. cit.*, pp. 125–155.

[139] Note that R. Smend, *op. cit.*, p. 478, conjectures that this line actually belongs before *Sir* 50:1, where it refers to the High Priest, V. Russel, *Die Sprüche Jesus', des Sohnes Sirachs*, in: E. Kautzsch, *Die Apokryphen und Pseudepigraphen des Alten Testaments*, Tübingen 1900, vol. I p. 236 and p. 467, accepts its present position in the "Praise" and wishes to deduce from it a pre-Danielic redaction date.

[140] On the basis of *Gen* 45:5.

[141] For a discussion of the problematic provenance and date of this document, see especially: *Schürer* III, pp. 567–68.

the biblical figures either as righteous or wicked. Alongside Adam, Noah and Abel Joseph is thus situated in the "good category" and the workings of Wisdom on him are subsequently demonstrated. The first example chosen is Wisdom's protection from sin, which presumably means from Potiphar's wife.[142] Her blessings are then said to culminate in Her promotion of Joseph to power.[143] Also this outline of Joseph's story follows a pattern in *Wis*'s "historiography". Thus Adam, for example, is also delivered from sin in order to be advanced to rule (*Wis* 10:1–2).

It emerges that the figure of Joseph is of no particular significance to the narrator of *Wis*. He mentions his story as another manifestation of Wisdom's effect in the world. It is nevertheless to be noted that in comparison with a previous interpretation of this sort in *Ps* 105 the focus has shifted from Joseph's trouble in prison to that in Potiphar's house.

Joseph also plays a role in Mattathias' alleged speech in which he recalls, for political purposes, the forefathers' praiseworthy deeds.[144] According to the Maccabean historiographer, the significance of the biblical figure can be summarized thus:

> Joseph in his distress kept the commandment (ἐφύλαξεν ἐντολὴν) and became king (κύριος) over Egypt.

Reflecting his own *Weltanschauung*, the narrator regards two aspects of Joseph essential: his religious devotion and his political achievement. The personal distress which Joseph is said to have successfully endured presumably refers to his challenge by Potiphar's wife.[145] This notice is then the earliest allusion to the concept of this 'affair' as a trial of religious steadfastness. In view of the narrator's

---

[142] See also: C.L.W. Grimm's lively formulation in: *Das Buch der Weisheit*, Leipzig 1860, p. 201: "ἁμαρτία ist die Sünde der verführenden Macht, die in der Person des buhlerischen Weibes ihre Schlinge um Joseph zu werfen suchte".

[143] Note that the phrase in vs 14 is not as precise as one would hope and it is thus not clear whether an actual royal position for Joseph himself is intended.

[144] For a background on I*Macc* and a discussion on its probable date in the first decades in the 1st century BC, see especially: *Schürer* III, pp. 180–85; J.A. Goldstein, *IMaccabees: A New Translation with Introduction and Commentary*, New York 1976, pp. 7–8 and pp. 238–42. I*Macc* 2,53.

[145] The reference to his keeping of the commandment makes sense only in the context of this distress. Similarly conjectured also e.g.: Oesterly, *I Maccabees*, in: R.H. Charles, *The Apocrypha and Pseudepigrapha*, Oxford 1913, p. 74; and E. Kautzsch, *Die Apokryphen and Pseudepigraphen des Alten Testaments*, Tübingen 1900, vol. 1 p. 39.

contemporary situation this interpretation does not seem surprising.

Also Joseph's political role is important to the Maccabean histo-riographer. It is likely that he enhances Joseph's status in the hope of providing a national model for his own party's aspirations to power.

In Stephen's speech in *Acts* 7:1 – 53 we have a source for the views of the Hellenistically oriented members of the early Jewish Christi-ans.[146] The comments on Joseph review the biblical story quite faithfully and no dramatic interpretations are advanced. Like the Psalmist, Stephen is said to present Joseph's story as a case of God's benign providence. By comparison to earlier interpretations it is perhaps remarkable that the hardship which is emphasized in this context is the selling of Joseph. Otherwise the narrator shows a lively interest in the events which happen to the family as a whole in Egypt. This focus corresponds to the narrator's general fondness of Israelite history in the diaspora.

The analysis of the above references to Joseph between the ac-count in *Gen* and the first full treatments of the story render impor-tant insights into early exegetical developments. It has thus emerged that the figure has been widely used and for very different purposes. In each rendering the particular concerns of the narrator are reflect-ed in his selection of the essentials and his reshaping of extant items.

The predominant feature, typical of all narrators, is the positive attitude towards the biblical figure. For one reason or another, Joseph seems to represent for each narrator a certain *Idealtyp*. Another factor common to most of these interpretations is their em-phasis of the Divine. God's providence tends to be stressed and the other elements of the story, including Joseph's personality, are often seen in the light of it. The precise outline of the details usually cor-responds to the narrator's topical concerns.

A distinction between the Greek and the Hebrew sources can only be drawn with difficulty; and there is no clear dividing line between

---

[146] For a background, see: *Stephen, IDB* vol. IV, pp. 441–42; *Freedman, Syna-gogue of,* IDB vol. II p. 325; *Hellenists, IDB,* vol. II p. 580; M. Simon, *St. Stephen and the Hellenists,* Longmans 1958, pp. 39–59; M. Dibelius, *Studies in the Acts of the Apostels,* London 1956 (1st ed. 1951), pp. 138–86; R.A. Knox, *A New Testament Commentary,* London 1958 (1st ed. 1953), pp. 16–17; K. Lake/H.J. Cadbury, *The Acts of the Apostles,* in: *The Beginnings of Christianity,* ed. F.J. Foakes Jackson, London 1933, pp. 72–74 (contains completely unjustified Christological interpretations); E. Hänchen, *Die Apostelgeschichte,* Göttingen 1956, p. 233–37; F.F. Bruce, *The Acts of the Apostels,* London 1953 (1st ed. 1951), pp. 18–21.

their respective interests in the story. It only emerges that the Greek speaking world is always concerned with Joseph's activities in Egypt, whereas the others are not necessarily so. Clearly idiosyncratic treatments of Joseph are found in the *Book of Jubilees* and *Artapanus*. Especially the former remains an isolated case in the history of exegesis. The themes which are addressed in the other documents are, however, also dealt with later. The various motifs resurface in complex combinations and interwoven with new ideas. It will be the aim of the following chapters to uncover these patterns.

CHAPTER THREE

PHILO'S FIGURE OF JOSEPH

Introduction: a Bios of the Statesman?

Philo introduces his treatise on Joseph as βίος τοῦ πολιτῖκου.[1] By Philo's time the term *bios* seems to have become a widespread label for the genre of biography, although few of its traits can be established with certainty.[2] It is therefore crucial to examine Philo's use of the term against this cultural background and to gather evidence for his personal concept of the category *bios*. For this purpose, I shall initially treat Philo's theoretical remarks extant in the various *Lives*. In addition, I shall then also briefly outline Philo's own political background and suggest how this might influence his biography of a politician.

While Philo's works on Jacob and Isaac have been lost, his *Lives* of Abraham and Moses are still available. Between these two biographies there is a remarkable difference in style and composition. In order to appreciate the significance of the *bios* of Joseph I shall begin with an analysis of the conceptual assumptions found in these two.

Philo's introduction to the *life of Abraham* is similar to that of Joseph (*Jos* 1). He refers also here to the three patriarchs and ex-

---

[1] The Mss vary between βίος τοῦ πολίτικου and βίος πολίτικός, but the former is better attested (see *C-W*, vol. IV, p. 61).

[2] The classical study which prompted much of the subsequent research on the subject is F. Leo's *Die griechisch-römische Biographie nach ihrer literarischen Form*, Leipzig 1901, especially relevant for the period in question pp. 85–136; see also: D.R. Stuart, *Epochs of Greek and Roman Biography*, Berkeley 1928, especially pp. 155–189; A. Dihle, *Studien zur griechischen Biographie*, Göttingen 1956; F. Wehrli, *Von der antiken Biographie*, in: *Theoria und Humanismus*, Artemis Verlag 1972 (1st published 1964), pp. 237–241; C. Schneider, *Kulturgeschichte des Hellenismus*, München 1967, pp. 469–478; A. Momigliano, *The Development of Greek Biography*, Harvard University Press 1971, who expresses severe doubt concerning the method and the results of preceding research on 'peripatetic biography', a concept which he himself questions; D.A. Russell's excellent summary of the techniques of characterisation in Plutarch's biographies in: *Plutarch*, London 1972, especially pp. 102–06. See also M. Pohlenz' study on the generally increasing interest in the essence of character, το πρεπόν, *Ein Beitrag zur Geschichte des griechischen Geistes*, in: *Kleine Schriften*, Hildesheim 1965, pp. 100–140; the proliferation of biographical works is also witnessed by the lists of book titles in *DL* IV:12, V:42, V:59, V:87, VII:4.

plains that Abraham, Isaac and Jacob represent respectively the lives which result from teaching, the life of the self-taught and the life of practice. In the context of Abraham, however, Philo adds a significant insight. He states that: "... these three (are) nominally men (λόγῳ μὲν ἀνδρῶν) but really (ἔργῳ), as I have said, virtues ... thus it is meant to indicate the three said values rather than actual men".[3] In this exposition it is conspicuous that Philo makes no attempt to justify the correlation between each figure and his virtue. Neither the approach as such nor the specific content are corroborated by theoretical considerations. It might indicate a familiarity on the part of Philo and his readers with this perception of character.[4]

When Philo subsequently begins to treat the actual life of Abraham, he does not follow the biblical account. He opens instead with a general statement in which the essence of the character is revealed: "... (to) begin with the first: Abraham, then, filled with the zeal for piety, the highest and greatest of virtues, was eager to follow God and to be obedient to his commandments" (Abr 60). In the course of his biography Philo implements this concept of Abraham in two years. On the one hand, he omits unsuitable biblical material,[5] and on the other, he allegorises scriptural items. For the latter he mainly uses three Greek terms, namely ἀλληγορία, σύμβολον and ὑπόνοια.[6] Especially ὑπόνοια, but increasingly also ἀλληγορία were standard terms in the Hellenistic exegesis of Homer.[7] They

---

[3] Abr 54–55. Note that elsewhere (e.g. Abr 52) he also speaks of τρόπους ψυχῆς.

[4] For a general background, see also: D.A. Russell, Literary Criticism in Antiquity, OCD, p. 611–12 and Theories of Literature and Taste, in: The Classical World, ed. D. Daiches, London 1972, pp. 417–434; M. Fuhrmann, Einführung in die Antike Dichtungstheorie, Darmstadt 1973, especially pp. 99–134;; G.M.A. Grube, The Greek and Roman Critics, London 1965, pp. 103–09; and W. Kroll, Studien zum Verständnis der römischen Literatur, Stuttgart 1924, pp. 382–84.

[5] Such as Abraham's real family circumstances (Gen 11–12) or his material profits from Pharaoh's interest in Sarah (Gen 12:16). In view of such omissions A. Priessning defines Abr as "eine echte Verheissungsschrift" (p. 147) in: Die literarische Form der Patriarchenbiographien des Philon von Alexandria, MGWJ N.F. 37/1929, pp. 143–155; Y. Amir, Scripture, op. cit., p. 125, also mentions Philo's tendency to idealize.

[6] For the use of these terms by Philo, see I. Leisegang's Index to C-W, vol. VII, 1 pp. 81–82, vol. VII, 2 pp. 733–35, ibid p. 806.

[7] F. Buffière, Les Mythes d'Homère et la Pensée Greque, Paris 1956, pp. 45–65, on υ. and α., see especially pp. 45–48 and on σ. pp. 54–58. For a general background, see also: J. Tate, Allegory in: OCD, pp. 45–46; K. Müller, Allegorische Dichtererklärung, in: RE Sup. bd. IV 1924, Sp. 16–22; Allegorie, Lexikon der Alten Welt, Artemis Verlag 1965, col. 121–126; R. Pfeiffer, History of Classical Scholarship,

referred to a method which allowed the interpreter to distinguish
metaphorical, and usually philosophical meanings in the classical
texts. Subsequently this approach also became a tool in the defense
of the classical heritage.[8] During Philo's era, this method appears
to have still been popular;[9] and there is evidence that even in Alexandria, the centre of philological research,[10] the production of allegorical commentaries flourished.[11]

Oxford 1968, pp. 237–42; H. Lausberg, *Handbuch der Literarischen Rhetorik*, München 1960, pp. 441–46. Cf. R. Hahn's study on *Die Allegorie der Antiken Rhetorik*,
Tübingen 1967, which is severely handicapped by an exclusive examination of the
later term α.

[8] The scope of the "positive" versus the "apologetic" allegory and their
chronological order have been the subject of much controversy. It is J. Tate's merit
to have (re)established fifth century allegorisation as a philosophical activity which
connected the interpreter's thoughts with the Homeric texts from which they were
inspired to no small degree, see especially: *On the History of Allegorism*, *CQ* 28/1934,
pp. 105–114; *The Beginnings of Greek Allegory*, *Classical Review* XLI/1927, pp.
214–15, *Plato and Allegorical Interpretation*, *CQ* 23/1929, pp. 142–54 and *CQ* 24/1930,
pp. 1–10. Already F. Wehrli (*Zur Geschichte der allegorischen Deutung Homers im Altertum*, Dissertation Borna-Leipzig 1928, especially pp. 3–64) and E. Zeller (*Die
Philosophie der Griechen*, 5th ed. Hildesheim 1963, vol. III, 1, pp. 318–355) had
shown the Stoics' positive attitude towards the myth and claimed that they used allegory "um die Kluft zwischen einer älteren und einer von ihr wesentlich ab-
weichenden neuen Bildungsform zu überbrücken" (p. 330). It is perhaps the latter's open disregard for a. which provoked further emphasis on its non-apologetic
nature; thus e.g. I. Heinemann, (*Die wissenschaftliche Allegoristik*, *Mnemosyne* Serie
4,2 1948, pp. 5–18, and *Altjüdische Allegoristik*, Breslau 1936, especially pp. 5–14)
identifies as apology also the use of classical material in support of new ideas and
mistakenly stresses the dominantly text-oriented, "scientific" nature of a. See also:
J. Pepin's mostly descriptive treatment of late antique material in: *Mythe et Allégory*,
Aubier 1958, especially pp. 152–167 and pp. 215–246; P. Rollinson, *Classical theories of Allegory and Christian Culture*, Duquesne University Press 1981, pp. IX–XX
and pp. 3–28; K. Reinhardt, *Das Vermächtnis der Antike*, Göttingen 1960, pp.
33–34; D.L. Clark, *Rhetoric in Greco-Roman Education*, Columbia 1957, pp. 90ff; cf.
also H. Rahner, *Griechische Mythen in christlicher Deutung*, Zürich 1945, pp. 355–61,
whose religious illuminations are singularly hypothetical.

[9] E.g.: Cornutus (mostly cosmological allegory) and later Pseudo-Plutarch; for
the general background, see: *Cornutus*, *OCD*, p. 292; U. v. Wilamowitz-Möllendorff's treatment of his work in: *Der Glaube der Hellenen*, Darmstadt 1959, pp. 448–
451; J. Tate's treatment of Cornutus in *CQ* 24/1930, pp. 1–3; and F. Wehrli's discussion of Ps-Plutarch in: *Geschichte*, *op. cit.*, pp. 3–40.

[10] For a background, see especially: P.M. Fraser, *Ptolemaic Alexandria*, Oxford
1962, pp. 447–79 (thorough assessment of the history of Alexandrian scholarship
in comparison to that of Pergamon and an evaluation of its influence on subsequent
research); J.W. Atkins, *Literary Criticism in Antiquity*, London 1952, vol. I pp. 1–10
and pp. 164–195; and G.M.A. Grube, *op. cit.*, pp. 122–132.

[11] Thus, e.g. the Jewish Aristotelian thinker Aristobulus (in: Eusebius' *PrepEv*.
VIII: 9–10) explains that "our lawgiver has made the word a beautiful metaphor"
(p. 407, ed. E.H. Gifford, London 1903, vol. XV) and condemns those "who cling

Philo himself assumes the recognition of this method;[12] and once he even refers to the νόμοι or θεωρία of allegory.[13] In *Abr* 88 he furthermore explains that the symbolical and the literal meanings are to be understood as complementary.[14] This congruence of the "man" and the "soul", though established theoretically, may not always have been followed by Philo in his expositions.[15] This we may also gather from the scattered evidence concerning Jacob.[16]

---

to the letter" as "devoid of power and intelligence" (*ibid*); and also the important Homer Allegories by Pseudo-Heraclitus (1st A.D.). For the general background, see especially: B.L. Mack's review of the research on the subject in: *Philo Judaeus and Exegetical Traditions in Alexandria*, ANRW II, 21,1, pp. 227–271; E. Zeller, *op. cit.*, III, 2, pp. 277–88; J. Pepin, *op. cit.*, pp. 215–246; and R. Hahn, *op. cit.*, pp. 35–55.

[12] See also: E. Zeller, *op. cit.*, III, 2, pp. 385–467; E. Bréhier, *Les idées philosophiques et religieuses de Philon d'Alexandrie*, Paris 1907 (also published in: Etudes de Philosophie Medievale, Paris 1925), pp. 35–45; C. Siegfried, *Der jüdische Hellenismus*, Zeitschrift für Wissenschaftliche Theologie, Leipzig 1875, especially p. 465ff and also *Philo von Alexandria als Ausleger des Alten Testaments*, Jena 1875, especially p. 164ff; E. Stein, *Die allegorische Exegese des Philon aus Alexandria*, Giessen 1929, especially pp. 1–19 and I. Heinemann's critical review of Stein's use of etymology as indicator for sources in: *Hellenica*, MGWJ N.F. 37/1929, pp. 426–445; cf. also L. Treitel, *Philonische Studien*, Breslau 1915, pp. 114–123, and *Ursprung, Begriff und Umfang der allegorischen Schrifterklärung*, *MGWJ* 55/1911, pp. 543–554 who wishes to argue for the exclusive origin of allegory in the "im jüdischen Volke lebender Genius" (p. 547).

[13] E.g.: *Abr* 68, "κατὰ δὲ τοὺς ἐν ἀλληγορίᾳ νόμους", and *Abr* 131 τῆς ἐν ἀλληγορίᾳ θεωρίας". Since these expressions do not recur in Philo's work, it is doubtful whether they can be regarded as technical terms. He probably used them in a rather vague sense (see also I. Leisegang, *op. cit.*, Vol. VII, 1, pp. 81–2).

[14] See especially P. Karni, היסודות ההגותיים של פרשנות פילון האלכסנדרוני 14/1985 רעת, who modified his teacher Y. Amir's conclusions (*Die hellenistische Gestalt des Judentums bei Philo von Alexandrien*, Neukirchen 1983, pp. 19–20; also in: *JE* XIII, *Philo* cols. 409–15 and *Philo and the Bible*, in: *Studia Philonica* II/1973) towards a more conciliatory view of the a. and the lit. sense; V.A. Nikiprowetzky's conclusion that "dans les vies l'allégorie est utilisée pour justifier le texte biblique et pour en souligner la dignité" (*op. cit.*, p. 201) seems too general to define the essence of a. and is also not always appropriate. For other examples postulating congruence between the a. and the lit. in the field of Halacha, see especially: *Mig* 88–91 and *SpecLeg* I: 135–39; cf. also I. Heinemann's sceptical conclusions of his research, *Philons griechische und jüdische Bildung*, Breslau 1929, e.g. p. 464: "wie wenig Selbstwert Philon der wörtlichen Innehaltung der Gesetze beimisst".

[15] For a fine discussion of these issues especially with regard to Abraham, see: S. Sandmel, *Philo's Place in Judaism*, Cincinnati 1956, and *Philo of Alexandria, An Introduction*, Oxford 1979; I. Christiansen's attempt to demonstrate the logical consistency of Philo's whole allegorical corpus lacks substantiation (*Die Technik der allegorischen Auslegungswissenschaft bei Philon von Alexandrien*, Tübingen 1969).

[16] The diversity of the image transpires, for example, from the following passages: *Leg* II, 2 Jacob was a man "full of wisdom" and subsequently (*ibid*, 88), already in the womb he was destined to become a ruler and a master; *Sacrif* 42 he

For an evaluation of the *bios* of Joseph in relation to this "allegorical biography"[17] it is important to note Philo's remark in *Cher* 40. There he mentions the "persons whose virtues the lawgiver has testified". He then lists Abraham, Isaac, Jacob and Moses. Joseph, on the other hand, is conspicuously missing. This might raise our awareness to the possibility that Joseph is considered a somewhat exceptional case among the Israelite forefathers.

The other complete extant *Life* is that of Moses, "the legislator of the Jews, the interpreter of the Laws and the greatest and most perfect of men" (*Mos* I, 1).[18] For this biography Philo provides a distinctly different setting. He opens by dealing with the political fame and the reputation which this leader has gained among the nations. Towards the end of the introduction, Philo even approaches a discussion of his sources (*Mos* I, 2 – 4).

We may furthermore gather that Philo had a clear concept of the structure of this biography. In *Mos* I, 5 he relates that he will begin "with what is necessarily the right place to begin", i.e. Moses' family background and childhood. Before Philo deals with the philosophical and intellectual sides of Moses,[19] he summarizes the stations of life contained in his biography. He names birth and nurture on the one hand, and παιδεία and ἀρχή on the other (*Mos* II, 1). This division corresponds closely to standards of (peripatetic) biographies[20] and we may assume a certain familiarity of Philo with this genre. Furthermore, the existence of this type of *Life* among Philo's works opens the possibility that Philo had a similar biographical concept in mind when he wrote on Joseph.

"overthrew the seat and foundation of passion"; *Fuga* 10 he was in charge of a variegated flock, and a general evaluation of Jacob as ideally implementing "life of practice" in *Leg* II, 15.

[17] A. Priessing, *op. cit.*, p. 148, rightly warns that the allegories in the *Life* of Abraham are so numerous that they: "die Form der regelrechten Biographie geradezu sprengen".

[18] See also: A. Barraclough, *op. cit.*, pp. 487 – 91, who distinguishes the Platonic ideal of the philosopher-king to which specifically Hebrew epithets, such as high priesthood, were added by Philo; whereas D. Winston, החכם בתורתו של פילון, דעת 11/תשמ״ג, presents Moses as the culmination of the Stoic wise man.

[19] A. Priessing, *op. cit.*, p. 153, overemphasises this aspects when he claims that the whole of Moses' biography resembles Suetonius' works.

[20] See e.g.: D.A. Russell, *op. cit.*, p. 115; F. Wehrli, *Biographie, op. cit.*, p. 240; C. Schneider, *op. cit.*, pp. 470 – 71; F. Leo, *op. cit.*, p. 99; and A.J. Podlecki's excellent study on *The Peripatetics as Literary Critics*, *Phoenix* 23/1969, pp. 114 – 37. For a general background, see especially: Zeller's detailed account, *op. cit.*, II, 2, pp. 797 – 934; A. Momigliano's sceptical evaluation, *op. cit.*, especially pp. 82 – 86.

Since Philo conceives of Joseph as a politician, some preliminary remarks on his attitude towards politics are in place. In this respect we have to distinguish between theoretical dispositions and historical involvement. Although little evidence of Philo's personal life has survived, it is known that he belonged to a prosperous and politically engaged family.[21] Despite his general preference for a *vita contemplativa* Philo himself became active in the issue of the Alexandrian pogroms; and he participated in the Jewish Embassy to Gaius in AD 39–40.[22]

Intellectually, Philo belongs to an age which had departed from the classical appraisal of political organisation for the development both of society and the individual.[23] Hellenistic schools, particularly the Epicureans,[24] but, to a lesser extent, also the more influencial Stoa, were hesitant to sacrifice the philosopher's *vita contemplativa* for involvement in state affairs.[25] Individual perfection had become a more prominent concern and, in the aftermath of Alexander's con-

---

[21] See J. Morris, in: *Schürer* III, p. 814ff; V.A. Tcherikover, *CPJ* vol. I, Harvard University Press 1957, p. 67, who wishes to reduce Philo's thought to an "expression of a mode of thought characteristic of a whole social class"; for passages which seem to suggest Philo's intimate familiarity with high life, see: *LegAll* III, 155ff; *Fuga* 28ff; *SpecLeg* IV, 74ff.

[22] See also M. Smallwood's controversial reconstruction of the precise historical circumstances and dates, in : *Philonis Alexandri Legatio ad Gaium*, 1961, especially pp. 47–50; and R. Barraclough, *op. cit.*, pp. 418–36.

[23] See especially: E. Barker, *The Political Thought of Plato and Aristotle*, Dover reprint of ed. 1906, pp. 1–16; T.A. Sinclair, *A History of Greek Political Thought*, London 1951, especially ch. VIII–X; V. Ehrenberg, *Der Staat der Griechen*, Zürich 1965, pp. 290–302; A.E. Taylor, *Plato: The Man and his Work*, Meridian 1956; J. Annas, *An Introduction to Plato's Republic*, Oxford 1981; G. Klosko, *The Development of Plato's Political Theory*, New York 1986.

[24] For a background, see: *Epicurus*, *OCD*, pp. 390–92; V. Arnim, *Epikurus*, *RE* vol. VI, cols. 133–55; R.D. Hicks, *Stoic and Epicuran*, London 1910, pp. 153–202; B. Farrington, *Science and Politics in the Ancient World*, London 1939, pp. 118–29. Cf. also E. Zeller's intensely hostile account, *op. cit.*, vol. III, 1, pp. 273–493, and N.W. DeWitt's unscholarly presentation in *Epicurus and his Philosophy*, Minneapolis 1954, pp. 3–35.

[25] The Stoic attitude towards politics has been the subject of much research and no little controversy. Whereas the school's principle reticence was postulated earlier, their involvement has increasingly been emphasized. The classical statement in this regard is to be found in E. Zeller, *op. cit.*, III, 1, pp. 263–78 and pp. 302–06 and pp. 547–609; see also: A.H. Armstrong, *An Introduction to Ancient Philosophy*, London 1965 (4th ed.), pp. 114–129; E. Bréhier, *The Hellenistic and the Roman Age*, Chicago 1965, pp. 127–47; P. Wendland, *Die Hellenistisch-Römische Kultur in ihren Beziehungen zu Judentum und Christentum*, Tübingen 1912, pp. 2–52; A. Dihle, *Ethik*, *Reallexikon für Antike und Christentum*, Stuttgart 1966, vol. VI pp. 646–796; A. Schmekel, *Die Philosophie der Mittleren Stoa*, Georg Olms Verlag 1974 (1st ed. 1892),

quest, government was more happily left to the hopefully ideal kings.[26] It is to be expected that Philo's description of Joseph the politician should reflect some of these intellectual currents of his time.

Joseph's Youth and Early Training

Immediately after Philo has placed Joseph's biography among those of the other patriarchs, he mentions his early training (*Jos* 1). The reference is in fact made so promptly after Joseph is introduced as the politician, that one is inclined to regard it as Philo's explanation for identifying Joseph thus. In the following, the theme of his early education, as related in *Gen* 37:2a, is further elaborated (*Jos* 2):

> Yet he began to be trained (συγκροτεῖσθαι) when he was about seventeen years old in the principles of shepherding which corresponds closely (συνᾴδει) to those of statesmanship. I therefore think the poets are accustomed to call kings (βασιλεῖς) "shepherds of people" (ποιμέvας λαῶν) for someone successful in shepherding is also likely to be[27] the best king[28] since he has been taught care of the noblest flock

whose detailed analysis of the complicated source material has provided the standard for scholarship, see also pp. 225–229 and pp. 356–79 on Paneatius' and later Stoic political theory; M. Pohlenz, *Die Stoa: Geschichte einer geistigen Bewegung*, Göttingen 1964 (3rd ed.), especially pp. 111–157 and *Antikes Führertum*, Leipzig/Berlin 1934, where he stresses the relatively positive attitude to civil duties; and states his controversial (and ill-founded) theory about Zeno's Ideal State as a portrayal of the lost Golden Age; H.C. Baldry's fine article on *Zeno's Ideal State, Journal of Hellenic Studies*, 79/159, pp. 3–15; J.M. Rist, *Stoic Philosophy*, Cambridge 1969, especially pp. 173–218; M.E. Reesor, *The Political Theory of the Old and Middle Stoa*, New York 1951, pp. 1–37; Barth-Gödeckemeyer, *Die Stoa*, Stuttgart 1946, especially pp. 35ff; cf. contrary evaluation of the Stoic attitude to politics by: G.J.D. Aalders, *Political Thought in Hellenistic Times*, Amsterdam 1975, pp. 1–38 and pp. 75–112; M. Avi-Yona, *Hellenism and the East*, Jerusalem 1978, pp. 50–70; J.M.C. Toynbee, *Dictators and Philosophers in the First Century AD*, Greece and Rome 13/1944, pp. 43–58; see also: J. Dillon, *The Middle Platonists*, London 1977; and H. Doerrie's fine study on *Der Platoniker Eudorus von Alexandria, Hermes* 79/1944, pp. 25–39.

[26] See especially: O. Murray, περί βασιλείας: *Studies in the Justification of Monarchic Power in the Hellenistic World*, Dissertation Oxford, especially pp. 211–235; *idem*, *Aristeas and Ptolemaic Kingship, JThSt* N.S. XVIII/1967; *idem*, review of F. Dvornik's book *Early Christian and Byzantine Political Philosophy, JThSt* 1968, especially pp. 673ff; T.A. Sinclair, *op. cit.*, ch. VII–VIII; W.Th. Smitten, *Zur Königsideologie während des Hellenismus*, in: *Bibliotheca Orientalis* 30/1973, pp. 10–13; for a useful collection of translated texts on this subject, see: E. Barker, *From Alexander to Constantine*, Oxford 1956.

[27] F.H. Colson translates the optative more affirmatively as: "for success in shepherding will produce" (ed. Loeb, *op. cit.*, p. 141). See also H.W. Smith on the particle ἄν, in: *Greek Grammar*, Harvard 1984 (1st ed. 1920), p. 407.

[28] Note that the Mss vary between ἄριστος and ἄκρος.

of living creature, man, through the charge of flocks which deserve less.

Philo highlights the subject of his interest already at the opening of this passage, when he paraphrases ''was a shepherd'' as ''was train-ed in the principles of shepherding'', thus replacing simple verbs by more technical terms. Philo then establishes a correlation between the biblical item ''shepherd'' and the concept of political training by inserting two authorial remarks. Initially, he supplies a short subor-dinate clause in which he compares shepherding to statesmanship. He does so by applying the verb συνᾴδω which, though not a techni-cal term for allegory, is frequently used by him when relating bibli-cal material to broader concepts.[29] Sometimes he also employs the term in the specific context of literal and symbolical interpreta-tion.[30] Philo thus introduces almost unnoticed an allegorical notion to the biblical account.[31]

This bucolic metaphor was a commonplace in Hellenistic political thought;[32] and it was known in Judaism, though more restrictedly and usually in a religious context, from biblical times onwards.[33] Philo's readers could therefore be expected to grasp and endorse it

---

[29] E.g.: CreMund, 3; SpecLeg I, 202; SpecLeg II, 130; Mos II, 52; DeEbr 48.

[30] E.g.: Deplan 113: ''Let me say then, that this again is one of the points to be interpreted allegorically, the literal interpretation being quite out of keeping (μη συνᾴδοντος) with the facts''; and also Deplan, 50 and Conf 59. For other Hellenistic terminology of comparison, see: M.H. McCall (jr), Ancient Rhetorical Theories of Si-mile and Comparison, Harvard University Press 1969, pp. 130–161.

[31] See also: S. Sandmel, Philo's Environment and Philo's Exegesis, Journal of Bible and Religion, 22/1954, especially p. 249ff where he asserts that ''Philo's literal in-terpretation is not always as literal as one would suppose''.

[32] See also: G.J.D. Aalders, op. cit., pp. 23–26; W. Bauer, ποιμήν, in: A Greek English Lexicon of the New Testament and Other Early Christian Literature, 2nd revised ed. Chicago 1979, p. 684; for an example of the image, see e.g. DL IX: 40 where it is applied to Democritus. For a background on the bucolic imagery in Homer, to whom the note of ''the poets'' mainly relates, see J. Duchemin. Aspects Pastoraux de la Poésie homérique, Revue des Etudes Grecques, 73/1960, pp. 362–415, where she enumerates references to nature and deals in particular with the motif of hunting.

[33] The locus classicus is the story of David: in ISam 17:15 he is described as guarding his father's flock and in IISam 7:7–8 he is called by God from the flock to be the shepherd of His people; in Ex ch. XXXIV God is furthermore depicted as reprimanding Israel's leaders for neglecting their flock, and in Jer 2:8ff and Gen 49:24ff and elsewhere God himself is called shepherd. On the other hand, the term מלך is used far more frequently both for the human and the Divine king (e.g., IKg 16:22, Ex 15:18); there are also prominent layers in Scripture which reject human leadership altogether and regard it as mistrust in God (e.g.: Jud 8:22–23; ISam 8:1–22); for the background, see also: J. Kaufman, תולדות האמונה הישראלית, Jerusalem 1956, vol. II, 1, pp. 160–61, where he affirms the principally real-

easily.[34] Nevertheless, Philo inserts a further, more expanded explanation.

In his second remark Philo elaborates the metaphor from a more directly authorial perspective and relates the biblical passage to contemporary literary notions. On the basis of the preceding identification of shepherding with statesmanship, he introduced a reference to "the poets" and further authorizes the metaphor by his own conjectures. Although he himself does not specify the reference, Philo might well have been thinking particularly of Platonic works.[35] This is corroborated by *Legatio* 44 and 76 where Philo not only describes the ἡγεμών as shepherd but also insists on the positive moral responsibility which this title implies.[36]

It is of great significance that Philo uses the shepherd imagery in the biography of Moses, too. Also the grand Israelite leader is said to have been trained thus for his later political career (*Mos* I, 60):

> Moses took charge of the sheep ... for the shepherd's business is a training ground and a preliminary exercise in kingship for one who is destined to command the herd of mankind.

It emerges from this parallel that Philo portrays Joseph's youth in conformity with his own standards of a "political biography", which he developed most, as we saw above, in the case of Moses.[37] We may gather how positive an understanding he had of the epithet

---

political orientation in Ancient Israel; B.D. Napier, *Sheep/Shepherd*, *IDB* vol. IV, pp. 315–16; S. Szikszai, *king*, *IDB* vol. III, pp. 11–17 and P. Weber-Schäfer's discussion in: *Einführung in die antike politische Theorie*, Darmstadt 1976.

[34] Cf. J. Jermias, ποιμήν, in: *Theologisches Wörterbuch zum Neuen Testament*, ed. G. Kittel, Stuttgart 1933, p. 488ff, where he mistakenly conjectures that Philo inserted the image in anticipation of condescending reactions on the part of his readers; for a conclusive evaluation of the *Wörterbuch*'s fundamental shortcomings, see: J. Barr, *The Semantics of Biblical Language*, Oxford 1961, pp. 206–262.

[35] E.g.: *Pol* 261D, 266E (statesman and king as guards of the herd), 267D (statesman as flock-tender); 275 (Divine shepherd superior to the human ones who resemble their subjects) and 365D; *Gor* 516A; cf. G.J.D. Aalders, *op. cit.*, p. 24, who mistakenly regards Plato's moderations of super-human attributes, which had apparently been attached to the image, as a "forceful" rejection of the whole metaphor. Consider also other classical uses for the image of the shepherd, e.g. in Homer's *Iliad* I, 263. For expressions of Philo's general admiration for Plato, which increases the likelihood of his borrowing from him, see e.g.: *Abr* 10; *Prov* II:42; *QuOmn* 867; *DeProf* 459.

[36] By imputing the idea of a human shepherd "of higher nature and destiny" to Silanius, Philo clearly distances himself from it.

[37] In this passage Philo stresses the royal claims of Moses, whereas concerning Joseph he had introduced the term 'king' only indirectly by reference to the poets.

shepherd, when we consider Philo's further elaborations on the topic throughout the biography of Moses. In *Mos* I, 61 – 63 Philo affirms that this title bestows the "highest honour"; he furthermore connects it with a "sense of duty and honesty" and concludes that the perfect king has to have knowledge in shepherding.[38]

If on the other hand, we compare Philo's interpretation of Joseph's youth with the Midrash it emerges that, although the shepherd image was attributed to Moses,[39] it was not used in this context of Joseph.[40] In distinct contrast to the midrasic emphasis on the sins of his early youth,[41] Philo even omits all negative biblical evidence[42] and thus idealizes the figure. It is thus obvious that in comparison with other exegetes, Philo attributes unusual importance to Joseph whom he describes in similar terms to Moses himself.

After this introduction Philo selects *Gen* 37:3[43] for further elaboration (*Jos* 4):

> So his father, observing in him a noble spirit (φρόνημα εὐγενὲς) which rose above ordinary conditions, rendered to him high admiration and respect, while his love for this child of his later years—and nothing condudes to affection more than this—exceeded his love for his other sons. And being himself a lover of excellence, by special and exceptional attentions he fostered the fire of the boy's nature, in the hope that it would not only smoulder but rapidly burst into a flame.

---

[38] See also *Mos* I, 64 where he eulogises the prosperity of Moses' flocks and *Mos* I, 217 where he expresses a general praise of kingship.

[39] E.g.: *ExR* 2:2 (God to Moses) "You have shown compassion in leading a flock of flesh and blood, by your life, you will guard my flock Israel", also *TanB* II, 1; see also: L. Ginzberg, *The Legends of the Jews*, Philadelphia 1969, vol. ii, pp. 300 – 01; vol. IV, pp. 82 – 83; vol. V, p. 114 n108 – 09; vol. VI, p. 248 n13 – 14, he cites numerous passages in support of a wide-spread use of the shepherd image; these are, however, usually very late and often even Christian. Ginzberg seems to have been guided by the conviction of a basic congruence of the different cultures.

[40] Also in later references such as *Tan Gen* 5 and *Shir Hashirim Zuta*, A, 15.4 the term רעה (*Gen* 37:2) does not acquire a political dimension although it is applied to the shepherd of human beings: as Joseph was a shepherd in his youth so he was later to become a nourisher of his brothers. For more details, see Chap. V and especially section three.

[41] For details see chap. V.

[42] I.e. Joseph's bad report about his brothers and the colourful coat which Jacob gives to him as a token of his special love (*Gen* 37:2 – 3).

[43] "Jacob loved Joseph more than all his children because he was the son of his old age".

In this passage, Philo mentions the biblical reason for Jacob's preference which he, as in the case of Abraham,[44] qualifies by a psychological generalisation. In addition, he inserts qualities of Joseph which demand in his opinion the father's respect and thus he justifies Jacob's otherwise perhaps wanton preference.

The exceptional φρόνημα which Philo attributes to Joseph, has to be appreciated in the context of Philo's praises of other patriarchs. In comparison to them, the description of Joseph seems rather more modest. In fact, the descriptions of Isaac and Moses, for example, are far more consummate. Thus the reader learns of Isaac's "great bodily beauty and excellence of soul" and of his "perfection of virtues beyond his age". His father Abraham is moreover said to be moved not only by "natural affection, but also by such deliberate judgement as a censor of character (ἠθῶν δικαστὴν) might make".[45]

Moses' talents are furthermore eulogized to an incomparably greater degree. Philo initially praises his "unusual comeliness",[46] then he gives examples of his quick childhood development[47] and finally extols his nous as almost divine and exceedingly rational.[48] Characteristically, Philo also describes in some detail the sort of education Moses received and how he astonished his teachers.[49]

By comparison to these two, Philo's Joseph is less hellenized and the topoi of political biography are not fully exploited in his case.[50] In this passage, as in numerous others,[51] Philo shows instead a keener interest in the figure of Jacob and the focalisation on the father's inner life overshadows the figure of Joseph. Highlighting

---

[44] Abr 195: "For parents somehow dote on their late-born children".

[45] The above quotations are to be found in Abr 168.

[46] Mos I, 9 "γεννηθεὶς οὖν ὁ παῖς εὐθὺς ὄψιν ἐνέφαινεν ἀστειοτέραν ἢ κατ' ἰδιώτην"; F.H. Colson's translation "goodliness" (op. cit., p. 281) misses the aesthetic dimension. See also: Mos I, 15.

[47] Mos I, 19.

[48] Mos I, 27.

[49] Mos I, 20–25.

[50] In Philo's list of the necessary attributes of a ruler (Mos I, 154) the term φρόνημα is also missing, although σωφροσύνη is mentioned; for the general background, see also: V. Tcherikover, The Ideology of the Letter of Aristeas, HTR 51/1958, pp. 59–85.

[51] E.g.: Jos 22–27 (Philo's expansion on Jacob's mourning over his son's alleged death); Jos 187–89 (Jacob's mourning over Simon's absence) and Jos 192–95 (where Philo's Jacob gives more extensive advice for the journey than his biblical counterpart does).

the *Vorlage* Jacob's hopes concerning Joseph is future development, nevertheless raise the reader's expectations and re-focus his attention on the protagonist.

Philo reshapes the biblical account of the open family tensions in accordance with the above characterisation of Joseph. Modifying *Gen* 37:4[52] he writes (*Jos* 5):

> But envy (φθόνος) ever the enemy of outstanding success set to work also in this case and created division in a household where all parts had been flourishing. They displayed ill will to Joseph as a counterpart to his father's good will.

In contrast to the biblical account, Philo's narrative is at this point not focalised on the brothers. He takes instead a more general look from the authorial perspective and thus prevents the reader from identifying with the brothers. Philo moreover stresses Joseph's innocence by applying a popular Hellenistic concept[53] to the biblical story. Envy is furthermore a standard item in Hellenistic biographies, where it usually figures as a challenge to the idealised protagonist at the initial stages of his career.[54] It is also highly significant that Philo inserts this element also in Moses's *curriculum vitae*,[55] and we gather from this to what extent Philo adapts the account of Joseph's youth to the standard of a political biography.

In the subsequent unfolding of the family drama Philo provides additional evidence in Joseph's favour. According to him, it was Joseph's naiveté which prompted him to relate his dreams in a slightly

---

[52] "And his brothers, seeing that his father loved him most of all his sons, hated him and could not talk to him in peace".

[53] Note that the term φθόνος has also no basis in the *LXX*; and the variant reading εζηλωσαν which would better corroborate Philo's interpretation belongs to a 13th Century MSS (see also: J.V. Wevers, *Genesis*, Göttingen 1974, p. 353); numerous book titles testify to the importance of the concept of envy in Hellenistic thought, e.g.: *SFV* III, 418; *DeTusDis* IV, 58ff; Epictet's *Diatribes* 3, 11, 2 and 4, 5, 7; for the background, see also: E. Milobenski, *Der Neid in der griechischen Philosophie*, Wiesbaden 1964, especially p. 118ff; for Philo's treatment of the subject in general, see e.g.: *SpecLeg* II: 141; *Abr* 151ff; *Vir* 223; *Prob* 13. Note that J. Laporte, *op. cit.*, p. 44 n4. emphasises that "l'Envie est presque personnifiée".

[54] See D.A. Russell, *op. cit.*, p. 115; A. Wardman, *Plutarch's Lives*, London 1974, especially pp. 69–78, where he discusses such passages as *Cato* I, 16:4; *Dion* 11:7ff and *Fab* 25:2–3; for other examples in Plutarch, see: *Tim* XXXVII:4 ("he did not expose himself to the jealousy of his fellow citizens, the rock on which most generals in their insatiable greed for honours and power make shipwreck"); *Coriolanus* XXIII:3 and XXXI:1–2.

[55] In *Mos* I, 64 he is said to be envied for his success in shepherding.

frivolous fashion to his brothers (*Jos* 6). Also, he is said to have approached his brothers with salutations while they looked at him "as though he was an enemy in battle" (*Jos* 14). These elucidations of Philo are very much in line with those of his exegetical predecessor Artapanus. Both interpret Joseph's position in the initial scenes of the biblical story in a very favourable light; and both show unusual sympathy for the plight of the talented individual among his "boorish" brothers. Yet while Artapanus seems to have been motivated by the simple desire to create an ideal fore-father of the Hebrews in Egypt, Philo's interpretation is likely to have been prompted more by his literary background.

The figure of Joseph thus emerges from the above passages by Philo as an idealised youth who betrays certain signs of a grand political future. These are introduced in a similar fashion, yet far more modestly than in the case of Moses.

Joseph's Career: Literally and Allegorically

As we know from *Mos* II, 1 Philo considers ἀρχή a standard topic of biography. Subsequent to early up-bringing and education, he conceives of career as a distinct phase in the life of the politician. Also in the case of Joseph he pays special attention to his rise to power and the climax of his career.[56] He expresses this interest in significant, literal and allegorical insertions.

The first focal point of Joseph's career naturally is his success in Potiphar's house. Reshaping the biblical account,[57] Philo describes this stage as follows (*Jos* 37–38):

> In a few days he gave proof of his nobility of character and nature (τῆς καλοκἀγαθίας καὶ εὐγενείας) and therefore he received authority over his fellow-servants and the charge of the whole household ... so while it seemed (τῷ μὲν οὖν δοκεῖν) that it was his purchaser who appointed him, in fact and truth (ἔργῳ δὲ καὶ ταῖς ἀληθείαις) nature was soliciting for him rule over cities, a nation and a land; for the future statesman

---

[56] Consider Philo's general concern in e.g. *Jos* 246 (rendered through the words of Joseph's brothers.)

[57] *Gen* 39:2–4: "The Lord was with Joseph and he became a successful man and he was in the house of his master the Egyptian, and his master saw that the Lord was with him, and that the Lord caused all that he did to prosper in his hands. So Joseph found favour in his sight and attended him and he made him overseer over his house and put him in charge of everything he had".

needed first to be trained and practised in house management . . . and household management may be called a small scale state management (οἰκονομία συνηγμένη τις πολιτεία).

In this passage, Philo substantially reshapes the biblical scene; and while moderating its emphasis on Divine providence[58] he presents his own, more philosophical understanding of this phase in Joseph's life.

Philo primarily accounts for Joseph's promotion by reference to his nature. He emphasises Joseph's morally noble character and his natural aptitude. Philo generally uses the term καλοκἀγαθία in its Hellenistic sense[59] but also in a more religious connotation.[60] Significantly, it is also in Philo's account of Moses's promotion to national leadership (*Mos* I, 148–50) that this quality is important. Philo stresses here that it was only on account of these inherent qualities that Moses was appointed. He further adds that this was "not like some of those who thrust themselves into positions of power by means of arms and engines of war and strength of infantry, cavalry and navy".[61]

His parallel portrayal of Moses suggests that it is Philo's notion of a "political biography" which provoked this standard, albeit more moderate presentation of Joseph's first step in "public life". It

---

[58] Note that Philo does not altogether omit the reference to God: the sentence not quoted in the above passage reads thus: "for his owner had already observed many signs that everything which he (i.e. Joseph) said or did was under God's directing care". It should also be mentioned that this reiteration of a biblical item by Philo does certainly not corroborate R. Barraclough's attempt (*op. cit.*, p. 493) to affirm E.R. Goodenough's claim that the biblical passage was accommodated to Hellenistic concepts of kingship under "Divine guidance and inspiration".

[59] E.g.: *SpecLeg* 215 (in connection with ἀρετή), *Agr* 135, *Leg* 5 (in connection with σώφρονος βίου ζῆλον), *DeCong* 31 (in connection with physical health and δικαιοσύνη), *Abr* 56 (refers in a wider sense to Moses's virtues), *Vir* 10, 52 (of Moses), 60, 201, 226, *Fug* 45. For a background, see especially Aristotle's discussion on the necessity of inherent good inclinations for the development of character, *NE* 1179b.

[60] E.g.: *Vir* 79, *SpecLeg* 101 (as requirement of the priest's wife and in connection with aristocratic lineage), *Abr* 98 (in connection with εὐσέβεια), *Mos* II, 189 (as a gift from God, particularly for the Jewish people), *VitCon* 90 (the Therapeutae are said to deserve a special friendship with God thanks to their κ.) and *Abr* 254.

[61] See also *Vir* 55–56, where Philo expresses himself in similar terms about Joshua: he is said almost to share Moses's power on account of his numerous virtues and his faithful assistance. In contrast to his treatment of Joseph and Moses, Philo then goes on to explain that, although Moses regarded him so highly, he did not appoint him διάδοχος because his judgement was only human and worth much less than Divine inaugurations.

emerges that Philo is for this reason highly sensitive to the fact of Joseph's growing responsibilities; and he wishes to assert that this development conformed to the ideal pattern of political advancement.

Philo further provides an allegorical interpretation which illuminates Joseph's progress at this stage from a slightly different angle. He introduces this exegesis as a metaphor and postulates the equivalence of house and state, thus stressing the value of house management in the future stateman's training. The image of the household is common in political thought both throughout Philo's work[62] and in Hellenistic theories.[63] Parallel to the shepherd-allegory Philo can thus be sure of his readers' familiarity and quick acceptance of it.

Joseph's career takes off when he is appointed by Pharaoh.[64] Philo describes this event in accordance with his earlier exegetical interests[65] (*Jos* 106–07; 116–18):

> The king, judging him by his appearance (ὄψεως τεκμηράμενος) to be a man of free and noble birth, for the persons of those whom we see exhibit characteristics (χαρακτῆρες) which are not visible to all, but only to those in whom the eye of understanding is quick to discern, said: ... Joseph, nothing awed by the high dignity of the speaker, spoke with frankness combined with modesty, rather as a king to a subject than the subject to a king ... Pharaoh said: shall we find another man such as this? ... And no one will condemn me for hastiness, for I am not actuated by self-confidence ... (but) great natures (μεγάλαι τῶν φύσεων) take no long time to prove themselves

---

[62] E.g.: *Fug* 36; *Mut* 149; *Ebr* 91 and *Praem* 113.

[63] See also: R. Barraclough, *op. cit.*, p. 494 (with examples in Hellenistic literature in n.705) and p. 498, especially n.747; consider particularly: Plato's *Pol* 259C (identification of kingship with household management and statesmanship, to be headed by the wise ruler); and Aristotle's *Politics* I, 2 (king's rule resembles the senior's presidency over the house), *ibid* I, 12 (types of household management resemble types of political rule), *ibid*, III, 6 (ruler's concern for his subjects' welfare resembles authority over the household).

[64] *Gen* 41:14–17: "... Pharaoh said to Joseph: I have had a dream and there is nobody to interpret it; and I have heard it said of you that when you hear a dream you can interpret it. Joseph answered Pharaoh: it is not me, but God will give Pharaoh a favourable answer ... And Pharaoh said to his servants: can we find such a man as this, in whom is the spirit of God? ..."

[65] Note, however, that after these secularised versions of Joseph's career, Philo also provides a profoundly pious interpretation of the events (*Jos* 122–24); vacillations of this sort are typical of Philo's heterogeneous works.

(δοκιμάζονται), but by the massiveness of their power force others to give them rapid and immediate acceptance.

We may clearly distinguish three parts in Philo's paraphrase, i.e., Joseph's calm posture with regard to Pharaoh which is bracketed by two more theoretical considerations on the part of the king.

Philo highlights two aspects in Joseph's behaviour, namely, his composure and his natural superiority. His point on Joseph's self-possession is all the more picturesque since he describes the situation from Joseph's perspective. In this way Philo encourages the reader's admiration for the protagonist. Although the precise qualities of "frankness and modesty" are not mentioned in Philo's list of a king's excellences (*Mos* I, 54), they would nevertheless appear to correspond to the more general requirement of temperance.[66] In this particular situation they establish Joseph as a person who neither flatters nor behaves arrogantly.

Assuming again the authorial perspective Philo then explicitly states the kingly nature of Joseph's demeanour. This comment develops further a theme of which we encountered earlier hints in the form of royal allegories. This exegetical line has a considerable tradition and is first attested in *IMacc* 2,53. It should nevertheless be noted that Philo remains sufficiently faithful to Scripture as to refrain from directly identifying Joseph as the king. He makes the most daring statement in *Jos* 119 where he affirms that, while Pharaoh kept the title, Joseph actually executed the power.[67]

Philo further uses the figure of Pharaoh to express important remarks of general import about Joseph. Focalising the biblical scene on Pharaoh, he is able to expand and expose his inner thoughts. Subsequently, he also embellishes the biblical account of Pharaoh's actual speech to Joseph. In these two indirect characterisations of Joseph a distinct concept of human personality transpires.[68] It becomes clear that according to Philo the character of a person can in

---

[66] Modesty and frankness furthermore belong to the canon of Hellenistic kingship whence Philo might also have drawn them (see also: O. Murray, *op. cit.*, pp. 211–221).

[67] As we saw above, this is a recurrent theme in Philo's descriptions of political relations, e.g. *Vir* 55–57 of Joshua.

[68] For a general background on the concept of person in Antiquity, see especially: F. Leo, *op. cit.*, pp. 85–118; A. Momigliano, *A. Mauss and the Quest for the Person in Greek Biography and Autobiography*, in: *The Category of the Person*, ed. M. Carrithers a.o., Cambridge 1985, pp. 83–93, his fervent affirmation of the concept of person

the main be deduced from the person's external expressions. We furthermore note the underlying assumption that particularly great natures are reflected in action and in visible wordly influence. This understanding of personality is in fact rather common in the Aristotelian traditions; and it is often reflected in biographical works.[69]

We may gather how essential these concepts are in Philo's "political biography" from a comparison with his description of Moses. Philo in fact relates the discovery of his portentous talents in almost identical terms (*Mos* I, 59):

> Their father was at once struck with admiration of his appearance (ὄψιν) and soon afterwards of his disposition, for great natures are transparent (ἀρίδηλοι γὰρ μεγάλαι φύσεις) and need no length of time to be recognized (οὐ μήκει χρόνου γνωριζόμεναι).

Philo moreover introduces the scene at the well, in the context of which the above comment is made, in truly biographical style.[70] In *Mos* I, 51 he stresses that he will "describe an action of his (Moses) at

---

is based mostly on fine intuitive evidence, but sometimes lacks clear definitions; K.J. Weintraub, *The Value of the Individual*, Chicago 1978, especially pp. 1–18, where he postulates anew G. Misch's arguments; R. Hirzel, *Die Person: Begriff und Name derselben im Altertum*, Sitzungsberichte der Bayrischen Akademie 1914, who presents a collection of the philological evidence; B. Bucher-Iser, *Norm und Individualität in den Biographien Plutarchs*, Stuttgart 1972, pp. 79–82. Cf. also W. Janke, *Individuum/Individualismus*, in: *Theologische Realenzyklopädie* XVI, Walter de Gruyter 1987, pp. 117–124 and H. Drexler, *Die Entdeckung des Individuums*, Salzburg 1966, who both claim a Christian monopoly on the origin of the concept.

[69] See e.g.: J. Barnes' introduction to Aristotle's thought, *Aristotle*, Oxford 1982, pp. 36–83; A. Oksenberg Rorty (ed.), *Essays on Aristotle's Ethics*, University of California 1980; D. Charles, *Aristotle's Philosophy of Action*, London 1984, especially his detailed discussion on pp. 57–108; in the *NE* the following passages are particularly relevant: IV: 1; VI: 12, IX: 3; X: 8; concerning the biographical tradition, see e.g.: Polybios' discussions (bk IX: 22–24; X: 2:1ff) on whether and to what extent a man's deeds disclose his nature and the example of Scipio Africanus (for a background on Polybios' biographies, see: F. Leo, *op. cit.*, pp. 242–53); some examples of Plutarch are to be found in e.g. *Timoleon* VI: 1–4; *Coriolanus* I: 2 and IV: 1–2; *Alexander* IV: 1–3 and XX: 1; *Demetrius* 1: 2–3.

[70] See also: A.J. Podlecki, *op. cit.*, especially p. 132, where he summarises his results concerning peripatetic biographical practices; F. Leo, *op. cit.*, especially pp. 184–90, on Plutarch's concepts as based on continuous Aristotelian traditions; E. Zeller, *op. cit.*, III, 2, pp. 198–205. For a background on Plutarch's anthropology and its application in the biographies; for Plutarch's practices, see also: J.H. Hamilton, *Plutarch. Alexander. A Commentary*, Oxford 1969, pp. XXXVII–XLIII; H. Erbse, *Die Bedeutung der Synkrisis in den Parallelbiographien Plutarchs*, Hermes 84/1956, pp. 384–424, see especially pp. 399–402 and p. 422ff; for examples, see: *Alexander* I, 2 where he categorically states that he will not present all the available facts but select those incidents which reveal character (ἔμφασιν ἤθους) and I, 3

this time which, though it may seem a petty matter, argues a spirit of no petty kind''. It becomes clear in this introduction that Philo relates that particular anecdote with a view to illustrate the protagonist's underlying character. His above quoted summary evaluation of Moses' nature must be considered in light of it and therefore be taken all the more seriously. Philo obviously has this more expanded notion also in mind when paraphrasing Joseph's promotion. It thus becomes clear once more that Philo adapts to the Joseph story certain biographical categories which he uses more explicitly in the *bios* of Moses.[71]

In the "literal" account the brothers' meeting in Egypt is the last subject which Philo clearly embellishes in terms of a political biography. He does so on many occasions and the accumulation of evidence offers another glance at Philo's understanding of Joseph's role in worldly affairs.

Philo's description of his brothers' first encounter with Joseph opens with the same concern for their failure to recognize him as does Josephus's later.[72] Also Philo explains this perplexing fact by reference to their excitement over the governor's high rank. However, after this brief focalisation on the brothers, Philo, in contrast to rabbinic exegesis,[73] paraphrases the remaining events with an exclusive view to Joseph.

Philo thus embellishes the brothers' reception with a unique aspect (*Jos* 166):

> Although he was still young he succeeded to such a high position, invested with the first office (διάδοχος)[74] after (along with)[75] the king,

---

where he compares this procedure to painting which catches but the essential, these principles are also stated in *Cimon* II: 3–5; for vivid examples, see e.g. *Alexander* VI: 1–5 and IX: 1–2.

[71] Note in this context also that only with regard to these two is the term φύσις employed in the biographical sense; for the common Philonic uses of the word, see e.g.: *Poster* 185, *Abr* 249, *Opif* 89 and 21, *Sacrif* 12 in the sense of Natural Law; *Cher* III: 10, *Opif* 149–50, *Sacrif* 75–77 in the sense of human nature as distinct from animal; for a general background, see also A. Mendelson's discussion of human types in Philo's *opera* (*Secular Education in Philo of Alexandria*, Cincinnati 1982, pp. 47–67), as far as I can see, however, he remains exceedingly faithful to S. Sandmel's conclusions.

[72] *JA* I: 97.

[73] Consider for example *GR* 1122 where the brothers' anticipation of and search for Joseph in Egypt is vividly described.

[74] Note that in Hellenistic Greek the term increasingly carries the notion of "deputy" rather than "successor".

[75] This is the reading of MSS Vatican Laurentianus plut. LXXXV cod. 10

to whom[76] the east and west was looking up;[77] he was flushed with the prime of life and the greatness of his power, having the opportunity of revenge, he might have born malice, but he exercised control over his emotion.

The impetus for Philo's expansion may be his urge to moderate the apparent harshness of the biblical Joseph by putting it into proper perspective. Yet his detailed portrait of Joseph's position also betrays his keen interest in the status of the individual. The terms he is using here in the description of royal power are indeed so lofty that they rather seem to reflect the status of rulers over great empires, such as Philo might have known from earlier or contemporaneous history.[78] Also his expressions of Joseph's self-discipline might be inspired by such a background in kingship, theory or practice.[79] Philo's account of the later relations between the brothers in Egypt essentially corresponds to that of Josephus. Yet unlike his Hellenistic colleague he phrases his interpretations in terminology with distinct political connotations.[80]

In addition to the above mentioned interpretations of Joseph as a politician Philo also presents what he himself describes as the allegorical meaning of those passages. The expositions are usually quite lengthy and interrupt the natural flow of the *bios*. In these expansions of the biblical text Philo is also concerned with the political aspects of Joseph. Here he illuminates them, however, at greater liberty and in more detachment from the *Vorlage*.[81] The first such

---

(μετά βασιλεως. For an evaluation of it, see *W-C*, pp. XX–XXV.

[76] The relative pronoun ''ov'' can be regarded as dependent on either the king or Joseph himself. P. Laporte, *op. cit.*, p. 109, assumes the former and F.H. Colson, *op. cit.*, p. 221, the latter. The context appears to support P. Laporte's interpretation.

[77] Note that the MSS vary between ἀπο- and ἐπιβλέπω.

[78] Note that the eulogistic Alexander traditions were at that time fully flourishing (see R. Lane Fox, *Alexander The Great*, London 1973, especially p. 11; pp. 25–27; p. 43ff); also consider that Philo himself witnessed the contest of the Roman *triumviri* for dominion over the vast empire.

[79] See *Mos* I, 154; O. Murray, *Aristeas, op. cit.*, p. 338; for the importance of this subject in biography, consider Plutarch's stress on Alexander's self-control in situations stimulating the opposite (e.g.: *Alexander* XXI: 1–5; XXII: 45; XXIII: 1ff); note also that Philo reiterates this motive when treating Joseph's confrontation with Benjamin (*Jos* 200–01).

[80] Note in this context also that when justifying Simon's imprisonment, Philo's exposition conspicuously reflects an awareness of inner-party struggles (*Jos* 175ff).

[81] A careful analysis of the allegorical material and its relation to the literal ac-

addition is to be found in *Jos* 28 – 31 and has widely been recognized as inspired by Stoic thought.[82] With this remark Philo sets a certain frame for his subsequent allegorical interpretations. In *Jos* 32 – 34 Philo presents an extended allegory of Joseph's colourful coat:

> He is further quite properly said to assume a coat of many colours,[83] for political life is a thing multi-coloured and varied, open to innumerable changes brought about by personalities, circumstances, motives, individualities of conduct, differences in occasions and places. The pilot is helped to a successful voyage by means which change with the changes of the wind and does not confine his guidance of the ship to one method. The physician does not use a single form of treatment for all his patients, nor even for one individual if the physical condition does not remain unaltered, but he watches ... all the changes of the symptoms and varies his salutary processes sometimes using one kind, sometimes another. And so also the politician must be a man of many sides and many forms.

In this passage Philo allegorises some items of the Joseph story and so presents one facet of the politician's role.[84] According to him the statesman's way of adapting to the changing circumstances of life is to be compared to that of a pilot or a physician. He furthermore

---

count is needed. Studies of this subject have been executed before and some of them tend towards too clear-cut generalisations. See especially: Y. Amir, *Griechische Gestalt, op. cit.*, especially pp. 19 – 20, where he summarises Philo's exposition of the figure of Joseph thus: "Es ist gewiss kein Zufall, dass die positive Bewertung im Bereich des Wortsinns herrscht, die kritisch-ablehnende dagegen in der allegorischen Deutung: solange Philo sich im gegebenen Rahmen der konkreten Welt hält, hat er Anerkennung für den relativen Wert des Politikers ... dagegen kann das Lavieren mit den wechselnden Umständen den Menschen nur fernhalten von seinem absoluten Streben nach absoluter Wahrheit"; his concept of Philo's "doppelter Buchführung" (private communication, Jerusalem March 1988) stresses perhaps too much Philo's separation between the two which, as we saw earlier, Philo himself does not always strictly keep; R. Löwe, *"Plain" Meaning of Scripture in Early Jewish Exegesis*, in: *Papers of the Institute of Jewish Studies London*, ed. J.G. Weiss, Jerusalem 1964, vol. I, regarding Philo p. 148ff; J. Pepin, *Remarques sur la théorie de l'exégese allégorique chez Philon*, in: *Philon d'Alexandrie, Colloques Nationaux du Centre National de la Recherche Scientifique*, Paris 1969, pp. 134 – 50; E. Brehier, *op. cit.*, pp. 14 – 18; G. Delling, *Perspektiven der Erforschung des Hellenistischen Judentums*, *HUCA* 45/1974, especially p. 144.

[82] Most recently, this point has been made by R. Barraclough, *op. cit.*, p. 492; see also: F. Geiger, *Philon von Alexandria als sozialer Denker*, Stuttgart 1932, p. 51, and G.J.D. Aalders, *op. cit.*, p. 88ff.

[83] Note that Philo uses in this allegorical passage the very item which he had conspicuously omitted from his "literary" account.

[84] R. Barraclough, *op. cit.*, p. 493, regards this passage as an indication of Philo's pragmatism and "sober realism". As we shall see below, such descriptions are perhaps somewhat too strong.

stresses that the politician thus benefits the whole community (*Jos* 34).

Philo builds this allegory on three metaphors. Initially he identifies one biblical item (colourful coat) as a reference to the variegated nature of political life. He then supplies two symbolic examples to elucidate the specific role of the statesman in it. Philo uses these metaphors of the pilot and the physician also elsewhere in his work. In the context of Abraham's allegorical (!) biography he likens the wise man both to the ruler of the city and to a pilot in a ship (*Abr* 272). From his subsequent comment we may further gather Philo's high regard for this function: he compares the position of the pilot and the wise man in society to the soul in its relation to the body.

The medical metaphor is furthermore treated in *Jos* 62–63 where the doctors are mentioned in the context of an allegory on democracy and the rule of law.[85] They are favourably contrasted with the cooks and their contribution to society is acknowledged. It is also clear that Philo expects his readers' familiarity with this image for he confidently refers to "matters of common knowledge".

Such references in addition to the details of Philo's image make it probable that Philo had Platonic terms in mind. In Plato's then highly popular political theory this medical metaphor is indeed a commonplace.[86] Thus the question is raised in *Pol* 295D whether the politician should not be allowed to change the rules in accordance with the patients' needs for, so Plato urges, "the wind or something else had, by the act of God, changed unexpectedly from their natural course". In *Pol* 297D he further writes:

> Just as the captain of a ship keeps watch for what is at any moment for the food of the vessel and the sailors, not by writing rules, but by making his science his law and thus preserves his fellow voyagers, so may not a right government be established in the same way by men who could rule by this principle . . .

---

[85] For a discussion of Philo's exceptionally positive and idiosyncratic conception of democracy, see also: E. Langstadt, *Zu Philos Begriff der Demokratie*, in: *Occident and Orient*, ed. B. Schindler, London 1936, pp. 349–64; R. Barraclough, *op. cit.*, pp. 520–23. Consider particularly *Immut* 176 where democracy is presented as the most desirable form of government.

[86] See especially F. Wehrli, *Der Arztvergleich bei Plato*, in: *Theoria, op. cit.*, pp. 206–214 (1st published 1951), he reaches the conclusion that Plato uses the metaphor differently from contemporary medical usage "um den bedingten Wert der Gesetze darzustellen, welche sich den der Einzelsituation angemessenen Vorschriften des Herrschers beugen sollen" (p. 207).

Not only do the above passages suggest Philo's borrowing from Platonic imagery, but there is a further indication in the fact that the ἱμάτιον ποικίλον frequently serves in Plato's works as a metaphor for the (dangerous) many-sidedness of political life in a democracy.[87]

It thus emerges that Philo probably draws this allegory of the statesman from Platonic traditions. It is Philo's tendency in the *Life*, to focus more on the positive role of the politician amidst instability of political life and to withhold his general, moral reservations about his function.[88] It is moreover significant that the topic of political instability recurs in the *Life* of Moses. In the case of the grand Israelite leader Philo uses even more univocal language. In place of using metaphors, he takes here the opportunity of the account of Israel's rebellion in the desert to praise Moses' political performance in subduing it (*Mos* I: 197–98).[89] Philo's attitude is thus highly complex and he expresses his ethical reservations towards politics more with regard to the minor figure of Joseph.

On the occasion of Joseph's confrontation with Potiphar's wife, Philo later revives the discussion on the statesman's struggle with the dangers of political life. He interprets here the licentious woman as an allegory for the human multitudes who ensnare their leaders and enslave them to pleasures (*Jos* 64–66).[90] Against this threat he then casts the behaviour of the "true politician" (*Jos* 67–68):

---

[87] E.g.: *Pol* 557C, 559Dff, 561D etc. For the background on Plato's thought on democracy and his condemnation of its diversity and instability, see especially E. Barker's discussion, *op. cit.*, p. 140, pp. 254–8, pp. 290–1, pp. 311–2; E. Zeller, *op. cit.*, vol. II, 1 pp 892–925.

[88] On other occasions, however, Philo expresses his reservations towards politics very clearly. In such passages, Joseph often comes to symbolize "the many-sided pride of wordly life" (e.g.: *Confus* 71; and also numerous passages in *Somn* I and II; *Vir* 15 etc.). These "hard-line" statements seem moreover to have been inspired by Hellenistic thought. For a background, see also: W.K.C. Guthrie, *A History of Greek Philosophy*, Cambridge 1978, vol. IV ch. VII; A.A. Long, *Hellenistic Philosophy*, London 1974, pp. 210–32; A.H. Armstrong, *op. cit.*, pp. 114–29; J.M. Rist, *op. cit.*, pp. 173–200; G.J.D. Aalders, *op. cit.*, pp. 97–102; E. Zeller, *op. cit.*, III: 1, pp. 263–78 and pp. 581–86; M. Pohlenz, *Zeno und Chrysipp*, in: *Kleine Schriften*, *op. cit.*, pp. 1–38; idem, *Philon von Alexandria*, ibid, pp. 324–76. For sources, see especially: *SVF* III, pp. 174–75; Cicero's *Acad* II, 44–136, *DeOff* I, 72; I, 90 and III,4: 16–18; and in *DL* VII: 179–202; Seneca *Ep* 120: 22; *DeTranq* I: 4.

[89] Among other things, Philo stresses in this context that "the mass by its very nature is an unstable thing".

[90] Note that in *Leg* 236–37 Philo allegorises Potiphar's wife as general pleasure which Joseph "the self-controlling character" surpasses.

Now the true politician knows quite well that the people have the power of a master, yet he will not admit that he is a slave, but regards himself a free man and [lacuna] to please his own soul. He will frankly say: I never learnt to cringe to the people and I will never practise it. But since the leadership and the charge of the state is put into my hands I will know how to hold it as a good guardian or affectionate father ... I will fear no tyrant's menaces even though he threatens me with death, for death is a lesser evil than dissimulation.

Still in the same context, Philo then reiterates the allegory of the physician and demonstrates how the true politician should educate the people rather than succumb to their flatteries. In these expositions Philo offers unusually concrete examples of proper behaviour in the different political institutions, such as the general assembly.[91]

Besides the reference to the danger of enslavement,[92] which is presumably of Stoic inspiration,[93] there are elements, in this fictitious speech of the politician, which are clearly of different provenance. Taken together, the monologue form, "the statesman's" concern about threats on his life and the rhetorical connotation of the passage suggest Plato's *Gorgias* as a background.[94] In *Gor* 521 an extended speech by Socrates is quoted in which he replies to an invitation for political office. This "Socratic" response must be understood in view of Plato's contemporary experience of the deterioration of democracy in Athens. Then we may also fully appreciate the similarities to the Philonic passage.

---

[91] Note that there is also mention of the politician as the free-born citizen "of that best and greatest state, this world" (*Jos* 69); R. Barraclough, *op. cit.*, p. 497, stresses this element and concludes that in the absence of O.T. terminology, the whole passage should be regarded as "dominated" by Stoic terms; it is, however, doubtful whether such generalisations are appropriate. Cf. also A.F. Dähne, *Geschichtliche Darstellung der jüdisch-alexandrinischen Religionsphilosophen*, Halle 1834, pp. 398–99, who interprets Joseph here as the "Symbol des rückfallenden Asketen".

[92] Note that Philo repeats this theme in *Jos* 35.

[93] See M.E. Reesor, *op. cit.*, p. 11 and pp. 50–51, where she emphasises that Philo's Stoic terms always have to be examined in view of their adaptation to Jewish concepts; see particularly: Cicero's *Acad* II, 44:136 where only the wise man is said to be "a citizen and a free man and (but) all those not wise are foreigners, exiles, slaves and madmen".

[94] For the popularity and wide-spread use of this Platonic dialogue in Late Antiquity, see E.R. Dodds, *Gorgias: A Revised Text with Introduction and Commentary*, Oxford 1959, pp. 58–62; see also I.G. Kidd, *The Impact of Philosophy in Greco-Roman Literature*, in: *The Classical World*, *op. cit.*, pp. 397–416.

Then please specify to which of these two ministrations of the state you are inviting me: that of struggling hard, like a doctor, with the Athenians of make them as good as possible or that of seeking to serve their wants and humour at every turn? . . . So it is to a flatterer's work that you invite me! I think I am one of the few, not to say the only one, in Athens who attempts the true art of statesmanship . . . as the speeches I make from time to time are not aimed at gratification but at what is best . . . for I shall be like a doctor tried by a bunch of children on a charge brought by the cook. Just consider what defence a person like that would make at such a pass, if the prosecutor would speak against him . . . I am sure you would see me take my death easily. For no man fears the mere act of dying, except he be utterly irrational and unmanly; doing wrong is what one fears.

Plato's account of Socrates is thus likely to have inspired Philo to offer another version of the relatively positive role of the statesman in a hostile, democratic environment. It is important to note in this context how little Philo's allegory is actually connected to the biblical Joseph story. The latter merely serves as a springboard for Philo's thought and is perhaps the most outstanding of the allegories in *Jos*.[95]

I have examined in this section that material of the *bios* which falls under Philo's category of the politician's "career". We have seen that he attributes exceptional importance to those biblical passages which deal with Joseph's promotion and that he shows a particular interest in his behaviour at the height of power. In the "literal" account Philo tends to embellish significant episodes both by biographical motives (such as the discovery of character) on the one hand, and by allegorical interpretation (such as the image of the household as a state on the other hand. In both of these Philo enhances the importance of the biblical figure significantly. In his expansions which conform to his notion of "political biography", Philo even describes the training and the career of Joseph in terms similar to those of Moses's course of development. In his "allegorical" commentary on the other hand, he presents much broader ideas behind which the

---

[95] This is further highlighted by the rare quotation of Euripides at the end of it (*Jos* 78). Also the allegory of the statesman as the interpreter of the dream of life (*Jos* 125–42) is an extended exposition; it has been properly analysed by H. v. Arnim, *Quellenstudien zu Philo von Alexandria*, Berlin 1888, pp. 94–100; his conclusions concerning Philo's sceptic sources for the above passage have been widely accepted and reiterated, see e.g.: J. Laporte, *op. cit.*, Paris 1964, pp. 33–36; for a background, see also: E. Brehier, *op. cit.*, pp. 207–25; other examples of Philo's "scepticism" are also to be found in: *Ebr* 166, 189, 192 and *Somn* I: 119, and II: 17 where Joseph is identified as the interpreter of life-dreams.

original subject matter recedes considerably. In these the figure of the statesman is drawn in more ambivalent terms. In both kinds of exegesis Philo shows little interest in the specific character of the biblical Joseph. He rather tends to identify in Scripture certain evidence for the preconceived types of the politician to which he then fully accommodates the biblical text.

In Late Antiquity it was not uncommon for a writer to engage both in biography and allegory. Yet in contrast to Plutarch fot example, and as opposed to his own writings on Moses and Abraham, where he clearly separates between historiography and allegory, Philo did not keep these categories strictly apart in his *bios* of Joseph.

Joseph and the Egyptians

Philo's view of Egypt is shaped by both the biblical account and his own experiences in the contemporary state. On both grounds he develops an ambivalent attitude. Based on certain scriptural injunctions,[96] which he understands in the context of his own religious and moral outlook, Philo regards Egypt as *the* symbol of licentiousness.[97] In his own days he not only enjoys the privileges of a Hellenistic city but also has to struggle for Jewish rights and against anti-semitism.[98] It moreover appears that the categories of biblical and contemporary Egypt are not always clearly separated in Philo's thought. Thus he often blends topical considerations with exegesis;[99] and he tends to apply similar moral criticism also to the Egypt in which he lives.

The confrontation between Joseph and the Egyptian woman, one

---

[96] E.g. *Ex* 7:11 (negative image of E. sorcerers); *Lev* 18:1–5 (exhortation not to imitate E. in its sexual transgressions etc.); *Lev* 24:10; *Is* chap. XIX.

[97] See especially: *Leg* II: 59 (Egypt as the body); II: 77 (E. as corporal mass); II: 103 (E. drowned in the sea of passions); III: 38 and III: 175 (E. given to human passions); *Sacrif* 48 (E. as passion-loving body); *PosterC* 155–58 (E. symbolizes bodily passions); *Attack* 46 (warning to avoid E. and the subjugation to irrational passions); *Agric* 64 (E. is τῇ σώματος καὶ παθῶν χώρᾳ); *MigAbr* 77 (E. is σύμβολον for sense perception and passion); *Abr* 103 (E. as συμβολικῶς νοῦς φιλοσώματος); for the background, see especially: P. Karni, מצרים המקראית בתפישתו של פילון, שנתון למקרא ולחקר המזרח הקדום, ה-ו, 1982.

[98] See especially the collection of documents in V.A. Tcherikover, *op. cit.*, vol. II.

[99] E.g.: *Virt* 106–08, after having quoted *Lev* 23:7 ("you shall not abhor Egypt . . .") Philo contemplates how this might be implemented in view of the present Egyptian maltreatment of and ill will towards his nation.

of the superb highlights in the biblical story, is generally de-emphasised by Philo. Although he must, like Josephus, have been familiar with the Hellenistic romance material he diminishes the erotic allusions of the bible.[100] He also refrains from stressing the scene as a typical time of hardship in the life of a politician; and he only briefly mentions the woman's false accusations in his summary evaluation of Joseph's troubles (*Jos* 270).

Against this background, Philo expands the chaste reply of the biblical Joseph.[101] He in fact turns this confrontation into an encounter of Hebrew and Egyptian culture.[102] He has focused the reader's attention on this aspect already by his introductory remark that Joseph's reply was ἀξίας τοῦ γένους (*Jos* 42). Also on the occasion of this speech Philo typically addresses both ethical and contemporaneous issues (*Jos* 42–53):

> What, he said, are you forcing me to? We children of the Hebrews follow customs and laws (ἔθεσι καὶ νομίμοις) hitherto lived an irregular life, drawn by the impulses of youth and following after the luxury of this land (τὴν ἐγχώριον ἐζηλωκὼς τρυφήν), I ought not to make the wedded wife of another my prey . . . Indeed I am to honour him not only as a master but also as a benefactor (ὡς εὐεργέτην) . . . A fine gift this would be, an appropriate return for preceding favours! The master found me a captive (αἰχμάλωτον) and an alien and he has

---

[100] Thus he replaces in *Jos* 40 the biblical reference to Joseph's beauty by a reminder that "he established exceedingly good repute in the household". This emphasis appears to respond to incipient criticism of Joseph's provocative behaviour, as already adumbrated in *LXX* (in *Gen* 39:6 the adverb σφόδρα is inserted). Note that Philo also omits the biblical reference to Joseph's unusual return to the empty house (*Gen* 39:11), which became one of the favourite items in midrashic exegesis. Note, however, that in the final summary of Joseph's life, he is described as κάλλος (*Jos* 269).

[101] *Gen* 39:8 "But he refused and said to his master's wife: lo, my master has no concern for anything in the house and he has put everything into my hands, he is not greater in this house (*LXX* MSS vascillate between a faithful rendering and amending the phrase to the more modest "there was nobody in the house" . . ., i.e. among the servants), nor has he kept back anything from me exept yourself because you are his wife; how can I do this great wickedness and sin against God?"

[102] Cf. E.R. Goodenough's conjecture that this "section (is) obviously inserted as a propaganda for the Gentile reader" (*Politics, op. cit.*, p. 50). Focussing on the issue of Hebrew vs. Egyptian culture I shall not discuss the notion of the soul/conscience which, though mentioned at the end of Joseph's speech, is a general Philonic subject which has been examined in its proper ideological context; compare a "Greek" to a "Hebrew" approach: R.T. Wallis, *The Idea of Conscience in Philo of Alexandria, Studia Philonica* 3/1974–75; J. Milgrom, *The Origin of Philo's Doctrine of Conscience, ibid.*

made me by his kindness a free man (ἐλεύθερον) and a citizen (ἀστὸν) as far as he could do it.

This speech is one of the rare cases where Philo actually invigorates biblical discourse.[103] The climax of this scenic description is reached when Joseph mentions his responsibility towards his master, Philo going so far as to use ironic rhetoric.

Many of the points discussed by Philo's Joseph remind us of the author's own concerns in his community. Thus the Jewisch νόμιμοι, which Philo specifies in unusual terms,[104] are known to have been a bone of contention in the discussion on Jewish rights in the πολίτευμα and Alexandrian citizenship.[105] Here Philo uses the biblical context to give an example for laudable adherence to this heritage. This type of exegesis is not uncommon in Philo and he treats other figures similarly, as for example Moses.[106]

When Philo furthermore contrasts Joseph's behaviour with the licentiousness of Egypt he may well have had contemporary mores in mind.[107] He after all lives at the time when Cleopatra and Mark Antony's romance agitates the whole civilized world. Both the woman's art of seduction and the triumvir's weakness were rapidly becoming a favorite topic of the creative imagination.[108] It is there-

---

[103] For a more typical solemn rendering of an originally lively conversation, see for example *Jos* 237–245 on the disclosure of Joseph's identity to his brothers.

[104] Philo's deviation from the biblical and mishnaic penal code regarding adultery has been carefully examined by B. Ritter, *Philo und die Halacha*, Leipzig 1879, pp. 68–94 (his solution, i.e. that local Jewish law courts caused these changes remains, however, controversial); for Second Temple injunctions of strict monogamy and male virginity before marriage, see also: G. Vermes, *Post-Biblical Jewish Studies*, Leiden 1975, pp. 52–53; and the *Damascus Document* of Qumran 4:20–5:2.

[105] See e.g.: V.A. Tcherikover, *CPJ* III, pp. 25–107; *idem, Hellenistic Civilisation and the Jews*, New York 1985, pp. 296–332.

[106] *Mos* I:32; R. Barraclough's conjecture (*op. cit.*, pp. 494–95) that such insertions might indicate "Philo's own orthopraxy" appears to be a possible but not necessary conclusion.

[107] For a background, see especially: C. Vatin, *Recherches sur le mariage et la condition de la femme mariée a l'époque hellénistique*, Paris 1970, pp. 40–50; F.H. Licht, *Sexual Life in Ancient Greece*, London 1932, pp. 256–76.

[108] See for example Plutarch's splendid account in *The Life of Antony*; in XXV:3–XXVI:4 he provides marvellous psychological insights into Cleopatra's beautifications; in XXVIII: 1–2 he dwells on how she ensnares him; in LIII: 3–6 he highlights C.'s rapturous seduction by comparison to A.'s prudent wife Octavia; throughout the biography Plutarch furthermore stresses the shameful enslavement of A.: in VI: 5 he is reported to have already established an "ill repute for his rela-

fore not impossible that Philo's version of Joseph's speech also coun-
teracts the reputation of foreign men of surrendering to Egyptian
women. We find additional evidence of this exegetical line in the biography of Abraham. Also in the relations between Sarah and Pharaoh, Philo highlights the problem of her being exposed to a foreign
land and to a "licentious and cruel-hearted despot" of Egypt (*Abr*
94–95).

Towards the end of Joseph's speech, Philo resumes more explicitly the subject of citizenship. Considerably transcending the *Vorlage*
he imputes to Joseph gratitude for social and political promotion.[109]

Also Philo's description of Joseph's subsequent interaction with
the Egyptians often betrays intimate familiarity with contemporary
customs. Thus Philo adds a picturesque scene to the biblical account
of Joseph's appointment to the government of Egypt. According to
him, Pharaoh did not discuss the matter freely with his 'staff' but:
"bade his companions come closer to him so that Joseph might not
hear" (*Jos* 109–13). This embellishment seems to reflect Philo's
familiarity with courteous behaviour which he presumably ex-
perienced in the environment of Alexandria. He refines in this way
the simple human contacts described in Scripture according to current etiquette.

In the same vein Philo presents Joseph's reception meal for his
brothers in terms of a Hellenistic *symposion* (*Jos* 201–06).[110] He
clearly expects his readers to grasp it in such light since he apologeti-
cally accounts for the lack of reclining in the biblical account (*Jos*

---

tions with women''; in XXV: 1 Plutarch concludes that he was C.'s "captive" and
in XXXVI: 1 he describes A.'s irrresponsibility in war: "and finally, like a stub-
born and unmanageable beast of the soul, of which Plato speaks, he spurned away
all saving and noble counsels and sent . . . to bring C."

[109] Consider also *Mos* I, 141 where liberty is extolled and praised as far superior
to material values.

[110] For a background on Hellenistic feasts and culinary habits, see also: *Sympo-
sion/Symposionliteratur*, *RE* Zweite Reihe, vol. IV cols. 1266–82; F. Ullrich, *Entste-
hung und Entwicklung der Literaturgattung des Symposion*, in: *Programm des Kgl. Neuen
Gymnasiums zu Würzburg*, Teil I 1908, pp. 3–49, Teil II 1909, pp. 3–73; R. Hirzel,
Der Dialog. Ein literaturhistorischer Versuch, Leipzig 1895, vol. I pp. 359–69; W.
Schmid, *Geschichte der griechischen Literatur*, München 1929, vol. II p. 53; C. Schneider, *op. cit.*, pp. 183–207. More generally on the impact of Alexander's conquest
on the social stratification in the Hellenistic cities, see: M. Rostovzeff, *Greece*, Oxford 1963, pp. 258–77.

203). He furthermore embellishes the *Vorlage* with many typical details, such as toasts and good wishes (*Jos* 206).[111] It is moreover significant that Philo does not reiterate the biblical emphasis on the complete separation of Egyptians and Hebrews. He has instead indigenous dignitaries participate in the festivities (*Jos* 201).

Towards the end of his account Philo also expresses himself in more general terms. He thus has Joseph's brothers suggest that he was in fact the inventor of these civilized customs in Egypt. This pride in the allegedly Jewish origin of Egypt's Hellenistic ways has, as we saw, a longer tradition and can also be encountered in Artapanus's interpretation of Joseph. In addition, Philo stresses that the feast was appropriate to the circumstances of the time, i.e. drought, and that it remained moderate. This emphasis on the spiritual nature of the *symposium* recalls classical idealisations of such gatherings;[112] and it also corresponds to Plutarch's almost contemporary neo-classicistic treatises.[113]

Conclusions

I have examined in this chapter the figure of Joseph in Philo's *bios*. This document is the earliest complete interpretation of the whole Joseph story. It also remains the only independent treatment which is specifically devoted to it. For this shape, but also for other features, Philo was inspired by his Greek background.

It emerged that Philo reshapes the biblical figure in accordance with his concepts of both the "allegorical" and the "political" biography. Thus, he shows a keen interest in the stages of Joseph's education and career. Significant aspects are embellished with biographical *topoi* and thus Joseph's importance is enhanced. Many of these features are stereotypical and also recur in the *Life* of Moses. But in the latter case they receive more detailed notice and greater attention. Those passages which Philo himself introduces as allegor-

---

[111] For a background on the δειπνα, see also: F. Ullrich, *op. cit.*, Teil II, pp. 18ff.

[112] Such as Plato's or the Epicureans': for the background, see especially: F. Ulrich, *op. cit.*, Teil I pp. 3–11 and pp. 19–20, Teil II pp. 6–8; R. Hirzel, *op. cit.*, pp. 363ff.

[113] E.g.: *Dinner of the Seven Wise Men* 150, 158 etc. For a background, see also: F. Ulrich, *op. cit.*, Teil II pp. 39–47; R. Hirzel, *op. cit.*, pp. 359ff. On Philo's general "Polemik gegen Tafelluxus und Gelage", see also: P. Wendland, *Philo und die kynisch-stoische Diatribe*, Berlin 1895, pp. 18–24.

ical incorporate diverse philosophical material on the role of the politician. The biblical story consequently recedes into the background and the function of the politician also receives more ambivalent notices. On the whole, Philo presents an idealised image of Joseph and accommodates the biblical material to his preconceived ideals of political personalities. He also presents him as an ideal Hebrew in Egypt.

CHAPTER FOUR

JOSEPHUS'S JOSEPH

In view of their same name[1] it is to be expected that the historian should have related in a special way to the biblical figure. Their lives were indeed so similar that even modern scholars inadvertently changed "Joseph" to "Josephus" when treating the biblical Joseph's promotion to Pharaoh's dream-interpreter.[2] How much more is Josephus likely to have taken this kind of typological approach to the story![3]

This will be one of the important issues which I shall address in my analysis of Josephus's paraphrase. Other questions to be addressed are the degree and the nature of Hellenisation, as compared to that in other Palestinian sources. In addition, the place of Joseph within *JA* needs to be assessed, especially in view of Josephus's portraits of other patriarchs.

Joseph and his Father

According to Josephus, it is only the nature of Jacob's attitude to Joseph which creates the latter's peculiar position among the brothers. Departing from the *Vorlage*,[4] he transforms Jacob's love into the initial setting of the story. In *JA* II, 9 he explains the reasons for Jacob's preference:

> Joseph, whom Jacob begat by Rachel, was beloved of his father above all his sons, alike for the beauty of person that he owed to his birth (τὴν τοῦ σώματος εὐγένειαν) and for virtuous qualities of the soul (ψυχῆς ἀρετήν), for he was endowed with exceptional understanding (φρονήσει γὰρ διέφερε).

---

[1] Note that Josephus even changes the Septuagintal and Philonic form of the biblical name (ιωσηφ) to ἰώσηπος.

[2] L.H. Feldman, *Use, Authority and Exegesis of Mikra in the Writings of Josephus*, in: *Mikra, op. cit.*, p. 488. For other treatments of Josephus as a bible exegete, see *idem, Hellenisations in Josephus' Jewish Antiquities: The Portrait of Abraham*, in: *Josephus, Judaism and Christianity*, Detroit 1987, pp. 133–153; *idem, Flavius Josephus revisited: the Man, his Writings and his Significance*, in: *ANRW* II, 21.2, pp. 763–861.

[3] For a discussion of the term and the exegetical method, see especially: D. Daube, *Typology in Josephus, JJS* 31/1980; and also H. Lausberg, *Handbuch, op. cit.*, p. 445, where he restricts the term typology in ancient rhetoric to an interpretation through analogy of the writer's historical reality.

[4] *Gen* 37:3; for details, see chap. II. See also: A. Schalit, קדמוניות היהודים, Jerusalem 1955; p. L–LII, where he gives other examples of Josephus's significant omissions of biblical material.

In this passage Josephus replaces the biblical expression "son of his old age" (*Gen* 37:3) by two alternative rationales for Jacob's favoritism: one has to do with Joseph's bodily advantages, the other with his spiritual talents.

Josephus does not only mention Joseph's physical beauty, as would be natural for a Hellenistic writer,[5] but connects it further-more with Rachel. He thus reminds the reader that Jacob begat this son from her and suggests by the term εὐγενής that Joseph's comeli-ness was an inherited feature.[6] In this way, Josephus introduces a more personal perspective to the biblical account and suggests Jacob's fond memories as a reason for his preference for Joseph. This emphasis of the sensual concords well with Josephus's general interest in the subject.[7] Throughout the *JA* he has shown moreover a particular liking for the romance between Jacob and Rachel. He extolled her beauty (*JA* I, 288) and stressed Jacob's devotion[8] much beyond the regular description of biblical engagement-scenes.[9] In addition, Josephus's insertion betrays a fine psychological under-standing of human affairs.[10]

The only other explicit link of Joseph's features with Rachel's is to be found in *GR*. In 1059 R. Isaac is said to compare mother and son in terms of their beauty and to highlight the hereditary factor. Despite their general similarity, we must distinguish the different

---

[5] This has already been pointed out by H. Sproedowsky, *Die Hellenisierung der Geschichte von Joseph in Ägypten bei Flavius Josephus*, Greifswald 1937, p. 17; it is also mentioned by H.L. Feldman, *op. cit.*, p. 486 (consistent with his general views of Josephus he links also this case with his alleged apologetics).

[6] For Josephus' description of Rachel's beauty, see *JA* I, 288.

[7] I. Heinemann, דרכו של יוספוס בתאור קדמוניות היהודים, *Zion* 5/1940; p. 186, mentions "erotic motifs" attributed to the protagonists as one of the four ways in which Josephus hellenizes his material. In this context he especially refers to the sto-ry of Joseph and Potiphar's wife; see also H.W. Attridge, *The Interpretation of Biblical History in the Antiquitates Judaicae of Flavius Josephus*, Scholars Press 1976, p. 19.

[8] *JA* I, 288. Note the exceptional strength of the term ἡττήθεις to render *Gen* 29:11 "(Then Jacob kissed Rachel) and wept aloud". Josephus's accentuation may further be gathered by comparison to his de-emphasis of Jacob's emotional response in *JA* I, 291.

[9] Compare for example: *JA* I, 246ff Rebecca is said to be chosen for marriage on account of her chastity; *JA* I, 255 Josephus laconically describes the personal en-counter between Isaac and Rebecca: "and Isaac married Rebecca"; *JA* I, 253 Moses's marriage to the Ethiopian king's daughter is related in terms of a business; and in *JA* I, 263 Moses is simply said to be given one of Raguel's daughters in marriage.

[10] For other example of Josephus' fine psychological insight, see: A. Schalit, *op. cit.*, p. LXIV.

narratorological functions of these two interpretations. The midrashic saying serves as a prelude to the attempt of Potiphar's wife at seducing Joseph (*Gen* 39:6). Following the *Vorlage*, R. Isaac is concerned with Joseph's inherited beauty as a catalysing factor in the dramatic action. Josephus, on the other hand, is more interested in character and mentions Rachel as a psychological explanation for Jacob's emotions.

The nature of Josephus's interpretation is further illuminated by contrasting it to other near-contemporary treatments of Joseph in the context of *Gen* 37:3. It emerges that his features are in the Palestinian exegesis predominantly likened to Jacob's,[11] and the more Hellenistically inspired *XII* also mentions their common beauty.[12] However, in contrast to Josephus, the awareness of their similarity is here attributed to Joseph. It is furthermore said to enable him to resist Potiphar's wife. Also the midrashic exegetes expand on Jacob's motifs for preferring Joseph. Yet their insistence on a physical likeness between father and son lacks the more complex erotic dimension which marks Josephus's paraphrase.

Josephus's portrait of Joseph must further be evaluated in view of his other biblical biographies which often dwell on the beauty of their heros. It is notable in this context that the ascribed εὐμορφίας especially to Moses (*JA* II, 231). Regarding him, Josephus embellishes the theme in the most glowing terms. He thus tells of a wonderous increase in Moses's stature at the age of three, describes him as παῖδα μορφῇ θεῖον[13] and, to give a picturesque illustration, he also invents a street scene where passers-by are astounded at the child's beauty (*ibid*). It transpires from these descriptions that Josephus is well familiar with Hellenistic techniques and uses them artfully in his presentation of the grand Israelite leader. Concerning Joseph, on the other hand, he seems to be satisfied with moderate literary means. He shows instead a greater interest in the personal and emotional aspects of this biblical scene.

It is Joseph's intellectual and spiritual virtues which Josephus adduces as a second reason for Jacob's preference. The quality of ἀρετή is the most general praise which Josephus generously bestows

---

[11] See for example *GR* 1010, where R. Jehuda is quoted as saying: שהיה זיו איקונין שלו דומה לו; also *TanB*, p. 179: אלא שהיה איקונין דומה לו.

[12] *TJos* 18:4 "ἐν δυνάμει καὶ ἐν κάλλει".

[13] *JA* II, 232.

on the biblical protagonists.[14] He uses the term in a variety of ways,[15] ranging from Greek notions of general excellence[16] and political virtue[17] to the specifically Jewish concept of piety towards God.[18] When applied to individuals, it describes an inherent quality of the person which manifests itself in decisive situations of life.[19] Josephus specifically characterises the youth of one other patriarch in terms of practising virtue. Isaac, also passionately beloved because he was the son of old age, is said to have "endeared himself to his parents by the practice of every virtue, showing a devoted filial obedience and a zeal for the worship of God".[20] In the description of Joseph, however, Josephus associates virtue with the soul and the intellect. Since on other occasions he contrasts the pious concept of virtue with beauty,[21] yet attributes both of these to Joseph, he must

---

[14] See for example: *JA* I, 256 Abraham is said to die as ἀνὴρ πᾶσαν ἀρετὴν ἄκρος; I, 280 Jacob's renown for δόξαν ἀρετῆς μεγάλης is mentioned; in II, 7 the virtues of all of Jacob's sons are mentioned (see also A. Schalit, *op. cit.*, p. LVII); III, 12 of Moses: ἀρετῆς καί σύνεσεως; III, 187 of Moses: τὴν ἀρετὴν τοῦ νομοθέτου (also: III, 322; IV, 196; IV, 331 etc.); V, 230 Gideon; V. 301 and VI, 292 of Samson; VII, 390 of David: ἄριστος ἀνὴρ ἐγένετο καὶ πᾶσαν ἀρετὴν ἔχων (also: VIII, 1); VIII, 49 and 53 and 165 of Solomon's surpassing virtues.

[15] Note H.W. Attridge, *op. cit.*, p. 20, who points to the inconsistent use of Greek terminology in Josephus and questions the validity of studies which generalize isolated occurrences of terms without taking into account the specific context of each.

[16] For example *JA* III, 302 in connection with the qualities of the land (also: IV, 97 and 200). For a background, see Aristotle's discussion in *NE* bk I.

[17] For example: *JA* IV, 214 rulers of each city are to exercise virtue and pursue justice; IV, 223 it is said to be the king's function to guarantee justice and virtue; in VI, 343 the pursuit of virtue is associated with aspiring to things which will procur reknown and social recognition.

[18] For example: *JA* I, 20 Moses is said to give moral instructions to Israel on the assumption that God "as the universal father and Lord who beholds all things, grants to such as follow Him a life of bliss, but involves in dire calamities those who step outside the path of virtue"; in I, 53 it is said of Abel that, "being believing that God was with him in all his actions he paid heed to virtue"; in II, 309 the virtuous are said to have extra strength, because they are supported in everything by God; in IV, 185 Israel is promised Divine protection as long as "she continues in the path of virtue"; in I, 113 it is considered a sin to attribute success to human virtue and not to God.

[19] For example: in *JA* I, 300 Jacob is said to give proof of his virtue by enduring to stay with Laban; in II, 257 moreover Josephus comments thus on Moses's assistance to the Israelite shepherd girls: "he was destined to play a part, arising out of the customs of the inhabitants, which exhibited his virtue (συστήσασα τὴν ἀρετὴν αὐτοῦ) and proved the opening of a better fortune".

[20] *JA* I, 222; note that also in *JA* XVII, 13 Josephus defines virtue and concern for justice as care for parents.

[21] E.g.: *JA* VI, 160.

have meant more generally Hellenistic notions in this case.

The specific attribution of φρόνησις, practical wisdom,[22] is comparatively rare for human protagonists in Josephus's *JA*.[23] Josephus uses the term almost exclusively, yet abundantly, with regard to Solomon. The latter is frequently praised for his φρόνησις καὶ σοφία,[24] which manifest themselves also in the beauty and the skilful arrangement of the palace buildings.[25] It is naturally also understood to imply the observance of the Jewish law (*JA* VIII, 190).

With regard to Joseph, φρόνησις describes his wise disposition to life in general and anticipates his successful coping with the imminent challenges. It is significant that both Potiphar's wife and Pharaoh mention this quality when impressed with Joseph's competence. Especially the latter stresses his wisdom as that trait which qualifies him for the interpretation of their dreams (*JA* II, 87). It is possible that Josephus perceives a likeness in this respect between Joseph and his more famous counterpart Solomon, the stereotype of a wise man at court.

The theme of Joseph's wisdom is moreover popular among ancient interpreters. Philo, as we saw, also depicts him as having φρόνημα εὐγενές and in *GR*[26] he is distinguished by halachic expertise which Jacob taught him. Josephus's account differs from the former in not connecting these virtues with Jacob and from the latter in being more generally humanistic.[27]

---

[22] See also *Vita* 92 where it is said of Simon, a distinguished Jerusalem Pharasee, that he "was highly gifted with intelligence and judgement, he could by sheer genius (φ.) retrieve an unfortunate situation in affairs of state.

[23] Consider also the following passages: in *JA* II, 270, φ. is mentioned more generally of Moses's mind as the receptacle of God's manifestations; otherwise the term is used of the Tree of Wisdom in the Garden of Eden (*JA* I, 37; I, 40 and 42); it is contrasted to the fear which coerced Pharaoh to accept certain decisions (*JA* II, 299); intellectual leaders are moreover qualified in terms of φ. (*JA* VI: 10; also *AgAp* II, 242 where the exact formulation of *JA* II, 9 recurs).

[24] Thus in *JA* VIII, 34 and 42 and 165 and 171; see also *JA* VIII, 23 where Solomon's "νοῦν ὑγιῆ καὶ φρόνησιν ἀγαθήν" are mentioned.

[25] *JA* VIII, 168 related from the point of view of the Queen of Sheba.

[26] E.g.: *GR* 1010 or 1195. For details, see chap. V.

[27] Note that S. Rappaport drew a parallel between Josephus's account and Targum Onkelos, where Joseph is described as בר חכים (*Agada und Exegese bei Flavius Josephus*, Frankfurt 1930, p. 22; he does not specify the quoted interpretation other than "aggada" but he must have had the targum in mind). Consistent with his aim to approximate Josephus and Midrash (p. XIV), he suggests that he has identified Josephus's source also in this instance. However, given the popularity of the motif this conclusion is not warranted.

A comparison to Josephus's treatment of Moses's youth shows that also the broader theme of wisdom is more developed there. He eulogises Moses as being φρονήματός τε μεγέθει καὶ πόνων καταφρονήσει ἑβραίων ἄριστος[28] and claims that his games displayed such maturity as to stimulate ambitious hopes (*JA* II, 230). Josephus further relates mysterious stories which foreshadow Moses's future power (*JA* II, 234). Reflecting the biblical framework, his description of Joseph's spiritual talents is far more moderate.

The above analysis has isolated the salient features of the story's starting point, as paraphrased by Josephus. His interpretation of Jacob's preference for Joseph parallels midrashic exegesis in its distinction of a physical and an intellectual aspect. Josephus, however, specifies these items in his own, often Hellenistic way and incorporates them in a distinct fashion into the biblical material. He also approaches the underlying text with greater freedom and omits certain narrative elements, such as the colourful coat. Josephus's characterisation is not atypical of his biographical style. We must nevertheless take into account that he does not fully exploit the means of characterisation as he did for example in the case of Moses. Regarding both the degree of Hellenisation and his alleged importance, Joseph remains a just-above-average figure in Josephus's biographies. The perhaps most important contribution of the above passage to Josephus's overall Joseph story is his modification of the starting point. The family situation is extracted from its primarily rural context (sheperding) and the beginning of the brothers' relationship is defined exclusively by reference to Jacob's love. In this way Josephus improves the image of Joseph significantly.

Joseph and his Brothers

Recent scholarship has established the significance of dreams in Josephus's theology, particularly with regard to his concept of prophecy.[29] He considers dreams as important indications of God's

---

[28] *JA* II, 229.

[29] See especially: J. Barton, *Oracles of God*, London 1986, p. 117: "The most striking feature in Josephus' understanding of the Old Testament prophets is his assumption that most of them received their inspired messages through *dreams*". Barton further mentions that Josephus sometimes adds to the biblical account references to dreams and mentions *JA* V, 215 (concerning Gideon) as an example. See also *JA* X, 266ff where Daniel is described as "one of the greatest prophets"; or *JA* XII, 300 where the story of Hyrcanus's nocturnal vision and communication

providence.[30] Some of them were taken to be self-evident,[31] but most of them seem to have required an interpretation.[32] In his own life, Josephus's ability to foretell the future, allegedly based on an earlier dream, proved vital. It enabled him to survive the siege of Jotapata and established him as a protege of the Romans under whose auspices he undertook his historical writing.[33] The similarity to Joseph's transfer from distress to the height of power, also prompted by a prognosis to the ruler, has long been acknowledged.[34] But the recognition of this obvious parallel has unfortunately prevented scholars from a closer examination of the function of dreams in Josephus's Joseph story. It has thus been overlooked that Josephus does not in fact treat the scene of Joseph before Pharaoh with special care, but merely paraphrases the biblical account.[35] It emerges that Josephus's experience of that stage of his career had no impact on his interpretation of the narrative.

I shall argue instead that Josephus was highly aware of the role of the dreams in the relationship between Joseph and his brothers. It will become clear that in rewriting the history of this affiliation, Josephus identified with Joseph. As a result, he interpreted the events of the biblical family in the light of his own relationship with co-leaders of the Jewish revolt in Galilee. Especially the brothers' jealousy, Joseph's dream and his later benevolent behaviour reminded Josephus of his own dealings with John of Gischala. More accurately, these items in the biblical narrative reminded him of how he would have liked them to have been! The issue of Josephus's early war record, and especially his co-operation with other leaders, remained a sensitive point throughout his life. His apologetic concern

---

with God is defined as prophecy. In this context, Josephus mentions also Hyrcanus's priestly origin. For a fine discussion on the status of *Dan* in Late Antiquity, see K. Koch, *Is Daniel also among the Prophets?* in: *Interpreting the Prophets*, ed. J.C. Mays/J. Achtemeier, Philadelphia 1987, pp. 237–49. He treats Josephus especially on pp. 241–43.

[30] E.g. *JA* X, 142.

[31] E.g. *JA* XI, 227 and 333.

[32] This is a function in which the Essenes are considered specialists, see for example: *JA* XVII, 345–54.

[33] *JW* II, 350ff.

[34] See H.St. Thackeray, *JW* II, p. 674 note b; this parallel has been more firmly established by D. Daube, *op.cit.*, p. 27.

[35] The scene is to be found in *JA* II, 80–87. The broader comment about dreams in *JA* II, 86 conforms to Josephus's general views on the subject and does not add anything to them.

was in fact so strong that even decades after these events he wrote an autobiography which deals almost exclusively with charges on those grounds.[36] It is thus not surprising that he should have been provoked by the Joseph story and treated it in terms of his own personal apology.

It is in Reuben's speech[37] before the selling of Joseph that Josephus presents his overall conception of the brothers' relationship.[38] In Josephus's version, Reuben highlights Joseph's innocence and reminds the brothers of his youth.[39] Whereas Philo focusses on fracticide as the most vicious (ethical) implication of their plot,[40] Josephus has Reuben stress the religious dimension. He thus insists that the brothers "would deprive God of the one to whom he had given these (favours) graciously".[41] It emerges that Josephus has the vision of a blameless young sibling who is promoted by the Deity, but hindered by his brothers who thus also commit a sin against God. In the following we shall examine how Josephus's general assumption influences his interpretation of the various passages.

In *JA* II, 10 Josephus summarizes the impact of Jacob's favoritism and introduces the brothers' envy. He does so from an authorial perspective, distancing himself from the events and thus claiming greatest objectivity.

> This affection of his father[42] aroused against him the envy (φθόνον) and the hatred (μῖσος) of his brothers, as did also his dreams, predictive of good fortune, which he saw (θεασάμενος) and made

---

[36] See especially S. Cohen, *Josephus in Galilee and Rome*, Leiden 1979, p. 126–27 and G. Misch, *Geschichte der Autobiographie*, Berlin 1949, vol. I p. 329ff and p. 340ff.

[37] For a discussion of Reuben's speech, consider: A. Schalit, *op. cit.*, pp. LXIV–V and p. 46, where he argues that many of "Reuben's" ethical expressions have a Greek flavour.

[38] Josephus is well known for using this technique in his historiography, see for example *JW* II, 345–401 (Agrippa's speech at the outbreak of the revolt) and a detailed analysis of it by O. Michel, *Die Rettung Israels und die Rolle Roms nach den Reden im Bellum Judaicum*, in: *ANRW* II, 21.2, 1984, especially p. 945 and pp. 952–56. See also: M. Braun, *Griechischer Roman, op. cit.*, p. 27, who points to the methodological similarities between rhetorical historiography and the romance.

[39] *JA* II, 26.

[40] *Jos* 12–13.

[41] H.St. Thackeray's translation (*JA* I–IV, Harvard/London, 1978, 1st ed. 1930, p. 181): "the recipient of his favours" diminishes the active part of God too much.

[42] H.St. Thackeray, *ad.loc*, translates "tender affection", which seems too soft a rendering for στοργή.

known,[43] both to his father and to them; so jealous (ζηλοτυπούντων) are men of the successes (εὐπραγίας) even of their relatives.

Here, Josephus associates the dreams with the father's love on the grounds that both are equally unjustified sources of the brothers' envy. In this initial description of their emotions, Josephus uses two terms where the biblical narrative is limited to ζηλόω. The inserted notion of envy expresses Josephus's criticism and highlights the tension.

On the basis of this term H. Sproedowsky[44] conjectured that Josephus used Philo who, as we saw earlier, also mentions envy in the context of the family tensions. We must, however, remain aware of the differents and evaluate the two versions in their own right. It is thus to be noted that Philo inserts the theme of envy as a general truism which he expands in philosophical terms. Significantly, he adduces it as an explanation only for the brothers' reaction to Jacob's favouritism. His idealisation of Joseph furthermore does not render him insensitive to his shortcomings. He still shows an acute awareness of the growing tension between the brothers' increasing hostility and Joseph's continuous talk about his dreams. Yet being sympathetic to the protagonist, he attempts to justify his extroversion by reference to his youthful ignorance. In contrast to Philo's account, Josephus does not appear to be conscious of Joseph's possible fault in relating his dreams. He thus applies the theme of envy also to this scene and in particular to the dream interpretations. He furthermore stresses in this connection the brothers' neglect of their family bonds.[45] It seems therefore less important for the understanding of Josephus's interpretation whether he knew Philo or not. The main feature of his narrative is distinctly his own and must be examined as such.

It is precisely this type of unjust envy with which Josephus frequently charges his arch rival, John of Gischala. In *Vita* 122 he claims that John was envious of his success (εὐπραγίαν) because he feared that it would impede his own career. Again in *Vita* 189ff Josephus describes John's envy in terms of his hatred of Josephus's

---

[43] The term ἐμήνυσεν carries perhaps a stronger connotation of disclosure and annunciation than H.St. Thackeray's translation, *ad.loc.* suggests.

[44] *op. cit.*, p. 19-20.

[45] Note that this motif is also to be found in Philo's *Jos* 10; but he imputes it to Jacob thus presenting it with far less authority than Josephus's authorial statement.

success.[46] On other occasions, he also accuses John of jealousy of his dreams.[47] We may conclude from these examples that Josephus describes both Joseph's and his own opponents in the same terms. In this instance, Josephus does not introduce major changes to the biblical story, but limits himself to one-sided paraphrasing. We shall have occasion to note a more substantial influence of his own experience on his subsequent paraphrase.

In *JA* II, 11 – 12 Josephus relates the events around Joseph's first dream. He introduces changes to the biblical material and is able, by focalising on the different characters, to suggest a new significance of the scene.

Josephus initially provides a reason for Joseph's report of his visions to the brothers. According to him, Joseph wished to thereby solicit an interpretation.[48] In this way Josephus replaces the ambiguity of the biblical character, created by Joseph's frivolous and provocative address to his brothers.[49] The family's reaction in the biblical story in fact suggests that Joseph is held responsible for the content of his dreams and thus indirectly accused of personal aspirations to power. Josephus, on the other hand, postulates Joseph's ignorance of the dream's meaning. He thus accommodates Joseph's behaviour to what he considered normal practices concerning dreams and their interpretation.[50]

We may moreover suspect that this improvement of the character was motivated by personal reminiscences of Josephus. In *Vita* 302

---

[46] For another example reflecting the same general atmosphere see *Vita* 204: "I was deeply distressed, both by the base ingratitude of my fellow-citizens, whose jealousy, as I could see, had prompted the order to put me to death ...".

[47] This point is to be further discussed below.

[48] Note in this context that Josephus did acknowledge the existence and the reliability of self-evident dreams. Also Th.W. Franxman, *Genesis and the Jewish Antiquities of Flavius Josephus*, Rome 1979, p. 222, identifies Josephus's version as a deviation from the *Vorlage*, but unfortunately he only mentions this fact without offering an explanation for it.

[49] See H.L. Ehrlich, *op. cit.*, p. 60, where he discusses whether in the biblical account the dreamer is held responsible for his dream and reaches the conclusion that Jacob's reprimand proves that Joseph was considered responsible; cf. H. Sproedowsky, *op. cit.*, p. 25, who conjectures that Josephus wished to idealize Joseph "im Sinne hellenistischer Heldendarstellungen". Compare also how the expression שמעו נא is construed in *GR* 1012.

[50] Josephus describes the cupbearer's reaction to his own dream in such standard terms (*JA* II, 63 – 5): Josephus presents the events as a normal occurrence and describes how the cupbearer naturally grasped the Divine origin of his vision, how he looked for a well-qualified interpreter and requested a "πρόρρησιν τῆς ὄψεως".

he defends himself against John's charges that he "was aspiring to make himself a despot and gaining a position of absolute power by deceitful speeches". These accusations correspond precisely to the brothers' feelings towards Joseph. By proclaiming Joseph's ignorance and thus rendering the brothers' accusation of personal ambition obsolete, Josephus accomplishes something which was unattainable in his own case: he extracts the protagonist's aspirations from the realm of a personal power struggle and includes it in the category of Divine providence. As a result, Josephus's Joseph appears remarkably passive and well-behaved.

In Josephus's narrative the hero is further victimized by the brothers' alleged refusal to render the desired interpretation. In thus withholding resented knowledge, they are presented as severely violating established norms.[51]

Against this background Josephus casts the scene of Joseph's second dream. In this central passage he adds two aspects which are crucial in his own apology: he emphasizes the Deity's impetus and advances the brothers' resolution to kill him, thus presenting it as a direct response to Joseph's dreams.

In *JA* II, 13 Josephus introduces the second dream with the following words:

> But the Deity, counteracting their jealousy, sent Joseph a second dream . . .

This paraphrase is based on the concise statement that "then he dreamt another dream and told it to his brothers . . ." (*Gen* 37:9). The biblical narrator focalises on Joseph. He does so from without, refraining from indicating Joseph's thoughts at the time. Philo, in his paraphrase of this passage, is obviously disturbed by Joseph's insensitivity to the prevailing situation. He is, however, able to present Joseph in a favourable light by focalisation from within. He thus attributes the appropriate mental disposition to the protagonist: "He, suspecting nothing, a few days later saw and told his brothers another dream" (*Jos* 8).

In contrast, Josephus drastically changes the original setting. He

---

[51] These are depicted for example in *JA* X, 245ff; see also: *JA* II, 80 for which H.L. Ehrlich, *op. cit.*, p. 83, unnecessarily assumes Philo as a source; and A. Schalit, *op. cit.*, p. 45, whose general interpretation it is that the brothers used curses in order to prevent the implementation of dreams.

relates the events from the authorial point of view, thus claiming more objectivity and greater knowledge. His embellishment avoids the issue of Joseph's culpability and instead presents this scene as another example of Divine protection against the jealousy of one's opponents. Also in this interpretation there is a striking parallel to Josephus's understanding of his own life. In *Vita* 208–9 Josephus mentions a dream which he had at the height of tension between him and other revolutionary leaders. According to him, this conflict was caused by the others' jealousy.[52] At the very moment when he considers withdrawing from his position, he claims to have "beheld a marvellous vision".[53] The Deity allegedly instructed him to remain in command and predicted important tasks for his future. It emerges that when paraphrasing the biblical story, Josephus is reminded of that phase in his own life. In retelling the Joseph narrative, he succeeds better than in his *Vita* to establish unassailable criteria in favour of the protagonist![54]

In *JA* II, 17 Josephus summarizes the significance of Joseph's dreams and mentions favourably Jacob's reaction to them. He then accentuates the brothers' disregard of their family bonds and adds that "they were eager to slay him". The biblical narrative provides a more complex characterisation of the brothers. They are depicted in their increasing opposition first to Joseph's special position and then to his provocative behaviour.[55] Their resolution to kill him occurs at a much later stage and crystallizes as a spontaneous reaction as Joseph approaches their pasturing site.[56] While Philo maintains the biblical image of the brothers,[57] the Midrash even embellishes Joseph's haughtiness.[58]

Josephus, on the other hand, designs this phase of the story differently. By advancing the brothers' plot, he not only vilifies

---

[52] For Josephus's explanations, see especially *Vita* 189 and 204; and also: G. Misch, *op. cit.*, p. 337.

[53] On the popularity of dreams and visions in Roman autobiographies, see S. Cohen, *op. cit.*, p. 109. Also Plutarch praises Sulla for ascribing in his own memoirs all his success to the intervention of the Deity (*Sulla* 6:5).

[54] This is further achieved by Josephus's unparalleled device of turning Jacob's response into a full-hearted enthusiasm (*JA* II, 14ff). This exegesis might perhaps have been inspired by the ambiguous term in *LXX ad. loc.*

[55] *Gen* 37:4, 37:5, 37:8.

[56] *Gen* 37:18.

[57] *Jos* 12ff.

[58] E.g.: *GR* 1019. For details, see chap. V.

them[59] but also raises the dramatic tension. The reader can now divine the subsequent events. He will even fear much worse for Joseph than that which actually occurs. Thus, Josephus skilfully exploits the dramatic possibilities of the material by creating a discrepancy between the reader's and the character's knowledge: the protagonists of the story remain ignorant of the imminent threat which Josephus has just outlined to the reader. Under these circumstances, Jacob's decision to send Joseph to the brothers is a tragic error,[60] of which Joseph is the victim. It emerges that Josephus has arranged the narrative elements with a view to ensure the reader's sympathy for Joseph.

Josephus's unique treatment of his scene can again be traced to his personal career. The almost fatal situation of him innocently falling into the hands of adversaries is a conspicuous theme in his autobiography. In *Vita* 276ff Josephus relates how, "suspecting nothing",[61] he agreed to attend a "general assembly" in Tarichaea at which other revolutionary leaders were also expected. As it turns out, this meeting had been planned as an ambush and Josephus was attacked by John's forces. He narrowly escaped and later comments: "the providence of God perhaps co-operating to save me, but for this turn of events I should undoubtedly have been murdered by John"[62] and, subsequently, that he escaped "beyond all expectation ... out of this perilous situation".[63] In numerous other circumstances Josephus also stresses his ignorance when being exposed to his enemies' different plots.[64]

---

[59] H. Sproedowsky, *op. cit.*, p. 32, also makes this point. Cf. A. Schalit, *op. cit.*, p. 46, who considers Josephus's addition of agricultural imagery to this passage as most significant.

[60] The notion of tragic error was first developed by Aristotle and has since been a topic of lively discussion in literary criticism. See especially: Aristotle's *Poetics*, chap. XIII–IV; S. Halliwell's recent discussion in *Aristotle's Poetics, op. cit.*, pp. 202–37; and in *Poetics, op. cit.*, pp. 122–39 (his analysis centres on the dramatic aspects and de-emphasises the conceptual value of ἁμαρτία); T.C.W. Stinton, *Hamartia in Aristotle and Greek Tragedy*, *CQ* 25/1975, pp. 221–54 (arguing for the ethical dimension of the term and the resulting notion of responsibility).

[61] This alleged ignorance is somewhat undermined by his own admission that he took precautions and posted guards to keep him informed of unusual events (*Vita* 276).

[62] *Vita* 301.

[63] *Vita* 304.

[64] E.g. in *Vita* 104 Josephus is described at Sepphoris where he innocently agreed to accept Jesus's "respects"; in *Vita* 189–218 Josephus, warned of his opponents' intrigues, is able to rectify his innocent behaviour towards them.

Let us turn now to Joseph and his brothers in Egypt. Josephus shares Philo's interest in the continuation of the brothers' relationship in Egypt, which the rabbinic interpreters leave mostly without comment. In this second phase the dreams play no part and parallels between Joseph and Josephus are less obvious. Nevertheless, Josephus introduces significant changes to the image of Joseph.[65] The brothers' first encounter is described thus (*JA* II, 97):

> He recognized his brothers but they had no thought of him, for he was only a lad when he parted[66] from them and had reached an age when his features had changed so as to make him unrecognizable to them. Moreover his exalted rank[67] prevented any possibility of his even entering their minds. So he was in a position[68] to test them (αὐτοῖς ... διεπείραζεν) with regard to affairs in general. Corn he would sell them none ...

Omitting *Gen* 42:7,[69] Josephus creates a new sequence of events. In his version Joseph does not act in any peculiar way until after the reader has been provided with the above account, including a convincing explanation. The reader's sympathy is thus again ensured.

The large first part of the above passage is inspired by *Gen* 42:8 which merely summarizes: "Thus Joseph knew his brothers, but they did not know him". Josephus focalises this scene on the brothers and offers reasons for their failure to recognize him. He first refers to Joseph's external features, which is also, though in more picturesque form, done in midrashic literature. Thus, in *GR* 1127 it is transmitted in the name of the rabbis:

> "And Joseph who parted from them when they had a trace of a beard recognized them; but they who did not part from him when he had the trace of a beard, did not recognize him".[70]

---

[65] Cf. Th.W. Franxman's judgement, that Josephus' rendering of the brothers' meeting in Egypt is "very faithful" (*op. cit.*, p. 248).

[66] The verb ἀπαλλάσσω also has the meaning of escaping, getting away. But since Josephus presents the scene here from the brothers' point of view, H.St. Thackeray's translation "part" (*op. cit.*, p. 209) is probably appropriate.

[67] Literally: "the greatness of his honour".

[68] H.St. Thackeray's translation of δυνάμενος as "proceeded" (*ibid*) loses the approving undertone of Josephus's account.

[69] "Joseph saw his brothers, and knew them, but he treated them like strangers and spoke roughly to them: where are you from?, he said. They said: from Canaan, to buy food".

[70] And similarly for example also in *b Yeb* 88a; note that S. Rappaport, *op. cit.*, p. 23, previously pointed to these parallels.

The second explanation rests on a fine psychological observation and shows how the brothers were caught in their own image of their sibling. The motive of Joseph's perplexing dignity is also to be found in Philo's account (*Jos* 164). It thus emerges that Josephus shared a general hermeneutic interest in the brothers' non-recognition.[71] He seems furthermore to have been familiar with both the Palestinian and the diaspora "solutions" of the issue.

In the last part of the above passage Josephus finally deals with Joseph himself. His remark replaces a longer biblical account in *Gen* 42:9: "And Joseph remembered the dreams which he had dreamt of them and he said to them: you are spies . . .". This is one of the rare cases where the biblical narrator discloses the inner life of his figures. Instead of developing this further,[72] Josephus distances himself and presents Joseph from an authorial perspective. We may conjecture that he did not find the biblical explanation for Joseph's behaviour helpful. Perhaps he also considered Joseph's self-awareness embarrassing because he had earlier made every effort to stress the protagonist's passive acceptance of Divine providence.

Philo, who shares this interpretation of Joseph's motives[73] is nevertheless more cautious to preserve the *Vorlage*. At this point of the story he merely remarks that Joseph acted "with a carefully considered purpose". He does not appear to be as anxious as Josephus to rectify the image. Rabbinic exegetes, on the other hand, were not in the least intrigued by the question of why Joseph behaved in such a way. For them the issue of *how* he made himself a stranger seems to have been of much greater concern.[74]

In *JA* II, 109 Josephus describes Joseph's emotional reaction to his brothers' confession of guilt towards the end of their first visit:

> Seeing them thus distraught, Joseph from emotion (ὑπὸ τοῦ πάθους) broke into tears and not wishing to be visible to his brothers withdrew, and after a while came back to them.

---

[71] Cf. H. Sproedowsky, *op. cit.*, p. 125, who identifies Josephus's concern as characteristically Hellenistic. But it is not clear on what evidence this interpretation is based.

[72] This is surprising since Josephus is known for his interest in character and especially for his insertion of motivations for particular deeds; see for example: I. Heinemann, *op. cit.*, p. 184; and A. Schalit, *op. cit.*, p. LXIII, who points out that Josephus's frequent characterisation through thought differs from biblical description through action.

[73] *Jos* 166 and 232–236.

[74] E.g. *GR* 1127.

This scene is based on the concise biblical statement that "he turned away from them and wept and returned to them" (*Gen* 42:24). Josephus focalises on Joseph from within and thus inserts psychological explanations for his behaviour. He furthermore exposes in this way the delicacy of Joseph's emotional constitution. For this purpose, Josephus also changes the sequence of events and in fact renders it implausible. According to him, Joseph was so overwhelmed by his emotions that he wept *before* he became self-aware and turned away. This emphasis on passion is paralleled in Philo's paraphrase, but the latter reconciles his interpretation with the biblical text: "Overcome by his emotion and on the point of weeping, (he) turned aside ..." (*Jos* 175). Josephus's insistence on Joseph's complete loss of control is consistent with his earlier embellishment on the brothers' sense of guilt.[75] Yet it is nevertheless remarkable in view of *JA* II, 184 where he stresses Joseph's composure when finally meeting his father.

In Josephus's description of the brothers' second encounter, he fervently reiterates his explanation for Joseph's sometimes harsh comportment. He thus clarifies that Joseph had his cup put in Benjamin's sack only in order to test whether the others would assist him (*JA* II, 125). This motif then influences disproportionately the final scenario, when Joseph actually reveals himself (*JA* II, 161):

> ... he made himself known to his brothers and said: I commend you for your virtue and that affection for your brother and find you better men than I had expected from your plots against me; for all this that I have done was to test your brotherly love ... I remember no more those sins against me of which you think yourselves guilty ...

The Joseph of this speech differs significantly from the biblical figure, which bursts out in genuine happiness and true concern for his family.[76] Not only does Josephus's presentation lack the vivid-

---

[75] Based on *Gen* 42:21–22, Josephus relates in *JA* II, 108 how the brothers' recognized their guilt and acknowledged that they were punished justly. This emphasis is not unique and also Philo (*Jos* 170) has the brothers' point to δίκη and their just chastisement.

[76] *Gen* 45:1–4: "... so nobody stayed with him when Joseph made himself known to his brothers. And he wept aloud, so that the Egyptians heard it and the household of Pharaoh heard it. And Joseph said to his brothers: I am Joseph, is my father still alive? But his brothers could not answer him for they were dismayed at his presence. So Joseph said to his brothers: come near to me, I pray you. And they came near. And he said: I am your brother Joseph whom you sold to Egypt".

ness of its *Vorlage*, but it also contradicts the narrative setting. Given the fact that he addresses his brothers, it is necessary for the inner logic of the plot that he should first identify himself. In Josephus's account, the speaker's identity remains a side issue and is to be inferred from his exhortation. It emerges that in reality Josephus's Joseph addresses the reader with a view to gain sympathy. Josephus's unsatisfactory style and apologetics become even more transparent when we compare Philo's narrative. As mentioned above, Philo basically shares Josephus's interpretation of Joseph. Yet he presents a summary reflection of Joseph's motives from the authorial point of view *before* the actual scene. The self-identification of Joseph is then related quite naturally (*Jos* 237–40). We may suspect that Josephus's awkward description was prompted by a personal concern.

Not surprisingly, charges of Josephus' atrocities and his revenge on the conquered cities is a recurrent theme in his *Vita*.[77] He attempts to disprove them by frequent reference to his exceptionally benevolent behaviour towards defeated opponents. Thus he boasts how mildly he treated Jonathan and his band despite the Galileans' outrage and their desire to kill them (*Vita* 262):

> To Jonathan and his colleagues I promised pardon for the past on condition that they showed their contrition and returned home ...".[78]

In direct response to accusations of this kind, Josephus furthermore insists that he punished the soldiers who dared to plunder Tiberias (*Vita* 333). He also claims that the city was saved by his "adroitness and considerate forethought" (*ibid* 389). Finally, he emphasises his benevolence by addressing his adversaries thus (*Vita* 353):

> Have you forgotten how, often as I had you in my power, I put none of you to death?!

It thus emerges from the above analysis that there probably is a personal background also to Josephus's overly keen justification of Joseph's behaviour towards his brothers in Egypt.

---

[77] In *Vita* 314, for example, Josephus explicitly mentions that he was accused of taking revenge on the Tiberians for their disloyalty towards him; they were "falsely implying that I had made such a threat"; see also S. Cohen's discussion of Josephus's aplogetics concerning his alleged vengeance on Sepphoris, *op. cit.*, pp. 122–24.

[78] Also in *Vita* 306 he claims to have calmed down the Galilaeans and restrained them from "exterminating" John; and in *Vita* 368–372 how he avoided bloodshed despite the Galilaeans' rage.

The biblical Joseph's relationship with his brothers emerges as that part of the story which is most similar to Josephus's own life. Thus, the paraphrase of this relationship naturally assumes the most autobiographical flavour. We have moreover seen that Josephus is especially concerned with the significance of Joseph's dreams for the brothers' relationship. The main hermeneutic impetus of this paraphrase corresponds to that of the *Vita*: in both expositions Josephus attempts to prove that the hero, far from initiating strife among brothers, did everything to avoid it.[79] Faithful to the tradition of Roman autobiography, Josephus focuses in his presentation on character. As in his *Vita*,[80] he presents the "relevant" facts of the hero's life in the "appropriate" order and then invites his readers to evaluate his ἦθος on the basis of them.

Joseph and Women

D. Daube established the importance in *JA* of Joseph's relation to Potiphar's wife and his marriage to Asenath. He argued that these items are the other two parallels to Josephus's own life and that they are used for a typological interpretation.[81]

It is, however, questionable whether these conjectures can be sufficiently corroborated. It seems primarily that neither the biblical nor the Josephan description of the 'affair' corresponds, as it is claimed, to *Vita* 424. In that passage Josephus mentions slanders based on envy of his career. The account lacks, however, any reference to charges of sexual harrasment[82] and can therefore not be adduced as a parallel to the biblical material.

Equally, the story of Joseph and Asenath, either in its biblical or its paraphrased form, does not exhibit a striking resemblance to *Vita* 414. Daube is right in pointing out that Josephus's Caesarean wife is said to be a virgin; and that marriage was arranged, too. Yet the attribute of virginity is a wide-spread literary topos[83] which does not therefore warrant a comparison. In addition, this marriage of

---

[79] For a summary statement in *Vita*, see especially paragraph 265.

[80] *Vita* 430: "Such are the events of my whole life; from them let others judge as they will of my character". See also: S. Cohen, *op. cit.*, p. 104.

[81] *Op.cit.*, pp. 27–28.

[82] Although these can be found for example in *Vita* 259.

[83] See especially: K. Kerenyi, *Die griechisch-orientalische Romanliteratur*, Tübingen 1927, pp. 206–229 and in particular p. 218, where he identifies the emphasis on the hero's virginity as a characteristic of the later romances.

Josephus's was very much a passing affair whereas Joseph's connection to Asenath is praised, especially by Josephus, as a major social achievement. We may therefore conclude that if Joseph's women reminded Josephus of his own, it cannot be detected in his paraphrase of the biblical stories. We must therefore search for other criteria to establish the significance of Potiphar's wife and Asenath in Josephus's narrative.

Josephus's account of the attempt by Potiphar's wife to seduce the youth has frequently been submitted to scholarly scrutiny. As mentioned above, M. Braun has conclusively shown Josephus's adaptation of the biblical material to the genre of romance.[84] He established the importance of Joseph's menial status as a background to the ethical issues,[85] highlighted the Greek-erotic features of the woman's psyche[86] and also isolated Stoic and Epicurian arguments in Joseph's responses to her.[87] It remains to be analysed how the

---

[84] *Griechischer Roman, op. cit.*, pp. 25–27. G. Tachauer, *Das Verhältnis von Flavius Josephus zur Bibel und Tradition*, Erlangen 1871, pp. 24–25, discovered previously that Josephus "stellt diese Thatsache auf eine mehr romantische Weise dar"; he, however, merely refers to the author's Greek education as a reason for this "poetische Ausschmückung" without further examining the motifs and their literary genre or origin. For a background on romance literature, see especially: K. Kerenyi, *op. cit.*, pp. 1–24 and R. Merkelbach, *Roman und Mysterium in der Antike*, Beck 1962, pp. 333–341 (both stress the religious origin and dimension of the romance); and R. Helm, *Der Antike Roman*, Göttingen 1956, pp. 32–52. Cf. also B.E. Perry, *The Ancient Romances*, University of California Press 1967, especially pp. 44ff. Consider also T. Haegg's interesting study of "*Narrative Technique in Ancient Greek Romances*", Stockholm 1971.

[85] *ibid*, p. 28 and p. 33–35.

[86] *ibid*, p. 37 and p. 48ff.

[87] *ibid*, pp. 41–47, p. 63 and p. 74ff. M. Braun also dealt with the *JA* in his important study of the Phaedra motive in *XII, op. cit.*, pp. 44–105, for Josephus see especially pp. 90–93. M. Braun's conclusions have frequently been reiterated in the secondary literature, see especially: A. Schalit, *op. cit.*, pp. LXVI–IX (he further emphasises the exposure of inner life and the rhetoric of Joseph's speech); H. Sproedowsky, *op. cit.*, pp. 55–73; I. Heinemann, *op. cit.*, p. 200 (he conjectures that the biblical seduction scenes appeared too naive in Josephus's eyes and was therefore embellished with Greek psychological motives); H. Schwarzbaum, *Studies in Jewish and World Literature*, Berlin 1968, p. 46 (repeating Braun's thesis he calls for further folkloristic investigations of the matter, but he himself does not offer these); E.W. Smith (jr), *Joseph material in Joseph and Asenath and Josephus' relation to the Testament of Joseph*, in: *Studies in the Testament of Joseph*, ed. G. Nickelburg, Montana 1975, pp. 133–39 (he draws unconvincing parallels between the two documents); Th.W. Franxman, *op. cit.*, p. 233 (he concludes that Josephus shows "a certain sympathy for the woman" because it is, according to him, suggested that she might be able to control her passion with a "little self-discipline"; however, given Josephus's general misogynism and his emphasis here on the feminine char-

image of "Joseph in speech" accords with Josephus's presentation of the scene as a whole.

In *JA* II, 39–40 Josephus introduces the Potiphar story by way of a summary preview. He relates how Joseph was sold to the "chief cook"[88] Pentephres and adds that he received exceptional treatment, including also "the education which befits a free man".[89] Josephus's insertion seems to reflect contemporary circumstances since in Late Roman times it was not uncommon for a talented slave to be educated by his master.[90] Josephus thus again transfers a biblical scene from its simple environment to a more elevated atmosphere. His embellishment, and particularly his emphasis on the aristocratic nature of Joseph's alleged education, has nevertheless further dimensions.

Culture, and thus education, were from early Antiquity linked to the nobility[91] and became the regular attribute of a "Volksheld".[92] Against this background it is notable that Josephus does generally not apply this quality to other eminent Israelites.[93] He furthermore

---

acter of the woman's infatuation and her slanders (*JA* II, 55) this cannot be corroborated!).

[88] Josephus construes the problematic biblical expression thus (for details, see chap. II). Compare also other exegetical solutions, e.g.: *LXX* on *Gen* 39:1; *GR* 1054–55 and *PJ* on *Gen* 39:1.

[89] H.St. Thackeray's translation (*op. cit.*, p. 185) "a liberal education" is thus perhaps slightly misleading. Cf. also L. Ginzberg, *Legends*, vol. V, p. 338, who postulates a parallel to Philo's account of Joseph in Potiphar's house (*Jos* 37). Against the background of chap. II it seems, however, clear that Philo's allegory is rather different from Josephus's insertion of a social status symbol.

[90] We may further infer from Josephus's remark in *JA* XX, 263ff that he expected his readers' familiarity with such customs. For a background on the education of slaves, see especially: M.P. Nilsson, *Die hellenistische Schule*, München 1955, p. 61; and more generally *education*, *OCD*, pp. 369–73; *Erziehung, Lexicon der Alten Welt*, p. 874. Cf. also A. Gwynn's account in *Roman Education*, Oxford 1926, especially pp. 22–34 (it suffers from an idealisation of Greek education).

[91] For an excellent account of the history of Greek education see: W.W. Jäger, *Paideia: the Ideals of Greek culture*, Oxford 1939 (translated from the 2nd German ed.), especially pp. 1–13, pp. 184–222 and pp. 300–311; cf. A.A. Bryant, *Boyhood and Youth in the Days of Aristophanes*, in: *Harvard Studies in Classical Philology*, 18/1970, pp. 73–122 (too enthusiastic). Concerning Josephus, see especially: A. Schalit, *op. cit.*, p. I, extensive footnote on π.

[92] See also: M. Braun, *Griechischer Roman, op. cit.*, p. 34 where he also mentions examples of Plutarch's historiography, such as Romulus in *Rom* 6,2.

[93] The exceptions are Joshua and Daniel who are relatively late and not formative figures. Joshua is said to have received π. in the form of νόμος from Moses (*JA* IV, 165); Daniel and his companions are said to have acquired a π. in Hebrew and Chaldean books (*JA* X, 194); see K. Rengstorf, *A Complete Concordance to Flavius Josephus*, Leiden 1979, vol. III, pp. 265–66.

rarely uses it in the context of Jewish learning.[94] Instead, he frequently imputes it to early Hellenistic or contemporaneous men of letters.[95] He in fact regards παιδεία as so prestigious in his own days that he accuses other historians of writing only with a view to gaining such a reputation.[96] He himself struggles to be exempted from the stereotype of Jewish parochialism, and often asserts his Greek learning.[97]

It thus emerges that the attribution of παιδεία to such an ancient figure as Joseph is unusual. Given his personal background, Josephus might have wished to provide his hero with qualities which he himself painfully lacked. More importantly, he thus enhances Joseph's embarrassing status in Potiphar's house and anticipates the issue, which he will present as the main background to the subsequent encounter.

Josephus them sums up his introduction to the Potiphar story by the following consideration (*JA* II, 40):

> Yet while enjoying these privileges, he even under this change of fortune (ὑπὸ τῆς μεταβολῆς) did not abandon that virtue which enveloped him (ἀρετήν ἥτις ἦν περὶ αὐτόν), but displayed how a noble spirit (φρόνημα) can surmount the hardships (δυσκόλων) of life.

In this passage Josephus inserts an authorial remark in which he presents his view of the story's overall message. According to him, this instance is to be generalised and regarded as one example of firm character confronting the vicissitudes of life (*JA* II, 42). Commenting on the woman's second approach, Josephus further writes (*JA* II, 50):

---

[94] In addition to the above mentioned, π. is cited also in *JA* IV, 261 where the parents' responsibility to provide the best possible training for their children is emphasised; in *JA* XVII, 149 where π. refers to the interpretation of ancestral law; *JA* XX, 263 and *Vita* 8 of Josephus's own Jewish education.

[95] Of Epaphroditus in *JA* I, 8; of Andreas and Aristeas in *JA* XII, 53; of Herod's sons in *JA* XVI, 203 and of Gaius in *JA* XVIII, 206, of king Ptolemy in *JA* I, 10.

[96] See for example *JA* I, 2. In *Vita* 40 Josephus furthermore acknowledges even his arch-enemy Justus of Tiberias' Greek π. Note also that Plutarch devotes a whole treatise to the subject of education which he self-evidently understands as pertaining to the free born (*Moralia* I, Loeb Classical Library 1969, 1st ed. 1927, pp. 4–71).

[97] E.g.: *JA* XX, 263–66. See also H.L. Feldman's critical evaluation, *Mikra*, *op. cit.*, p. 481: "Josephus was out to impress his readers with his knowledge of Greek literature". For a general background on Josephus's education, see: T. Rajak, *op. cit.*, pp. 26–32, where she discusses his training in the context of the rabbinic sources; and *Schürer* I, p. 40 and II, p. 80.

he resisted her entreaties and yielded not to her threats choosing to suffer unjustly (παθεῖν ἀδίκως) and to endure (ὑπομένειν) even the severest penalty, rather than take advantage of the moment.

This authorial remark by Josephus invokes an image of martyrdom. In this new framework the Potiphar story emerges as a trial and as a challenge for the Just. Josephus subsequently enhances Joseph's courageous steadfastness by turning the woman's intention to denounce Joseph into a public declaration. Josephus's Joseph consequently accepts consciously the results of his righteousness.

This pietistic interpretation of Joseph in the 'affair' has, as we saw earlier, a notable tradition in Palestinian exegesis. The most detailed parallel of Josephus's account is to be found in *TJos*. The dying patriarch allegedly derived the following moral from his experience with Potiphar's wife (*TJos* 2:7):

> In ten testings He showed that I was approved and in all of them I persevered (ἐμακροθύμησα), because perseverance is a powerful medicine and endurance (ὑπομονή) a good thing.[98]

In *TJos* 9:2 the patriarch's sayings are further reported in a more pious tone: "not even in my mind did I yield to her, for God loves more the one who is faithful in self-control . . ."[99]

Despite the greater degree of abstract formulation in Josephus's account, it is obvious that his interpretation corresponds closely to the image of Joseph in *XII*. It is possible that in addition to sharing this overall Palestinian exegesis Josephus is also happy to avoid biblical references to the national dimension of the confrontation.[100] Highlighting other aspects, such as the social and religious significance of the encounter, Josephus's narrative elegantly bypasses these issues.

Josephus interprets also the culmination of the Potiphar story in accordance with the above pietistic outline. He thus offers the following explanation for Joseph's silent acceptance of his prison sentence (*JA* II, 60):

---

[98] See also H.W. Hollander's discussion of this passage, *op. cit.*, pp. 28–30: identifying it as an "individual thanksgiving" (p. 20), he concludes that the "basic element of Joseph's temptation is to be found in his being forsaken".

[99] Consider further: *TJos* 10:2 "The Lord loves self-control" (ἠγάπησε τὴν σωφροσύνην); *TJos* 10:1: "how great are the things that endurance (ὑπομονή) and prayer with fasting accomplish" and *TJos* 4:8 "but I devoted myself the more to fasting and prayer that the Lord might rescue me from her".

[100] Consider especially *Gen* 39:14–17, where Potiphar's wife is shown to exploit the household's xenophobia.

> Joseph, on his side, committing his case entirely to God, sought
> neither to defend himself nor yet to render a strict account of what had
> passed, but silently underwent his bonds and his confinement, trust-
> ing that God, who knew the cause of his calamity and the truth, would
> prove stronger than those who bound him; and of His providence he
> had proof forthwith.

In this passage Josephus embellishes *Gen* 39:20, where the fact of
Joseph's imprisonment is laconically related. Since the biblical
description is furthermore focalised from outside most Ancient exegetes supplied motifs for Potiphar's rash decision. While Philo is
thus concerned with the violation of legal principles (*Jos* 52 – 3), it
is conjectured in *GR* 1074 that Potiphar acted against his better
knowledge and only with a view to this family's reputation.

Josephus's treatment is characteristically personal[101] and pietistic. He particularly illustrates Joseph's perspective in this scene[102]
and thus demonstrates an ideal human disposition towards Divine
providence. Not surprisingly, also this aspect of the figure of Joseph
has been precedented in *TJos*, where Joseph's denunciation is num-
bered among his trials (1:3). However, by comparison to this earlier
version, Josephus stresses human devotion rather more than Divine
trustworthiness.

The image of Joseph which emerges from the above authorial passages has a conspicuously religious flavour. It concurs in crucial
aspects with traditional Palestinian exegesis and must be appreciated as a significant frame of Josephus's largely Hellenised story of
Joseph and Potiphar's wife.

Josephus adds three important elements to the biblical account of
Joseph and Asenath:[103] he firstly praises the relation as a most distinguished marriage (γάμον ἀξιολογώτατον), then he describes
Asenath as a virgin and finally conjectures that Pharaoh assists in
bringing about the match.

---

[101] Note that in *JA* II, 28 Josephus also explains Potiphar's behaviour by reference to his overriding uxoriousness.

[102] Note that also Philo shows some interest in Joseph's point of view and in *Jos*
80 he remarks that he "did not have an opportunity to defend himself". It has been
suggested by M. Braun, *op. cit.*, p. 113, that Josephus's emphasis had been inspired
by Hellenistic romance stories where the hero's reaction to misjudgement is a wide-
spread theme. However, in view of the religious nature of Josephus's interpretation
such an impetus can at most be very remote.

[103] *JA* II, 9 cf. *Gen* 41:45: "And Pharaoh called Joseph's name Zaphenath-
paneah; and he gave him in marriage Asenath, the daughter of Potiphera, priest
of On. So Joseph went out over the land of Egypt".

Most of these notions are echoed in other Greek documents on the Joseph story. Regarding the marriage as a social distinction it is most notable that Philo expresses himself in similar terms.[104] Moreover, in *JosAs* 21:8–9[105] even the emphasis on Pharaoh's support is paralleled and we learn that he prescribes a general seven day vacation in honour of the wedding. Pharaoh is furthermore said to be eager to arrange the festivities and he is prevented from doing so only by Joseph's consideration for his natural father (*JosAs* 20:9). As well known,[106] rabbinic Midrash is instead concerned with Asenath's alien origin and this disturbing fact is accounted for in numerous ways. It should finally be mentioned that also Josephus's claim of Asenath's virginity is paralleled in the Hellenistic exegesis of the Joseph story. The most obvious recurrence is yet again to be found in *JosAs* (1:4 and 1:6).[107]

It thus emerges that Josephus's account of Joseph and Asenath differs quite significantly from its *Vorlage*. Like other Hellenistic writers he primarily attributes to it much more importance than the biblical narrator. Perhaps the most characteristic feature of Josephus's embellishments is a certain openness to foreign culture and an underlying sense of being an integral part of Gentile society.

Joseph and the Egyptians

In his apologetic of Judaism,[108] Josephus shows an acute awareness of the influence historical records have on contemporary relations between Jews and Egyptians. He complains that many of his Egyptian contemporaries betrayed prominent anti-Semitic tendencies and

---

[104] *Jos* 121.

[105] For an up-to-date and well documented discussion of the document's (Egyptian) provenance and (the possibly late) date see: M. Goodman, *Schürer* III, pp. 546–552; for a detailed review of the issues, see: Ch. Burchard, *The present state of research on Joseph and Asenath*, in: *New Perspectives on Ancient Judaism*, ed. J. Neusner a.o., University of America 1987, pp. 13–51; and on the document's genre see: S. West, *Joseph and Asenath: A neglected Greek Romance*, in: *CQ* 24/1974, pp. 70–81.

[106] See especially: V. Aptovitzer, *Asenath, the Wife of Joseph*, HUCA 1/1924, pp. 239–306.

[107] See also Ch. Burchard, *Joseph and Asenath*, in: *The Old Testament Pseudepigrapha*, ed. J.H. Charlesworth, New York 1985, p. 203 note j, "Asenath's virginity, not mentioned in the bible, plays a great role in JosAsen, as virginity generally does in the romances".

[108] *AgAp*, especially I, 224–25.

that they were influenced by the distorted history of the Israelites in their country. He furthermore accuses some of them of having a vested interest in misrepresenting Hebrew traditions and in attacking its representatives.

Josephus frequently attempts to dismantle calumnies of this kind. Usually he does so by giving detailed explanations of his heritage.[109] In addition, he also proceeds indirectly through calculated modifications of Scripture.[110] In the light of Josephus's commitment on this level it is to be expected that the biblical Joseph's activities in Egypt are of considerable interest to him. It is with this question in mind that we shall now examine the pertinent passages.

As we may gather from Josephus's abridgement of *Gen* 47: 14–22,[111] he is not particularly interested in Joseph's administration as such. His concern focusses instead on the relations between Joseph and the indigenous population. It is important for him to envision these two peoples in harmony. For this purpose Josephus on occasion changes the biblical scenes.

He thus insists on Joseph's humanitarian universalism which he is said to exercise even at the height of his power and in time of hardship. In this vein Joseph is described in *JA* II, 94 as σωτὴρ ὁμολογουμένως τοῦ πλήθους; and Josephus adds that he provided also strangers with corn. This he did, Josephus emphasizes, because

> he held that all men, in virtue of their kinship (κατὰ συγγένειαν ἀξιοῦντος), should receive succour from those in prosperity".[112]

These authorial insertions correspond to statements in Josephus's apologetic where he repeatedly defends the broad humanitarian values of Judaism.[113] This line of interpretation is shared by other diaspora writers, such as Philo.[114] *GR*, on the other hand, grasps

---

[109] E.g.: *AgAp* II, 121–159.

[110] See for example also: H.W. Attridge, *op. cit.*, pp. 65–69; L.H. Feldmann, *Use, op. cit.*, pp. 494–95; *idem, Flavius Josephus Revisited, op. cit.*, pp. 796–97; *idem, Hellenisations, op. cit.*, pp. 140–41.

[111] Josephus's concise, yet faithful account is to be found in *JA* II, 189–91.

[112] This is repeated by Josephus in *JA* II, 95 and 101. Note that Th.W. Franxman, *op. cit.*, p. 252, mentions this embellishment also. Consider also: A. Schalit's conjectures of a Stoic background to this universalism, *op. cit.*, p. 49.

[113] E.g.: *AgAp* II, 210ff.

[114] See especially *Jos* 157, where Philo describes how Joseph endeared himself on his inspection tours to the Egyptians. It should, however, be remembered that in contrast to Josephus he refrains from making a more general, theoretical statement on the issue.

the situation from an entirely Jewish perspective; and it is claimed that Joseph "put them [the Egyptians] to shame by circumcising them" (*GR* 1106).

Further completing this picture of co-operation between the Israelites and the Egyptians, Josephus inserts more details. Thus, he embellishes Jacob's advice for his sons' journey South by the admonition that "they should integrate themselves with the Egyptians" (*JA* II, 186). In the same vein he also minimizes the Egyptian plight which they suffer, according to the biblical account, at the hands of Joseph.[115] Josephus emphasizes instead that Joseph restored to each city its land and that he "might have reserved [it] for his own benefit" (*ibid*).

It is furthermore remarkable that Josephus shows how Joseph not only increased his own reputation but, and perhaps predominantly so, also that of the king.[116] In view of Josephus's own history, it seems likely that he thereby wished to accentuate aspects which were at the time subject of acute political concern. He thus asserts that despite contemporary accusations[117] the Jews are not to be considered as rebellious by nature. Their leaders, so argues Josephus now, are also capable of a conciliatory policy.

It thus emerges that Josephus' portrait of Joseph in Egypt reflects to a certain degree concerns of a diaspora writer.[118] In anticipation of certain prejudices, he highlights Joseph's humane decrees as a governor. More specifically, he presents him as the kind of leader that the Romans might wish to have encountered in Judaea prior to the revolt.

Concluding Remarks

In the above chapter we have examined Josephus's Joseph story which is part of his historical narrative on Ancient Israel. We have seen that when Josephus reaches the life of his namesake, he reacts in a special way to the biblical material.

A close examination of the treatment of Joseph's four most impor-

---

[115] *JA* II, 191 reflecting *Gen* 47:23–27.

[116] *JA* II, 193 τὴν εὔνοιαν τῷ βασιλεῖ.

[117] Throughout Josephus's *Vita* the responsibility for encouraging the uprising is a prominent yet painful subject; and the former leaders of the revolt are frequently reported as accusing each other of instigating the people.

[118] For a general background, see also: *Schürer* I, p. 48; and T. Rajak, *op. cit.*, pp. 224–25.

tant relationships has rendered highly interesting insights into Josephus's hermeneutics. It has thus emerged that according to Josephus the role of Jacob is the most crucial in establishing the protagonist's peculiar position among his family. This highly sympathetic treatment of Joseph's youth is further developed by attributing to him typical qualities of Israelite heros.

In Josephus's narrative Joseph's relations to his brothers are of the greatest interest. Because of the numerous parallels to his own life, Josephus has paraphrased them in distinctly autobiographical terms. The exegetical impetus is here astonishingly similar to that of his *Vita*: he is concerned in both works with the character of the protagonist and defends his impeccable behaviour by reference to divinely inspired dreams.

Regarding the biblical Joseph's relations with the two foreign women mostly two conclusions can be drawn from the above analysis. First, Josephus paints also a pietistic image of Joseph in the story with Potiphar's wife. It has typically Palestinian features and should not be overlooked besides the more overt Hellenistic motifs. Secondly, in his description of Joseph's wedding Josephus shows a relaxed openness towards foreign culture.

It is especially Joseph's connection with the Egyptians which Josephus shapes in accordance with his apologetics of Judaism against contemporary anti-semitism.

It emerges both from the centrality and the nature of these four relations that Josephus's paraphrase of the biblical story is the most personal one. In contrast to Philo and *GR*, his interpretation often reflects the narrator's own concerns. Being a man of the world, Josephus also refrains from creating an overall ideological framework. He appears instead to be more fascinated by the complexity of the characters and by the literary potential of the story. And he has also shown himself to be a master in the art of manipulation by introducing almost imperceptible, yet highly influential, changes to the biblical material.

CHAPTER FIVE

THE FIGURE OF JOSEPH IN GENESIS RABBAH

Among the sources discussed here, *GR* is the most heterogeneous and associative interpretation of the Joseph story. It thus lacks over-all coherence, even more than Philo's literal and allegorical account. Most obviously, the exegetical elaborations here on the figure of Joseph are not presented as part of an overall story but rather as direct interpretations of small units of biblical text. An examination of the figure of Joseph in *GR* therefore needs to seriously take into account the more dynamic nature of the presentation. This implies that a meaningful picture of the figure of Joseph has to be construct-ed from scattered, yet not wanton references. The question of how exegesis and *Weltanschauung* are interwoven also becomes a domi-nant concern.

Certain focal points in the Midrashic treatment of the figure of Joseph can be identified in the above graph. It is thus distinctly noticeable that *GR* is particularly concerned with Joseph's youth, his encounter with Potiphar's wife and, finally, with his image in Egypt. The exposition in *GR* on these issues needs to be further examined by comparing it, on the one hand, to the interpretation of other bib-lical figures in *GR* and, on the other hand, to images of Joseph in different midrashic works.

Joseph's Youth

The treatment of Joseph's personal history begins,[1] as in Philo, at the biblical introduction scene of *Gen* 37:2.[2] In view of this parallel,

---

[1] In *GR* the Joseph story is introduced by two long interpretations in which the significance of the figure for Israel's history and his relation to Jacob are empha-sized. It is mostly pointed out that it is because of Joseph that Israel came to Egypt. It is furthermore conjectured that it was also thanks to him that the Red Sea split during the Exodus. See also M. Emanuel, לדמותו של יוסף, *Beit Mikra* 47/1971, who sees Joseph from a "Zionist" point of view and criticizes the figure for having caused Israel to emigrate into the diaspora. This introduction differs significantly from that of the previous two interpretations. In *Tanhuma* this topic is not only men-tioned but also developed further.

[2] "This is the history of the family of Jacob. Joseph, being seventeen years old,

it is particularly significant that a different item is in fact selected for comment it moreover emerges that the exegetical intention in *GR* varies distinctly from the two Hellenistic paraphrases (*GR* 1008):

> Joseph was seventeen years old (*Gen* 37:2), and you say: that he was a youth (נער, *Gen* 37:2)?
> This means he was behaving childishly (עושה מעשה נערות). He pencilled his eyes, curled his hair and lifted his heel.

Parallel to the biblical scene, Joseph is depicted in this passage from the authorial perspective; and also here it is his actions which characterise him. However, the midrashic narrator replaces the biblical reference to Joseph's standard occupation by a report of a few individual deeds.[3] These inserted aspects of Joseph's behaviour indicate the narrator's understanding of his main traits: he is envisioned as complacent and vain.

In the above passage the narrator explains the exegetical impetus which inspired the interpretation.[4] It is said to respond to the two references in the same verse to Joseph's age. The assumption in *GR* of thirteen as the age of maturity might thus have supported this exegesis.[5] In the light of it the statement that Joseph was seventeen years old and yet still a youth must have appeared unusual and thus required elucidation.

It is remarkable that the term youth is here taken as an indication of Joseph's childish behaviour whereas it does not usually receive particular notice in *GR*.[6] This negative connotation of the term is paralleled by some more explicit biblical statements[7] and was perhaps also inspired by them to a certain degree.

---

was shepherding the flock with his brothers; he was a lad with the sons of Bilhah and Zilpah, his father's wives ...''

[3] On the distinction between conventional actions and those which originate from the individual himself, see: Y. Ewen, *op. cit.*, pp. 56–99; see also O. Meir, 1977, pp. 372–4, where she emphasizes that actions in the Aggadah tend to be clearly categorized as ''good'' or ''bad''.

[4] On the technical use of the term אתה אמרת in *GR*, see especially: Ch. Albeck, *op. cit.*, vol. III, p. 22.

[5] See especially *GR* 570 and 965. See also: Ch. Albeck's commentary *ad.loc.*, H. Freedman, *Midrash Rabbah*, London 1939, vol. II, p. 774 n.5; cf. also A. Mirkin, *Midrash Rabbah* (Hebrew), Tel Aviv 1956–67, vol. IV, p. 15 n.7.

[6] Compare for example: *GR* 569 on *Gen* 21:12 and also on *Gen* 21:17–20; 22:12; 34:19; 43:8; 44:22 and 44:31–32. For a general background, see also: S.H. Blank, *IDB*, vol. IV, p. 925.

[7] E.g.: *Prov* 22:15: ''Folly is bound up in the heart of the child but the rod of discipline drives it far from him''. For more neutral references to the term, see espe-

These considerations, however, corroborate only partially *GR*'s exegesis on Joseph. Most notably, they do not account for the two distinct features of this interpretation, namely its severely critical attitude and the independence of its contents from the *Vorlage*.

It is significant in this context that a reference to the same activities, i.e., pencilling the eyes, curling the hair and lifting up the heel, recurs elsewhere in *GR*. This motif is thus used to illustrate the principle that the evil inclination overcomes man not covertly but in the open (*GR* 211–12).

We may further gather the narrator's motivation for this picturesque insertion when we consider *GR* 1063. There we find a coment on *Gen* 39:7 which explains the peculiar position of the reference to Joseph's beauty:

> What precedes this passage (the attempt of Potiphar's wife to seduce Joseph)? 'And Joseph was handsome and good-looking' (*Gen* 39:6). 'And his master's wife cast an eye' (*Gen* 39:7). This is to be compared[8] to a man who was sitting in the street, pencilling his eyes, curling his hair and lifting his heel, saying: I am indeed a man! They (passersby) said to him: if you are a man here is a bear, up and attack it!

The midrashic narrator enhances here a biblical allusion and establishes a causal connection between Joseph's behaviour and his fate, a theme which we shall fully explore below.[9] For our discussion of *GR* on *Gen* 37:2, it is important to note that exactly the same actions of Joseph are mentioned here. In this context their provocative impact is furthermore made fully explicit. It seems likely that the same concept underlies, and perhaps even provoked, the midrashic insertion to the introduction of the Joseph story.

The above interpretation of Joseph's family circumstances is unusual in the rabbinic tradition.[10] In *TanhumaB*, *Vayesheb* 20, for example, the term youth is associated with I*Sam* 2:21 and Joseph's prophetic inclinations are thus inferred. The overall positive image

---

cially: I*Kg* 5:20 and II*Sam* 13:17, where it means "servant" or *Ex* 2:6, where it refers factually to very young age.

[8] In MSS Adler/London the technical term "משל ל" is used; the other MSS just employ a simple "ל" of reference.

[9] Note that Rashi in his commentary on *Gen* 39:7 is highly sensitive to this connection. He also uses some of the midrashic material, but places it within the scriptural narrative context, thus betraying a greater awareness than the midrash to the structure of the biblical story.

[10] Naturally, however, the interpretation of *GR* is preserved in *MHG*, *ad.loc.*.

of Joseph becomes in fact so popular that the medieval exegete S.
Yafe,[11] confronts the problem of how to reconcile this midrash in
GR with the image of The Righteous.

We saw previously that Philo and Josephus, each for his own reasons, omit Joseph's defamations of his brothers. In distinct contrast
to these, *GR* pays great attention to this aspect of his character and
embellishes it significantly (*GR* 1009):[12]

> 'And Joseph brought evil report against them' (*Gen* 37:2). R. Meir said:
> your sons are suspect of (eating) limbs (torn from) the living (animals).
> R. Judah said: they despise the sons of the handmaids and call them
> slaves.
> R. Simon said: they cast their eyes on the daughters of the country.
> R. Judah b. Simon said: with respect to these three 'a just balance and
> scale are the Lord's (*Prov* 16:11).
> The Holy One, blessed be He, said to him:[13] you said they are sus-
> pect of (eating) limbs (torn from) the living (animals), by your life!
> Even at the time of (their) sin they will slaughter ritually, as it is said
> 'and they killed a he-goat' (שחט, *Gen* 37:31). You said: they despise
> the sons of the handmaids and call them slaves, 'Joseph was sold as
> a slave' (*Ps* 105:17). You said they cast their eyes on the daughters of
> the country, I will incite a bear against you, 'his master's wife cast her
> eyes upon Joseph' (*Gen* 39:7).

The midrashic narrator withdraws in this passage behind the enumeration of exegetical traditions. He thus asserts the popularity and
the importance of this verse throughout the generations of scholarship.[14] The sayings collected here form two units. While the first
consists of three interpretations of the biblical item "ill report",[15]
the second is based on these and develops them further by introducing another narrative figure, namely God.

The sayings in the first unit offer three possible versions of
Joseph's defamations, since each rabbi is presented as directly quoting Joseph's speech to his father.[16] The biblical situation is thus im-

---

[11] יפה תואר, Venice שנ"ז, pp. 1062–63.

[12] Also to be found in *GR* 1062.

[13] See also H. Freedman, *op. cit.*, p. 774, who translates more freely "rebuked him".

[14] On the individual rabbis quoted, see: H.L. Strack/G. Stemberger, *op. cit.*,
pp. 82–83 and p. 98.

[15] On the midrashic convention of embellishing biblical items which are not
closely defined, see: I. Heinemann, *op. cit.*, pp. 23–26.

[16] Note that H. Freedman, *op. cit.*, p. 774, rightly inserts a clarification to this
effect.

plicitly retained; and also the focalisation on the figure from without is the same.[17] The innovation of these sayings is that they make more vivid the biblical scene and provide extra, negative "facts" about Joseph.

In his commentary on *GR*, M.A. Mirkin[18] wishes to demonstrate how each of Joseph's alleged accusations emerges from the biblical expression "ill report". For this purpose he proposes a linguistic connection between each interpretation and this biblical item. He thus maintains that the reproach of non-ritual slaughtering and pursuit of foreign women derives from the epithet bad[19] and that Joseph's concept of his brothers as slaves is based on the expression "the wives of his fathers" (*Gen* 37:2). It seems, however, that Mirkin's adduced proof-texts are too vague and do not correspond factually to the precise accusations. Some of his conjectures furthermore appear to be inspired by later midrashic traditions.[20] Instead, the above passage in *GR* is far more complex both with regard to its inspiration and its significance.

In the first version of Joseph's reports, i.e., that the brothers ate flesh from living animals, he is presented as accusing them of violating even the basic Noachic laws.[21] This motif existed independently of and prior to *GR*. It is first attested in *TGad* 1:4–9:

> He saw that I had set free a lamb from the mouth of the bear which I then killed but I had killed the lamb when I was saddened to see that it was too weak to live and we had eaten it. And this he told our father.

---

[17] Joseph's motivation thus remains unexplained in *GR*, too. This lack of insight has been acutely felt by later interpreters of *GR*; and S. Yafe, *op. cit.*, p. 1063, for example, conjectures that Joseph was motivated by halachic concerns and only related what he considered his duty. Abraham ben Asher, אור השכל, p. 164, on the other hand, attempts to account for the way in which Joseph discovered his brothers' sins (according to him, he noticed the absence of animals combined with a lack of blood from ritual slaughter.

[18] *Op.cit.*, pp. 15–16 n.7.

[19] This is "corroborated" by reference to *Gen* 28:8–9, where it says that "when Esau saw that the Caananite women did not please Isaac his father, Esau went to Ishmael and took to wife . . . ''

[20] For example, *TanhumaB Vayesheb* 6 rephrases the material found in *GR* thus: "they lifted their eyes to the Canaanite women". This amendment is likely to have been made in view of *Gen* 28:8.

[21] For the halachic background of this exegetical tradition, see especially: אבר מן החי, *ET*, pp. 48–51; J. Bowker, *The Targums and Midrashic Literature*, Cambridge 1969, p. 241; G. Friedländer; *Pirke de Rabbi Eliezer*, New York 1965 (1st ed. London 1916), p. 291; S. Gronemann, *Die jonathanische Pentateuchübersetzung in ihrem Verhältnis zur Halakha*, Leipzig 1879, p. 97; and *bSan* 59a, *PJ* on *Gen* 9:14.

Here the incident is related from the perspective of one of the brothers, namely Gad; and sensible motives are consequently provided for his behaviour. He is presented is such a way as to arouse the reader's sympathy without, however, directly criticising Joseph. Also, the whole incident is firmly placed within a pastoral background in this version and it emerges as an everyday problem of rural life.

It is of great interest that two midrashic corpuses which are known for their preservation of earlier, and pseudepigraphic material, PRE[22] and PJ,[23] present only this version of Joseph's defamation. PJ on Gen 37:2 in fact remains linguistically close to the earlier tradition which he abbreviates to: "Joseph brought evil report about them for *he saw them* eating meat torn from a living animal".[24] It therefore seems possible that the narrator of GR was, at an earlier stage, also familiar with one form of this tradition.[25] This supposition is further corroborated by the fact that this alleged defamation differs from the subsequent two in that no direct linguistic connection is drawn to the corresponding punishment in the Joseph story. Yet in distinction to other rabbinic works, the narrator of GR further accommodates this tradition to an extended and complicated exegetical framework.

The other two alleged defamations of Joseph are not attested independently. They do, however, recur in similar form in contemporaneous or later Midrash.[26] In order to evaluate the significance of these two traditions, we have to examine their place in the overall frame.

The second exegetical unit is presented as a later tradition and attributed to an Amoraic teacher of the fourth generation. As previ-

---

[22] G. Friedländer, *op. cit.*, p. 291.

[23] A. Shinan, אגדתם של מתורגמנים, Jerusalem 1979, pp. 242–88.

[24] Note that L. Ginzberg, *op. cit.*, vol. V p. 326 note 8 and 9, suggests that PJ describes only the tension between Joseph and the handmaidens' sons. There seems, however, no indication to this effect in the text.

[25] On the possibility of folkloristic and pseudepigraphic traditions penetrating the rabbinic corpuses despite the official ban on them, see especially: E. Yassif's recent article on *Traces of Folk Traditions of the Second Temple Period in Rabbinic Literature*, *JJS* 39/1988, pp. 212–33, where he points to some examples of transmission of previously written material in oral form into the midrash. See also: M. Hengel, *op. cit.*, pp. 110–15; A. Shinan, עולמה של ספרות האגדה, Tel Aviv 1987, pp. 21–29; and N. de Lange's introductory treatment in *Apocrypha: Jewish Literature of the Hellenistic Age*, New York 1978, pp. 1–40.

[26] E.g.: *jPeah a,3, MHG ad.loc.* and partially also in *TanhumaB Vayesheb 6*.

ously mentioned, it presupposes the preceding sayings which are now given a new dimension. An intellectual framework for this evaluation is initially provided by a quotation from *Prov* 16. Thus the relevance in this context of the widespread rabbinic belief in God's exact and trustworthy retribution is stressed.[27] The application of this idea to the figure of Joseph must be seen as a further stage of development in the Hebrew exegesis of the story, which had from early on stressed Divine providence (*Ps* 105).

Then another literary figure, God, is introduced as Joseph's counterpart in an imaginary conversation. This dialogue takes the form of three pairs of speech in each of which one of Joseph's alleged defamations is repeated and then juxtaposed by God's response. It emerges that, according to *GR*, Joseph's three troubles, namely his brother's assault, their sale of him and the advances of Potiphar's wife, are in reality Divine punishments for each of his slanders. The causative link between Joseph's conduct and his later fate is further stressed by proof-texts which establish linguistic links between the charges and their respective outcomes. Thus, the calumny of the brothers' servile status is shown to result in Joseph's being sold as a *slave* and his accusation of their "lifting their eyes to foreign women" allegedly lead to the woman's *lifting her eyes towards Joseph*. Not surprisingly, the connection between the first charge and its respective outcome is of a more general nature. Also, the corroborating

---

[27] For a background, see especially: E.E. Urbach, *op. cit.*, pp. 227–54; *idem*, אסקזיס ויסורין בספרות חז״ל, *Jubilee Volume on the Occasion of I. Bear's seventieth Birthday*, Jerusalem 1960, pp. 48–68; A. Heshel, תורה מן השמים באספקלריה של הדורות, Jerusalem, Vol. II pp. 93–106 S. Schlechter, *Some Aspects of Rabbinic Theology*, New York 1961, pp. 242–264; A. Büchler, *Studies in Sin and Atonement*, New York 1961, pp. 156–211; A. Marmorstein, *The Doctrine of Merits in Rabbinical Thought*, London 1914, pp. 8ff; G.F. Moore, *Judaism in the First Centuries of the Christian Era*, New York, vol. I; *idem*, *Fate and Free Will in the Jewish Philosophies to Josephus*, HTR 22/1929, pp. 371–89; *idem*, *Simon the Righteous*, in: *Jewish Studies in memory of Israel Abrahams*, New York 1927, pp. 348–364; R. Mach, *Der Zaddik in Talmud und Midrasch*, Brill 1957, pp. 32–35; E. Fackenheim, *God's Presence in History*, New York 1972; S. Lowy, *The Motivation of Fasting in Talmudic Literature*, *JSS* 9/1958; M. Lazarus' apologetic treatment in: *Ethik des Judentums*, Frankfurt 1898 vol. I, pp. 272–80; cf. J. Wochenmark's problematic study *Die Schicksalsidee im Judentum*, Stuttgart 1933; R. Akiba is particularly important for the formulation of the theodicy problem, see: L. Finkelstein, *Akiba: Scholar, Saint and Martyr*, New York 1970, pp. 195–215; For a treatment of this theme in rabbinic midrash, see especially: Y. Frankel, עיונים בעולמו הרוחני של סיפור האגדה, Tel Aviv 1981, pp. 13–22; the most relevant talmudic sources are to be found in: *bBer* 5b; *bShab* 55a; *bKid* 40b.

key-word does not correspond precisely to the accusation.[28]

The above evidence confirms the special treatment of the two defamations which are not attested independently. The artistically perfect structure leads me furthermore to suggest that they in fact developed parallel to the existing tradition of Joseph's calumny. They were inserted so as to provide reasons for Joseph's later hard fate.[29]

These results have important implications for the technique of characterisation in *GR*. Firstly, an originally human conflict is turned into an issue between the individual and God. The figure is furthermore understood not in its specific situation but from the theological lesson which is deduced from the overall story. As a result, character is clearly subordinated to theme and the details of the former are accommodated to the latter. This is also corroborated by the obvious neglect in *GR* of the brothers' crimes, which might well be considered more severe than Joseph's.[30]

By comparison to the other two midrashic versions of this interpretation, the material is presented in *GR* in a didactically highly effective fashion. Thus, the form of dialogue and exclamations such as "by your life", which are lacking in *jPeah* a.3, greatly animate the scene. They also facilitate the reader's identification with Joseph and ensure that his example will be influential. In *TanhumaB Vayasheb* 6, by comparison, the material has been reshaped with greater formality. Joseph's sins are presented in more conceptualized terms and aspects of the tribes and dietary precepts are also

---

[28] Cf. J. Kugel, *op. cit.*, pp. 81–84; he wishes to draw a distinction between the first two and the last of Joseph's alleged defamations. He argues that only in the latter case does there exist a true correspondence between crime and punishment because only regarding Potiphar's wife is Joseph's accusation retributed by another (false) accusation. Several facts should however not be overlooked: it is primarily to be noted that a symetry does exist in the second case of crime and punishment when Joseph falsely accuses his brothers of their servile state, since he is later sold *as though he were a slave* himself. He is thus considered to be slave just as he earlier considered his brothers. Moreover, the midrashic narrator himself does not establish the fact of being accused as the basis for a correspondence between crime and punishment. He instead points out that Potiphar's wife *lusted* after Joseph (corresponding to his accusation of the brothers "casting their eyes on the daughters of the country), not that she accused him wrongly.

[29] For a background on "ethical exegesis" in the Aggadah, see especially: I. Heinemann, *op. cit.*, pp. 87–95.

[30] See for example the casual comments in *GR* 1016–20 on *Gen* 37:18–24; Cf. on the other hand *TZeb* 2 which shows a great sensitivity to Joseph's suffering at his brothers' hands.

mentioned. Joseph's punishment is moreover seen mostly in his exile in Egypt. Set against this, the version in *GR* springe more spontaneously from a profound personal piety.

The concept of fate as the individual's responsibility is a recurrent exegetical theme in *GR*. In the case of the Joseph story it is for example also applied to *Gen* 42:24 which is taken as a just retribution for Simon's allegedly outstanding cruelty earlier on.[31] Otherwise, the interpretation of the Tamar-Judah story provides an example which parallels almost *verbatim* the exegesis on Joseph's youth (*GR* 1045).[32] The starting point of this interpretation is Tamar's request that Judah may recognize his possessions and thus also his guilt towards her. With regard to this request the midrashic narrator presents the saying of a second-generation Amora. Also in this case, he "quotes" God's speech to Judah. Using the same expressions "you said" and "by your life", God is said to demonstrate the connection between Judah's earlier conduct and his present fate.[33] In this interpretation the same theological principles are applied to the biblical narrative. It is also structured similarly and uses identical keywords. Yet by comparison the passage on Joseph is significantly more artistic and complex. Also, *GR*'s view of Joseph's youth dominates to a greater extent the exegesis of the whole story. This theme becomes in fact a standard *topos* which is inserted on numerous occasions.[34]

The next important modification of the biblical figure is *GR*'s interpretation of Joseph's relationship with his father. In *GR* 1010 it is presented in the following terms:

> 'And Israel loved Joseph more than any other of his children, because he was the son of his old age' (*Gen* 37:3). R. Judah said: because the expression of his face was similar to his.
> R. Nehemiah said: because he passed on to him all the halachot which Shem and Eber had taught him.

---

[31] *GR* 1020; in order to corroborate this interpretation Simon is also identified with the biblically anonymous "they" who took Joseph and threw him into the well (*Gen* 37:24). For another example of this type of exegesis, see also *GR* 1018.

[32] It is based on the previous identification of Judah as one of the anonymous brothers in *Gen* 37:32, as formulated in *GR* 1024.

[33] For a different interpretation of *Gen* 38:25 in a theologically more neutral context, see *GR* 1214.

[34] E.g. *GR* 1051 and 1061–62. It should be noted that this concept of Joseph's youth differs also from some earlier Palestinian traditions, such as *TJos* 10:4–6, where the figure is eulogized as an exemplary brother.

The misdrashic narrator offers two tannaitic sayings[35] which might explain the somewhat inappropriate nature of the expression "son of his old age".[36] Both postulate a certain resemblence between Jacob and Joseph and elucidate this aspect from the authorial perspective.

In the first saying Jacob's preference for Joseph is justified on the basis of their physical likeness. The explanation is linguistically connected to the *Vorlage* in that זיו אקונין is a *notaricon* of the expression "בן זיקונים." The style of this interpretation is not unique to the figure of Joseph, but constitutes a theme by which *GR* likes to describe the relation between father and son. Thus, also in the case of Isaac it is conjectured, this time in an anonymous saying, that: "son of his old age, this means that his countenance (איקונין) was similar to his" (*GR* 561).

We may further compare this midrashic notice of Joseph to Hellenistic references to his beauty as a reason for Jacob's preference.[37] It emerges that while these point to his comeliness as a universal value, *GR* highlights through their resemblance the connection between father and son. In the midrash Joseph's external appearance is thus not of interest in its own right but only in so far as it reflects the family bond.

In the second interpretation Joseph is placed in the *Traditionskette* of halachic exegesis.[38] Here a tradition is established from Shem and Eber, the two midrashic pioneers of rabbinic teaching,[39] down to Jacob and then Joseph. This exposition on Joseph conforms to the more general theme in *GR* of the youngest child being the most talented.

It is significant that this saying in *GR* corresponds to late biblical

---

[35] On R. Judah and R. Nehemiah, see: H.L. Strack/G. Stemberger, *op. cit.*, pp. 83, p. 246 and p. 151ff.

[36] The age gap between the sons was so large as to justify Joseph's distinction on these grounds. In any case, this title would have been more appropriate for Benjamin.

[37] See above in the relevant chapters.

[38] On the technical term מסר/מסורת, see: W. Bacher, *Tradition und Tradenten*, Leipzig 1914, pp. 1–2; for its use in *GR*, see: Ch. Albeck, *op. cit.*, vol. III, p. 36; see especially *GR* 975 where the term is applied to the continuous tradition from God through Moses to Joshua.

[39] For a general background on Shem, see *Shem*, in *EJ*, vol. XIV, cols. 1368–70, and L. Ginzberg, *op. cit.*, vol. I pp. 161–74 and p. 274 and p. 332, vol. V pp. 181–82 and p. 187 and p. 192ff, vol. VII p. 434; on the tents of Shem as Beit Midrash in *GR*, see especially *GR* 342 and 693.

interpretations of Joseph. But while *Ps* 105:22 presents him as generally wise, *GR* expresses his talents in rabbinic terms. A similar formulation may be found in *PJ* on *Gen* 37:2 where Joseph is said to leave the Beit Midrash at the age of seventeen. This expression appears to assume a tradition such as found in *GR*, which is now expressed in more technical and concise terms. If we compare this Hebrew exegesis to Hellenistically inspired narratives, we find that they construe Joseph's spiritual gifts in universal, Greek terms.[40] It emerges again that *GR* interprets the story in light of distinctly rabbinic concepts and thus affirms Joseph's connection to his father and forefathers. Joseph's belonging to a larger family context is furthermore a popular theme in *GR* and recurs on other occassions too.[41]

Interesting conclusions about *GR*'s characterisation of Joseph emerge also from the above embellishments on Jacob's special love for him. We saw that the narrator presents two sayings each of which interprets the biblical item "son of his old age" and construes accordingly the reasons for Jacob's love. These suggest various qualities in Joseph and thus create different images of the biblical figure. Although similar motifs occur in the earlier traditions *GR* shapes them in its own way and simply places them side by side, without indicating their inter-relationship or their relevance to each other.

In what remains of the story of Joseph's youth the midrashic innovations on the biblical figure are of a more subtle nature. They do not shape the biblical figure in a new fashion but enrich it in various dimensions. In the following I shall examine three of them more closely and also analyse how the new details relate to our previous impressions of the Midrashic Joseph.

---

[40] See the relevant chapters above.

[41] E.g.: *GR* 1005–08 lists the similarities in personality and life between Jacob and Joseph; and in *GR* 1237 and 1195 great sensitivity is shown to the special relationship between father and son. There is a biblical background to this line of interpretation; see especially: B.J. van der Merve, *Joseph as successor of Jacob*, in: *Studia Biblica and Semitica*, Festschrift Th.C. Vriezen, Wageningen 1961, pp. 221–32 (Not all of his inferences can be corroborated by the biblical text; e.g. his assumption of Jacob's princely status is surely exaggerated; and the brothers' fear of Joseph after their father's death must be understood from the family context.)

GR 1016:
'And he (Joseph) said to him (Jacob): Here I am' (*Gen* 37:13) R.
Hama son of R. Hanina said: our father remembered these things and
he was deeply upset:[42] I know that your brothers hate you and yet say
'here I am'.

The narrator introduces here a saying which he presents as a continuous tradition. It is likely that it was Jacob's apparent insensibili-
ty to the prevailing situation which prompted this interpretation. He
is in this way shown to be in fact aware of the significance of his request.

We may further raise the question whether this passage may also
be regarded as a characterisation of Joseph through another
figure.[43] In order to establish this, it is necessary to determine
whether Jacob's thoughts actually express something about Joseph
himself. It appears that it is through Jacob's worries that the reader
is able to better appreciate Joseph's devotion.[44] For Jacob's saying
to be meaningful it would furthermore be reasonable to assume that
Joseph too is aware of the imminent dangers. Through this indirect
characterisation the level of this figure is thus also raised.

If we consider the above passage in the context of the passages
analysed so far, its positive evaluation of Joseph is notable. It
emerges that GR is capable of being sympathetic to some aspects of
Joseph's personality while severely criticising others. In this sense,
GR's use of Joseph as an educational example, though reiterated frequently, does not preclude other insights into his personality.

In GR 1019 the scene is described where Joseph approaches the
brothers near Shechem. As we know from the biblical account, this
meeting was not friendly and we are well familiar with the brothers'
hostility towards Joseph. GR, on the other hand, shows an unusual
interest in Joseph at this stage:

'And it happened when Joseph came ...' (*Gen* 37:23)
R. L'azar[45] said: he came with (self-?) praise.

---

[42] Literally: "his innermost was cut".

[43] Note that Rashi, presumably inspired by the Midrash, highlights the significance of the biblical scene in *Gen* 37:13 for the character of Joseph. For a background on this type of indirect characterization, see: Y. Ewen, *op. cit.*, pp. 96–99;
S. Rimon-Kenan, *op. cit.*, p. 70; S. Bar-Efrat, *op. cit.*, pp. 99–112.

[44] Note the emotive style!

[45] The MSS vary between this abbreviated form and the full spelling of his
name.

In this interpretation Joseph's neutral action is qualified by a reference to the manner of his approach. The addition בקילום is crucial to the characterisation of Joseph because it discloses the midrashic understanding of his attitude at this decisive moment. It is therefore highly unfortunate that the term itself is ambivalent and can refer to self-praise, praise of others and praise towards a divinity.[46] As a result, modern scholars have tended to refrain from judgement and leave the question of its precise meaning in this context open.[47] Perhaps the medieval commentator S. Yafe was right in connecting this laconic statement with the earlier expansions and concluding: "he was all praise and adornment with which he was showing off as was his custom when he curled his hair and exalted himself over his brothers".[48] Although *GR* is generally well capable of presenting disconnected facets of characterisation, this conjecture from the overall context seems the most likely. The aim of this addition then appears to consist in the emphasis of Joseph's provocative behaviour. The brothers' reaction is in this way rendered more understandable and the reader is encouraged to sympathize with them even more than in the biblical account. It should be noted in conclusion that the above embellishment is peculiar to *GR* and may not be found in other early sources.

Finally, in *GR* 1021 we find an interpretation which reflects on the biblical scene of the Arab traders' unexpected arrival at the brothers' site. They are said to carry precious goods, and the brothers are able to sell Joseph to them. In *GR* the following conclusions are drawn from this arrangement:

'And they (the brothers) lifted their eyes' (*Gen* 37:25)
R. Abba bar Cahana said: but is it not the custom of the Ishmaelites to carry anything but skins and itran?[49] Instead consider the following: the Holy One, blessed be He, has arranged for that righteous man at that moment sacks full of perfume so that their aroma may waft around them against the smell of the Arabs.

---

[46] M. Yastrow, *op. cit.*, p. 1360.
[47] H. Freedman, *op. cit.*, p. 781 n4: "either, in the spirit of self-praise in accordance with his usual ideas of his future greatness; or, with praise of his brethren, i.e. with friendship and brotherly love''; Ch. Albeck, *op. cit.*, p. 1019, enumerates the three possibilities of meaning and corroborates them by reference to later commentators on *GR*.
[48] *Op.cit.*, p. 1064.
[49] See H. Freedman's explanation, *op. cit.*, p. 782 n.4.

The admitted starting point of this Amoraic tradition[50] is the astonishment about that event which is, according to the biblical narrator, a fortunate coincidence. In the eyes of the interpreter the traders' arrival is instead to be regarded as the result of Divine providence. On the assumption that there are no real coincidences, further conclusions are drawn. Most significantly, Joseph is labelled "the righteous". In this passage there is no evidence of his righteous behaviour or anything on his part which might provoke or only justify this title. Its only connection to the *Vorlage* is the theological assumption that God promoted the biblical events and that He must have done so on behalf of a worthy person. The brevity of the reference might also indicate the presupposition of earlier traditions which are now applied to this specific verse. The expression "Joseph the Righteous" is inserted on numerous occasions in *GR* and often in the same loose manner.[51] It clearly is indicative of *GR*'s subordination of character to theme.

In the above passages I have examined *GR*'s presentation of Joseph's youth. It has emerged that the midrashic narrator is highly critical of Joseph's behaviour in the family. Instead of reducing Joseph's shortcomings, he advances embellished exegetical traditions to highlight the protagonist's faults. He presents these faults in the theological framework of divine retribution and insists that it is they that caused Joseph's subsequent hardship. The midrashic narrator often employs traditions which reflect on Joseph from the authorial perspective. But within the didactically most important passage a highly emotive dialogical scene is created.

Scattered references to "Joseph the Righteous", relating to the remaining story of Joseph's youth, appear not to be based on his specific personality. They are rather derived from concepts of Divine action towards biblical figures. They can therefore not be directly used in the analysis of Joseph's character in the Midrash.

---

[50] R. Abba bar Cahana is an Amoraic teacher of the third generation; for a background, see; H. Strack/G. Stemberger, *op. cit.*, p. 96.

[51] E.g.: *GR* 1978, 1979, 1161, 1170, 1190. Note that this label is on the same theological grounds also applied to the brothers, e.g.: *GR* 1129. For the use of the term in midrashic literature, see also: R. Mach, *op. cit.*, pp. 1–13.

In Potiphar's House

According to the biblical narrative two crucial episodes take place in Potiphar's house: Joseph excels in his work and Potiphar's wife attempts to seduce him. In *GR* a considerable interest is taken in both of them.

Besides establishing that Joseph was not an ordinary slave in Potiphar's house,[52] the midrashic narrator adduces some interpretations which elucidate Joseph's relationship with his master (*GR* 1057–58):

> 'And his master saw that the Lord was with him' (*Gen* 39:3) R. Huna said in the name of R. Aha: he whispered (God's name) whenever he entered and whenever he came out . . . If his master bade him 'mix me a hot drink', and behold! It was hot; 'mix me a tempered drink', and behold! It was warm. He said to him (Joseph): What does this mean? Would you bring straw to Afraim and pots to Kefar Hananiah, fleeces to Damascus and witchcraft to Egypt? Witchcraft in a place of witchcraft. How long (did he suspect him of witchcraft)?
> Said R. Hunia in R. Aha's name: until he saw the Shechina standing over him. Hence it is written 'and his master saw that the Lord was with him' and 'Joseph found favour in his sight'.

The midrashic narrator presents here two sayings by a Tiberian teacher of the fourth Amoraic generation. His own presence is nevertheless to be felt in his question of how long Potiphar had suspected Joseph of witchcraft. This curiosity about how he, as a non-Jew, could have recognized God's presence provides the frame and the guideline for the two interpretations. This exegetical intuition is obviously radically different from Philo's reaction to this and similar scenes. He tends, as we saw, to concentrate on the human aspects and to stress the individual's personality which is responsible for the promotion.

The question of how Potiphar was able to recognize Divine providence behind Joseph's success is ultimately settled by reference to the physical appearance of the Shechina.[53] But before that, a fas-

---

[52] In *GR* 1054 both an anonymous tradition and a saying in the name of R. Joshua highlight those qualities which distinguish Joseph from slaves. We saw earlier that Josephus also shows an interest in Joseph's status. In his interpretation this issue becomes in fact the most important background information for Joseph's encounter with Potiphar's wife.

[53] For a background on this rabbinic concept, see especially: E.E. Urbach, *op. cit.*, pp. 31–32 and 40–45, where he discusses the attachment of the Shekhina to places and people; A. Goldberg, *Untersuchungen über die Vorstellung von der Schekhina*

cinating passage is inserted which describes in picturesque terms the relations between Joseph and his master. Parallel to the biblical account, these scenes reflect Potiphar's perspective. In addition, they depict how he, with his Egyptian religious concepts, decoded his servant's "mumbling" and his extraordinary abilities. For this purpose Joseph is also made to recite the Divine Name, thus providing a convenient impetus for Potiphar's enquiries. The vivacity of the situation is stressed by the quick succession of Potiphar's orders and his innocent exclamations of astonishment ("behold!'").

The above passage is a prime example of how lively the creative imagination of *GR* can be and how the biblical figures are employed to elucidate some belief of *GR*.[54] By comparison with the later midrash *Tanhuma*, the version in *GR* still expresses a more spontaneous piety. The above tradition is preserved there in a more ritualised form: Potiphar is labelled, without evident reason, "the Wicked" and Joseph recites liturgical prayers (*Vayesheb* 8).

I shall now turn to the analysis of 'the affair' in Potiphar's house as interpreted in *GR*. Parallel to other early Hebrew interpretation[55] this episode is regarded as the highlight and the turning point of the Joseph story. As a result, significant conclusions are drawn from it and it receives many different notices. I shall now treat in detail the most significant ones.

Initially, *GR* shows great sensitivity to the biblical introduction of the encounter as outlined in *Gen* 39:7 (*GR* 1063–64):

> 'And it came to pass after these things' (*Gen* 39:7)
> There were some reflections about things there. Who was contemplating?[56] Joseph.
> He said: when I was in my father's house, my father would check whether it is a goodly portion and offer it to me and (as a result) my brothers were jealous.[57] Now I give thanks to you that I am at ease.

---

in der frühen rabbinischen Literatur, Berlin 1969, especially pp. 486–521.

[54] For other examples of *GR*'s exegetical interest in theological issues in the Joseph story, see: *GR* 1056, where the expression "God was with Joseph" gives rise to an extended discussion on the presence of the Shekhina with the tribes and/or individuals; and *GR* 1058, where the biblical affirmation that Potiphar gave Joseph the responsibility for everything provokes the statement that the Shechina accompanies the righteous wheresoever they go.

[55] For details, see chap. I. Note also that this topic is increasingly de-emphasized in the *Tanhuma* traditions.

[56] Cf. H. Freedman's translation, *op. cit.*, p. 808.

[57] Note that some MSS use the expression "looked at me with an evil eye".

Said the Holy One, blessed be He: Empty words![58] By your life, I will incite a bear against you!
Another interpretation: my father was tried and my grandfather was tried, but I am not put to the test.
Said the Holy One, blessed be He: by your life! I will try you even more than them!

Before presenting two interpretations of the biblical passage, the midrashic narrator clarifies the exegetical impetus: דברים, in the above biblical expression meaning "things", can also be taken as thoughts or words. Such words are then attributed to Joseph and his inner life just before the encounter is illuminated. In this way a completely new scene is created. The brief biblical introduction from the authorial perspective is replaced by a description from Joseph's point of view. The flow of the events is thus arrested and the attention of the reader is focused on Joseph.

Also in this case another literary figure, namely God, is introduced. His alleged responses to Joseph's words do not only raise the biblical issue to a theological level but also forshadow the subsequent events. It thus becomes evident that these extensive insertions are made in view of the whole story. By means of these dialogues the narrator applies his understanding of the broader context to this specific situation of his own creation.

In the first interpretation we find a variation of the theme of Joseph's provocative complacency. In contrast to previous versions, Joseph is not characterised by his actions but by his mental disposition. He is shown to be conscious of his father's favouratism and instead of feeling uneasy about it, he is said to enjoy the privileges. He is furthermore portrayed as misunderstanding his present good luck in Potiphar's house. As a result, his gratitude towards God appears as gross pretentiousness.

The midrashic attribution of such thoughts to Joseph changes the biblically ambiguous figure into a clearly bad type. Instead of "just" misbehaving Joseph does so knowingly and even with pleasure. It is obvious that the narrator is highly unsympathetic to the figure. It is moreover to be expected that he pursues specific aims when he recalls Joseph's intricate family position at precisely this points of the story.

---

[58] On the problematic term הטלים, see: Ch. Albeck, *op. cit.*, p. 1064; and M.A. Mirkin, *op. cit.*, p. 56.

As in previous instances, God's hostile response is introduced and the 'affair' is presented as an appropriate punishment for Joseph's attitude. This form of an altercation is again used to demonstrate the theological principle that human arrogance leads to retribution.

The second exposition of Joseph's inner life follows the same structural pattern as the first. The narrator thus again presents the figure's thought so as to account for the following events. But in this interpretation Joseph is no longer understood on the basis of his personal history; neither is the 'affair' presented as a punishment for the past. Instead, the narrator imputes a rabbinic consciousness to Joseph. He is shown to be aware of his family history and of the paramount importance of his forefathers' trials. As a result of his complaint, the 'affair' is now viewed as a trial of the just and thus as a distinguishing challenge.[59]

The technique of using the expression אחר הדברים האלה to expose the protagonist's inner life before significant events is not uncommon in *GR*. Thus, for example in *GR* 578–88, this method is skilfully employed in preparation for the sacrifice of Isaac. We even find that almost identical thoughts about human trial by God are attributed to the figures of that story, too. Also there it is conjectured that "there were reflections about things there" and the question is subsequently raised "Who was contemplating?". This is then answered by a similarly concise reference to Abraham. It is moreover shown that he was haughty about not having made offerings to God. The narrator then juxtaposes in his well-known fashion a response by God. It is thus announced to Abraham that he will sacrifice his son. It emerges from this parallel treatment that the midrashic narrator greatly enhances the theological significance of "the affair" and consequently also Joseph's importance.

GR shares with other exegetes a lively interest in the first reported encounter between Joseph and Potiphar's wife. Like Philo and Josephus, the midrashic narrator greatly embellishes Joseph's reply and conjectures the precise reasons for his refusal to sleep with the woman.

---

[59] For *GR* concept of trial, see: *GR* 584–87 and 599. For a wider background, see especially: ניסיון, *EB* pp. 879–83; S. Spiegel, *The Last Trial*, New York, pp. 1–152; A. Sommer, *Der Begriff der Versuchung im Alten Testament und Judentum*, Breslau 1935. Note that the narrator of *GR* applies the idea of Joseph's trial also to other points of the biblical story. Thus Joseph is presented for example in *GR* 1065–66 as responding to Potiphar's wife by reference to the possibility of his having been chosen as a burnt-offering.

The biblical account mentions this point quite briefly, emphasizing Joseph's responsibility towards his master and God.[60] The midrashic narrator focuses on the expression הן אדוני which in the *Vorlage* refers to Potiphar himself (*Gen* 39:8). He furthermore adds the explanation "he said to her: I am afraid of . . .", which subsequently serves as the opening of each version of Joseph's reply to Potiphar's wife. Each of these presupposes a different identity of the master and thus indicates another reason for Joseph's resistence.

In the second of these interpretations the term master is taken as a reference to Jacob; and Joseph's speech assumes the following form (*GR* 1066–67):

> I am afraid of my father; because Reuben slept with Bilhah his birthright were taken and granted to me. Should I consent to you I should be deprived of my first-born rights.

In this alleged speech of Joseph his motivations for his critical decision are presented as family concerns. His affiliation is shown to impose on him clear ethical duties of which he is painfully aware. Joseph's further worries about the loss of his birthright[61] draw on the interpretation of the family story in I*Chron* 5:2. In *GR* earlier material is thus integrated into the midrash by way of attributing it as direct speech to one figure.

GR's conjecture of Joseph's rationale is to a certain extent paralleled in earlier Palestinian interpretations of the Joseph story. The first witness is *Jub* 39:6 where it says: "he remembered the Lord and the words which Jacob his father used to read . . ." and we also read in *TJos* 3:2–3: "I recalled my father's words . . .". These traditions are similarly preserved in the rabbinic works, such as *PRE*.[62] A direct dependence between the above traditions, however, cannot be conjectured because they clearly differ too much in detail; and the

---

[60] *Gen* 39:8–9: "But he refused and said to his master's wife: lo, having me my master has no concern about anything in the house, and he has put everything in my hand; he is not greater in this house than I am; nor has he kept anything back from me except yourself, because you are his wife; how can I then do this great wickedness and sin against God?"

[61] For a background on the biblical notion of first-born rights, see: *Firstling*, *IDB* vol. II, pp. 270–72. Regarding Reuben's status in Scripture, consider especially: *Gen* 35:22 and 49:3–4; and see also *GR* 1205 where the transfer of Reuben's rights to Joseph is mentioned.

[62] *Op.cit.*, p. 305: "When he wished to accustom himself to sin, he saw the image of his father and controlled his passion".

peculiarity of *GR*'s version must be taken seriously. It is nevertheless noteworthy that the Palestinian exegetes agree in their emphasis on the figure of Jacob for Joseph's decision. In this respect they clearly diverge from the Hellenistically insprired interpreters, such as Philo and Josephus.

In *GR* 1067 another interpretation of Joseph's response to Potiphar's wife is presented:

> I am afraid of my master. She replied: I'll kill him. He said to her: Is it not enough that I should be counted in the company of the adulterers, but am I to be counted among the murderers, too?!

This is the only case in *GR* where the term "master" is taken in the sense of its biblical context. Instead of just offering an insight into Joseph's motives, the midrashic narrator creates an additional dialogue between the two protagonists.

We saw above that the biblical Joseph expresses his gratitude towards Potiphar. Whereas Philo expands this theme in political terms, the reference to the master serves here merely as a spring-board for the woman's reply. Her proposal of murder remains conspicuously unexplained and the details of her intentions are not disclosed. Instead, Joseph is given ample opportunity to proclaim his indignity and to affirm his moral convictions. It is also noteworthy that this dialogue is not, like most others in *GR*, constructed in such a way as to culminate in a direct reference to God.

The accumulation of these traits leads me to suggest that the narrator uses, in abbreviated form, an existing tradition about Potiphar's wife and Joseph. He accommodates this material to his spiritual concerns and links it provisionally to the respective biblical item.

An earlier and more complete form of this altercation between Joseph and the woman is to be found in *TJos* 5:1. There the proposal of Potiphar's wife is not yet taken for granted and is thus presented in some detail. We learn the following from Joseph's perspective:

> Again on another occasion she said to me: if you do not want to commit adultery, I shall kill my husband by a drug and take you as my husband.

Still closely conforming to its Hellenistic models,[63] the narrator of the *Testament* then continues to explore the psychological ramifica-

---

[63] See M. Braun's research quoted above.

tions of this discussion. He thus describes how Potiphar's wife fears discovery and how her attitude changes as a result of it.

In the above passage in *GR* this material is only adumbrated. But the structure of the interpretation and the brevity of the reference to the woman's proposal indicate that it is indeed presupposed. Also at this last stage of Judaising originally Greek material, interesting changes are introduced. The most conspicuous alteration consists of replacing the dramatic psychological insights by moral admonition. The focus is moreover completely shifted from the woman to Joseph.[64] Among the midrashic works, *GR* remains the last one where such traditions are still preserved in any detail. It is thus highly significant that in the corpus of the *Tanhuma* midrash, these stories about Joseph and Potiphar's wife are increasingly subdued.

Joseph's second and more dramatic encounter with Potiphar's wife receives also detailed notice in *GR*. Based on the biblical opening scene we find the following collection of interpretations in *GR* 1071–73:[65]

> 'And it came to pass on a certain day ...' (*Gen* 39:11)
> R. Juda said: there was a celebration in honour of the Nile and everybody went to watch, but he came to the house to check the accounts of his master.
> R. Nehemia said: it was a day of theatrical performance but he came home to check the accounts of his master.
> R. Samuel bar Nahman said: to do his work, certainly! But (it is written) 'and there was no man'; this means upon examination he found himself not a man for R. Samuel said: the bow was drawn but relaxed, as it is written 'and his bow returned with strength' (*Gen* 49:24).[66]
> R. Isaac said: and his seed was scattered and issued through his fingernails, as it is written 'and the seed of his hands was scattered' (*ibid*).[67]
> R. Huna said in R. Mattena's name: he saw his father's face and his blood was cooled, as it is written 'by the hands of the Mighty One of Jacob, from there from the shepherd, the rock of Israel' (*ibid*). Who achieved this? Even by the God of your fathers who helped you.

These five interpretations are arranged in two groups. The first two sayings relate to the textually difficult expression כהיום הזה and construe the verb "to do his work" favourably with regard to Joseph. In the other three interpretations the passage is by contrast under-

---

[64] Note that in other scenes, such as *GR* 1068, the woman is focussed on for longer.

[65] Parts of these are to be found in *GR* 1270.

[66] The midrash reads תַשֵׁב instead of תֵשֶׁב.

[67] The midrash reads יפזרו instead of יפזו; see W. Kittel, *Biblia Hebraica, op. cit.*, p. 77; H. Freedman's note, *op. cit.*, p. 812, is slightly misleading.

stood in view of the Blessing of Jacob, to which they were probably
originally attached. Based on variant readings of the relevant verses
on Joseph, his erotic motivation is conjectured. While the narrator
attributes the first two sayings to Tannaitic teachers, he presents the
latter three as Amoraic traditions.[68] He thus suggests a substantial
development in the exegesis of this verse.

The initial interpretations reshape the biblical scene from an authorial perspective. They improve the image of Joseph in two
ways:[69] they highlight that he was industrious while the Egyptians
were enjoying festivities; and they also stress that his work was ad-
minstrative (and not manual). Both aspects affirm Joseph's innocence when entering the house, proposing that nothing special was
on his mind. Like the version in *Targum Onkelos*,[70] they appear to
answer a growing scepticism concerning this point.

The subsequent sayings by R.S. barNahman and R. Isaac both
apply the risqué details of *Gen* 49:24 to the biblical verse in question.
R.S. barNahman is presented as drawing the connection between
these two *loci*. He offers what he considers the only realistic
interpretation[71] of the term מלאכה, namely intercourse; and he
supports his view by reference to the biblical item 'no man' which
he also takes as a euphemism.[72] He then mentions as an authoritative corroboration R. Samuel's erotic understanding of *Gen* 49:42,
which appears to have been known independently. R. Isaac's interpretation follows the same model, except that it is shorter and pre-
sumes the erotic interpretation of the scene.[73]

---

[68] For a background on the rabbinic authorities, see: H.L. Strack/G. Stemberger, *op. cit.*, p. 8, p. 246 and p. 83, p. 151f and pp. 93ff and p. 85.

[69] For a discussion on the various festive occasions, see: M.A. Mirkin, *op. cit.*,
p. 61.

[70] See M. Niehoff, *The Figure of Joseph in the Targums*, *JJS* 39/1988, p. 238.

[71] The expression והיי, used by R. Nahman, is not unproblematic because it is
usually employed "zur Betonung der wörtlichen Bedeutung des Textwortes" (W.
Bacher, *Die exegetische Terminologie der jüdischen Traditionsliteratur*, Leipzig 1899–
1905, p. 48). For a discussion, see especially: Ch. Albeck, *op. cit.*, p. 1072; H.
Freedman, *op. cit.*, p. 811.

[72] Note that the medieval commentator S. Yafe suggests another sense of the
reference in *GR* to 'no man' (*ad.loc.*). He infers that Joseph considered his intentions and concluded that intercourse with Potiphar's wife would be an act below
human honour ("he would not have been worthy to be called a man"). This comment, however, clearly neglects the midrashic context.

[73] Note that M.A. Mirkin, *op. cit.*, p. 62, suggests II*Sam* 6:16 as a source of inspiration.

Both of these sayings are again reported in *GR* 1270 (relating to *Gen* 49:24). It is significant that R.S. barNahman's interpretation is here presented only after R. Yohanan, the first generation Palestinian Amora, is said to have established the erotic meaning of the scene in Potiphar's house. In this context the midrashic narrator thus presents these traditions as of clearly earlier origin.

This is paralleled in a collection of sayings in b*Sotah* 36b. Relating to *Gen* 39:11, R. Yohanan is here said to have conjectured both Joseph's and Potiphar's wife's erotic intentions. It is furthermore mentioned that R. Yohanan also interpreted *Gen* 49:24. He is reported to have suggested in the name of R. Meir that the motif of the returning bow means that Joseph's passion subsided. In the context of *GR* 1071–73 these insights were, as we saw attributed to R. Samuel and R.S. barNahman. We may furthermore note that in the above passage of b*Sotah* 36b there is to be found a more expanded version of the exegesis on "there was no man". It is explained here in greater detail than in *GR*'s saying attributed to R.S. barNahman. According to this version the euphemistic interpretation originated from astonishment over the fact that there should have been literally no one in Potiphar's huge house. More significantly, these conjectures are attributed to the "school of R. Ishmael".

It thus emerges that the narrator of our passage in *GR* chose to present the risqué interpretations of *Gen* 39:11 as later than was customary in other treatises. He attributes them to later Amoraic teachers instead of Tannaitic or early Amoraic ones. He also presents the contents of the sayings in a form which suggests that they presuppose earlier traditions.

Regarding the contents, a radically different image of Joseph emerges from these two interpretations. The nature of these conjectures is far more extreme than similar ones in other rabbinic works and the question of their purpose may be raised. It seems impossible that they could have been intended for educational or religious purposes. It is instead likely that they spring from a certain sensationalism and are inserted to edify. It is therefore perhaps not surprising that *PJ*'s version of *Gen* 49:24 comes very close to the above formulation:

> And his erect organ returned to its previous condition so as not to have intercourse with his mistress and his hands were withheld from voluptuous thoughts ...

It is, on the other hand, natural that these traditions are not transmitted to such midrashic works as *Tanhuma* or Rashi's commentary
on *Gen* 39:11.

The fifth saying, presented as a tradition handed down from R.
Mattena to R. Huna,[74] appears to have been placed last because it
assumes the state of the previous discussion. It also uses the last part
of *Gen* 49:24 as a proof-text and reconnects the exegetical process
with theological issues.

Its immediate starting point is Joseph's inner life at that critical
moment. The interpreter imagines that the face of his father appeared to him and that this memory prevented him from sinning.
The terms in which this mental process is described are unusually
psychological and realistic.[75] In this respect they differ markedly
from the earlier reference to Joseph's calculations concerning his
father. They seem highly appropriate to the situation and reflect a
penetrating knowledge of human nature.

Expanding on the expression "the rock of Israel" (*Gen* 49:24),
taken as a reference to God, the interpreter then completes his analysis. He highlights that not only the dominant father influenced
Joseph but that he was on the whole guided by Divine providence.

It emerges from the above analysis that the midrashic narrator
compiled various characterisations of Joseph on the occasion of his
second encounter with Potiphar's wife. They differ with regard to
their alleged age, their focalisation and, most significantly, with
regard to their content. It is only through the last interpretation that
the narrator introduces a religious dimension, while he otherwise
appears to be free to choose highly risqué interpretations of Joseph.

In *GR* the 'affair' between Joseph and Potiphar's wife does not
terminate, as in the bible, with his escape from the house and her
accusations. It is instead embellished by a further confrontation in
which she threatens to enhance his hardship in prison (*GR* 1075):

> 'But the Lord was with Joseph' (*Gen* 39:21) and 'the goalkeeper com-
> mitted to Joseph's hands' (*Gen* 39:22) R. Huna said in R. Aha's name:
> his service was pleasing to his master; when he went out he washed

---

[74] Note that in *GR* 1270, where this tradition is also preserved, another saying
is inserted after R. Huna's interpretation and the biblical proof-text. It reads as follows: "R. Menahema said in R. Ammi's name: he saw his mother's face which
cooled his blood."

[75] For a convincing explanation of the origin of the motif of Jacob's countenance, see J. Kugel, *op. cit.*, pp. 106–112.

the cups, lay the tables and made the beds; and she (P.'s wife) would say: in this affair I have made you suffer unduly. By your life! I will make you suffer in other ways, too!
And he answered and said: '(God) executes justice for the oppressed' (*Ps* 146:7).
I will have your food rations cut down. He answered her: 'He gives bread to the hungry' (*ibid*).
I will have you chained. 'The Lord frees those who are bound'
I will make you bent and bound. 'The Lord raises those who are bowed down (*ibid*).
I will blind you. 'The Lord opens the eyes of the blind'
How far (did she go)?
R. Huna said in R. Aha's name; so far as to place an iron fork under his neck so that he would turn his eyes and look at her. But despite of this he did not look at her, as it is written 'his feet they hurt with fetters, his person was laid in iron' (*Ps* 105:18).

The midrashic narrator introduces this scene by another embellishment on Joseph's extraordinary services to his master. Also in this case, the interpretation is imputed to R. Huna. But unlike the exegesis of *Gen* 39:3 the above passage serves only as an opening and has no theological purpose of its own. The examples of Joseph's devotion are therefore also more down-to-earth, being taken from every day life.

The subsequent altercation between Joseph and Potiphar's wife is based on late biblical interpretations of the Joseph story (*Ps* 105) and on the assumption of Divine assistance to the righteous in need (*Ps* 146). The dialogue is constructed in such a way that Joseph is each time to answer with an appropriate verse from *Ps* 146. The exchange is accelerated by increasingly shorter answers and replies which finally amount to a provocation followed by a biblical quotation. The tension is then resolved by an affirmation of Joseph's perseverance. In this way Joseph's behaviour is presented as the ideal reaction to suffering.[76] The narrator further highlights his theological interests by asking the question of how long Joseph's sufferings continued. This line of interpretation is typical of Palestinian sources and it is first attested in *TJos* 2:3 – 4.[77] Not surprisingly, it is also preserved in *Tanhuma Vayasheb* 9.

---

[76] It is of interest that the expression "Joseph the Righteous" is not developed in the interpretation of the 'affair' itself.

[77] "I was jailed, I was whipped, I was sneered at, but the Lord granted me mercy in the sight of the prison-keeper. For the Lord does not abandon those who

It emerges from the above analysis that Joseph's encounter with Potiphar's wife was a central concern in *GR*. It is embellished partly in fanciful, partly in apologetic fashion, both from the authorial and from Joseph's point of view. In this way different possibilities of human behaviour are associated with the figure of Joseph, without ultimately forming one coherent image. But the recurrent theme which frames the interpretations of the 'affair' in *GR* is the conviction that it is a type of suffering imposed on the righteous and thus constitutes a significant trial.

Other aspects of Joseph's life in Potiphar's house, such as his services to his master, are dealt with more briefly. In obvious contrast to Philo's rendering, the religious background of Joseph's success is highlighted and thus used as a further illumination of the nature of God.

Joseph in Egypt

GR shows a more selective interest in the remaining parts of the story. It is moreover noticeable that the exegesis no longer concentrates on the figure of Joseph. Other subjects, such as the various blessings or Jacob's journey to Egypt, often take precedence.[78] In my discussion of Joseph in Egypt I shall therefore treat aspects which are only marginal in the overall exegesis of *GR*. I shall deal specifically with the relationship between Joseph and his brothers and with Joseph as the governor of Egypt.

GR de-emphasizes the brothers' initial meeting in Egypt. Whereas Philo and Josephus are painfully aware of Joseph's harshness and insert various explanations, *GR* does not appear to consider this passage in any way problematic.[79] This is all the more noteworthy

---

fear him, neither in darkness nor chains nor tribulation or direct need''. Note that this tradition is also in live with Josephus's interpretation and *Ps* 105:17–22.

[78] Note that *GR* does not, however, emphasize Jacob's descent as much as, for example *Tanhuma Vayesheb* 18 where it is highlighted as the beginning of Israel's exile (This issue is dealt with in *GR* also in 1016 in the context of Joseph's departure from Hebron.).

[79] In *GR* 1127 the biblical expression ''he made himself a stranger'' (*Gen* 42:7) is only given a clearer linguistic formulation; and the subsequent biblical remark that while he recognized his brothers they did not identify him (*Gen* 42:8) provokes a picturesque conjecture about the change of their facial features. Note that there is an allusion to Joseph's motivation in *GR* 1170 where Joseph's testing of the brothers is compared to that of human beings by God; cf. also *GR* 1171 and 1214). Note that Rashi treats this verse with similar brevity in his commentary on *Gen*.

in view of *GR*'s heigtened sensitivity to Joseph's shortcomings as a youth. The reason for this must be seen in the fact that Joseph's later behaviour towards the brothers does not fit the theological pattern of crime and punishment which had prompted the earlier exegesis. In this spiritually insignificant part of the story, *GR* even appreciates the brothers' criminality and sympathizes with Joseph in fearing their brutality.[80] Since *GR* is furthermore a literature for insiders' use only, there is no need to justify biblical items which might appear parochial and embarrassing to the outside world.

GR is instead interested in the brothers' journey and their eager anticipation of Joseph.[81] His preparation for their arrival is also conjectured in order to account for the "coincidence" of their meeting at the corn market.[82] In a continuous effort to illuminate both sides in a balanced fashion, *GR* also interprets *Gen* 43:34 to mean that each party had been mourning and refrained from wine for 22 years.[83] The final recognition scene of the brothers again receives longer notice in *GR*. Prompted by an intellectual curiosity about how exactly Joseph proved his identity to them, a picturesque and later rabbinic idea is imputed to him: he is said to have shown them his circumcision.[84]

At one point *GR* also deals in detail with Joseph's administration in Egypt. The midrashic interpretation, made from a Palestinian point of view, evidently differs from comments made on this subject by Philo and Josephus. An encompassing exposition of the midrashic attitude is to be found in *GR* 1118–1120. It is an alternative interpretation of the biblical expression "and Jacob saw that there was grain" (in Egypt, *Gen* 42:1); and it is based on matching this verse with *Prov* 11:26.

---

[80] E.g.: *GR* 1159 where it is discussed whether Joseph behaved wisely then he ordered the Egyptians to leave him alone with his brothers; some rabbis consider Joseph's decision reckless because he thus exposed himself to their mercy and possibly violence. As we have seen in the earlier analysis, such insights regarding the brothers' guilt were suppressed in the context of the selling of Joseph when he was stereotyped as "the wicked".

[81] E.g.: in *GR* 1122 we find an expansion on the biblical expression "the ten brothers of Joseph went down"; the emphasis on ten is taken as an indication that each of them now came with love for Joseph.

[82] E.g.: *GR* 1122–23.

[83] E.g.: *GR* 1143 and 1166.

[84] *GR* 1160 and 1170.

"A blessing upon the head of him who sells (corn)", alludes to Joseph
the Righteous who nourishes the world like a shepherd. Concerning
him David said: 'Give ear, oh shepherd of Israel, who leads like
Joseph a flock' (Ps 80:2). What is meant by 'lead like Joseph a flock'?
When the famine began in the days of David he thus beseeched The
Holy One Blessed Be He for mercy: Sovereign of the Universe! Lead
your flock like Joseph who led and sustained the world during the years
of famine. When the famine became severe in Egypt, the Egyptians
went to him and said: give us bread. He answered them: Woe to me
that I should feed the uncircumcised! Go and get circumcised!
So they went to Pharaoh, crying out before him. He bade them: Go
to Joseph.
They answered him: we went to him, but he told us to go and get circumcised. Did we not tell you from the beginning that he is a Hebrew
and that it is not fitting for a Hebrew to rule over us?!
He retorted: fools! Did not a herald during all the years of plenty an-
nounce before him: famine is ahead, famine is ahead?! Why did you
not keep in reserve the produce of two or (even only) one year?
At that moment they started to weep, saying: even the corn which we
left at home has rotted.
He asked them: Has no flour remained from yesterday and the day
before?
They answered him: Even the bread in our baskets has rotted.
He said to them: You Fools! If the corn rots at his decree what if he
decrees against us and we die! Go instead to him even if he tells you
to cut something of your flesh, listen to him and do all he bids you.

This is the only passage in the midrashic Joseph story where the narrator identifies Joseph as the shepherd of humanity. We saw earlier
that while the political use of this label enjoys popularity among
Hellenists, it is limited in Hebrew culture. It is therefore of interest
that this midrashic interpretation is associated with David, the biblical paradigm of a shepherd-king.[85] In this way an opportunity is
provided to expand on Joseph's administration in Egypt.

It is noteworthy to begin with that, as opposed to Philo's account,
the midrashic narrator does not treat the technical details of Joseph's
administration. Parallel to Josephus, they do not engage his imagination. We furthermore saw that both Philo and Josephus minimize
the tension between the Egyptian people and Joseph by either omitting "unsuitable material" or by enhancing his beneficent influence
on Egyptian culture. GR by contrast dwells on the tension between

---

[85] Based on an amended Psalm (assuming צאנו כיוסף, rather than כצאן יוסף, as
in the massoretic text of Ps 80:1) the narrator conjectures David's prayer that God
may take care of the world just as Joseph did.

Joseph and the Egyptians and embellishes this point extensively. As in *GR* 1106, the narrator has Joseph insist on the Egyptians' circumcision. This being one of the main initiation rites, we have here a case where the conversion of Gentiles is indeed supported.[86]

He furthermore illustrates their plight by directly presenting their desperation and their urgent request for help. When they are depicted in discussion with Pharaoh, who fully supports his administrator, their problems are even shown to be foolish. In all of these scenes the superiority of Hebrew culture is asserted with uninhibited self-confidence. The innocent nature of these characterisations suggests that it is not anticipated that outsiders will read these remarks.

An apprehensive awareness of the Hebrew as a minority in a foreign environment does nevertheless transpire. When the Egyptians are said to reproach Pharaoh for having employed a Hebrew in the first place, they express clearly xenophobic or anti-semitic beliefs. The Hebrews are here shown to be pressed into the role of the scapegoat in times of national plight.

The above scenes thus reflect *GR*'s concepts of Hebrew experience in the Diaspora. In comparison with the Hellenistic exegetes of the biblical story, Joseph's superiority and his Hebrew values are asserted with greater confidence. But also in this interpretation one can sense a certain amount of uneasiness concerning the status of the Hebrew in a foreign land.

Conclusions

In the above chapter I have examined the figure of Joseph in *GR*. Despite the exegetical nature of midrash certain characteristics emerge which are very different from those of Philo's and Josephus's expositions. These subdivide into matters of content and of method.

In *GR* Joseph is not idealised, but some of his shortcomings are

---

[86] For a background on the question of proselytizing, see especially: *Schürer* III, pp. 150–76; M. Simon, *Verus Israel*, Paris 1948, pp. 315–55 (where he argues against the scholarly consensus that prosletytizing ceased in Judaism after the destruction of the Temple and the loss of national independence); B.J. Bamberger, *Proselytism in the Talmudic Period*, HUC Press 1929, for example of conversion see especially pp. 221–66, on circumcision pp. 42–43; S. Sandmel, *Judaism and Christian Beginnings*, New York 1978, pp. 228–35; W.B. Braude, *Jewish Proselytizing*, Providence 1940; pp. 74–78; P. Dalbert, *Die Theologie der Hellenistisch-Jüdischen Missionsliteratur unter Ausschluss von Philo und Josephus*, Hamburg 1954, pp. 21–26; D. Gorgi, *Die Gegener des Paules im Zweiten Korintherbrief*, Neukirchener Verlag 1964, pp. 83–186 (overestimation of the numbers of proselytes to Judaism).

highlighted instead. In *GR* particular attention is paid to Joseph's youth and his unworthy behaviour towards the brothers. This is understood in view of Joseph's subsequent hardship. Recognizing the principle of Divine retribution in the plot of the story, the midrashic narrator describes Joseph's faults in such a way as to account for the following events.

As in other Palestinian sources, *GR* presents Joseph's encounter with Potiphar's wife as the climax of the story. Some of the exegetical elements are based on earlier Palestinian adaptations of Hellenistic romance material. The midrashic narrator furthermore suggests that a change took place with regard to the understanding of this confrontation. According to him, earlier teachers defend Joseph's complete innocence and highlight his righteousness, while later ones indulge in fanciful conjectures about Joseph's real intentions. These interpretations are framed by various presentations of this 'affair' as a trial.

Like Philo and Josephus, *GR*'s description of Joseph's administration in Egypt also discloses some perceptions about the Hebrew in the Diaspora. *GR*'s straight affirmation of Joseph's position and his alleged enforcement of circumcision reflects the self-confidence of a literature for insiders only. But in *GR* a sense of disillusion about relations with foreigners also transpires.

Regarding the method of characterisation, *GR* varies significantly from earlier presentations of the biblical story. These differences partly derive from the exegetical nature of this midrash, which limits the use of authorial remarks or explanatory insertions of thoughts and feelings in the flow of the narrative. *GR* has instead developed its own appropriate ways of presenting the figure. The most important of these is dialogue. *GR* often takes one or two figures out of the immediate context of the biblical verse in which they are mentioned. Creating an additional scene, the narrator then juxtaposes their views and intentions, thus exposing the specific character of each. Such expressions of 'inner life' are usually closely connected to the action of the biblical context and tend to provide a certain background for it.

Another feature of *GR*'s characterisation is the predominance of religious themes and their application to the characters. This line of interpretation continues early Hebrew exegesis and is frequently directly based on it. The form of presentation is, however, specific to *GR*: the most frequent literary figure is God who on numerous

occasions intervenes with the human agents. In this way, most ethical issues receive a religious dimension. In contrast to later midrash,
such as *Tanhuma*, the theological concerns of *GR* are expressed with
charming directness and thus further serve educational purposes. It
emerges that once the theological message of the story is identified,
it is applied to numerous *loci* in the text. The theme is then presented
in various styles.

CHAPTER SIX

SUMMARY AND CONCLUSION

It is now appropriate to conclude our study and to examine how far it has contributed to the solution of the problems raised earlier. We may ask which new insights we have gained into the hermeneutics of characterization in post-biblical Jewish literature.

We saw initially that the biblical narrator sketches a very vivid image of the figure of Joseph. Using mostly scenic means of description, especially direct speech and internal focalisation, he outlines the development of Joseph's personality. In the initial stages, the narrator is less sympathetic to him and stresses his questionable behaviour towards his family. Yet as he accompanies Joseph throughout his turbulent life, the narrator increasingly highlights also his prudence and moral steadfastness. Joseph's growing maturity is furthermore shown in his dawning awareness of Divine providence. These features become particularly prominent in the climaxes of the biblical story, namely Joseph's encounter with Potiphar's wife, his imprisonment and his administration of Egypt. Numerous aspects of the biblical character nevertheless remain conspicuously opaque. Thus the reader can only conjecture Joseph's reasons for the way he behaved towards his brothers. It also remains open to what extent the narrator considered Joseph himself provocative and thus responsible for the 'affair'.

In the fragments of early exegesis on the Joseph story a few lines of development can be identified. In the Palestinian sources, clearly beginning with *Ps* 105, there is a tendency to enhance the theme of Divine providence. As a result Joseph's life and his personality are understood in the light of the pattern of suffering followed by Divine delivery. Growing significance is attributed in this context to the 'affair'. Whereas late biblical exegesis concentrates on Joseph's imprisonment as the quintessence of his trouble, the 'affair' increasingly assumes this place. In I*Macc* this process reaches a provisional climax when Joseph's encounter with Potiphar's wife is, for the first time, depicted in terms of a trial of the just.

The fragments of early interpretation are not, however, a homogeneous corpus; and numerous idiosyncratic insights are also advanced. Most notable among these are *The Book of Jubilees* and *Artapanus*'s account. Whereas the former introduces various halachic and theological peculiarities, the latter creates a fantastic image of Joseph as the originator of Egypt's Hellenistic culture. Yet these two deviating views of Joseph also conform to the general appraisal of the figure in early exegesis.

Philo's *Life of Joseph* is the first extant paraphrase of the whole Joseph story. It is in addition the only independent treatment which is explicitly dedicated to it. It has emerged from our analysis that this special consecration as well as other features of this treatise is inspired by Philo's Greek background. We saw that Philo is familiar with at least two distinct types of biography, namely the allegorical such as the *Life of Abraham* and the political, exemplified in the *Life of Moses*. His treatment of Joseph is a peculiar mixture, showing characteristics of both.

This has significant repercussions for his presentation of the figure of Joseph. He creates an idealised image which he derives from the biblical text by inserting both allegories and standard items of political biographies. In this way, Philo is able to identify Hellenistic political metaphors in the biblical story. On the basis of authorial remarks to this effect, Philo thus shapes the figure of Joseph in accordance with a certain *stereotype* of the political personality.

We have moreover been able to distinguish in Philo's paraphrase an underlying, more individual concept of character. It is most prominent in those passages where Philo relates Joseph's successful career. It is significant that modifications of this kind tend to be paralleled in similar stages of the *Life* of Moses. According to this concept, personality and especially that of great figures, can in the main be deduced from external appearance. It is furthermore held that a person's inner character will manifest itself in action and outward behaviour. These concepts and the way in which they are incorporated into the narrative are strongly reminiscent of the biographical genre whence Philo is likely to have borrowed them.

Among the ancient interpreters Josephus is most acutely aware of the narrative potential of the Joseph story. He is thus able to modify it substantially by introducing minute changes on the level of narrative perspective and the order of events.

Unlike Philo, Josephus's description of character is less inspired by philosophical and literary concepts. He rather reshapes the figure of his namesake according to his own personal experience. Reflecting his apologetics about his relationship with other leaders of the early Jewish Revolt, Josephus attempts to extricate Joseph from all ambiguity. He thus highlights the innocence of his behaviour among his family and emphasizes Joseph's dreams as an indication of Divine support against the brothers' envy. Parralel to his autobiography, Josephus presents the "relevant" aspects of the protagonist in an "appropriate" fashion so that the reader may draw more comprehensive conclusions about his character.

In *GR* we receive the most diverse picture of the figure of Joseph. Similar to Philo, its main features are shaped by the work's ideological concerns. Yet its contents and literary implementation are very different from Philo's.

A central interest of *GR* is the character of Joseph in relation to the story's plot. On the principle assumption of Divine retribution Joseph's life is examined in terms of crime and punishment. His youth is consequently reinterpreted so as to account for his later misfortune. As a result, the personality of his youth emerges as especially negative.

In accordance with early Hebrew exegesis, the 'affair' assumes even further centrality in *GR*. It is regarded as the turning point in Joseph's life and numerous interpretations are associated with it. The heterogeneity of the images of Joseph naturally becomes most prominent at this point; and conflicting views of Joseph's culpability are available. It is also crucial to note that fragments of the Phaedra material are integrated in this collection. The fact of their occurrence sheds new light both on the exegetical processes of *GR* and on the availability, presumably in a Semitic language, of traditions attested in *XII*.

The literary techniques of *GR* primarily reflect the exegetical and thus atomistic nature of the midrash. The most prominent means of characterization is the insertion of speech and in particular of dialogue. "Inner life" or an essential personality are not attributed to the literary persons. It is furthermore a decisive feature of *GR*'s presentation of character that the human figures are usually juxtaposed with God. In this way, biblical issues are turned into disputes of far-reaching theological import. It emerges that a midrashic figure is primarily a *homo religiosus* who mirrors the nature of the deity.

It has thus emerged that there exists a variety of ways in which character is depicted in post-biblical Jewish literature. These differ regarding their homogeneity and also regarding the degree of their personhood. Nevertheless, we can find in none of these expositions an interest in character for art's sake. The aesthetic or literary dimension always remains overshadowed by some ideological agenda or other topical concerns. In this respect, Jewish literature differs from other cultures in Antiquity.

We have furthermore examined the hermeneutical cycle which fostered each interpretation of the story. We have seen how the figure of Joseph functions in the different intellectual environments and how it is employed for the individual purposes of each exegete. This aspect had become particularly clear in the analysis of the reflection on Joseph in Egypt.

I thus hope to have provided in this study some methodological tools for a new comparative approach to the study of midrash. It will in the future be of great value to widen the scope of this investigation and to examine other literary figures according to the same criteria. Ultimately, it should be possible to establish more clearly the way in which character was grasped in Jewish Literature in Late Antiquity.

THE FIGURE OF JOSEPH IN THE TARGUMS*

In this part I shall delineate the specifically Targumic image of
Joseph and contrast it with the other interpretations. Given the
prolonged controversy over the precise date and the nature of the
Targums,[1] such an attempt might at first appear problematic. Indeed, a strictly diachronic treatment of the material does not suggest
itself; and we shall not attempt a neat chronological categorisation,[2]
nor shall we primarily contribute to the question of the Targumic
genre (synagogue reading or midrashic exegesis).[3]

Acknowledging the heterogeneity of the Targums, a typological
approach will be taken instead. We shall examine how each of the
extant Targums treats specific items of the biblical text and how each
construes the inherent exegetical problems. This will then be compared to other interpretations, such as the Midrash, on the one hand,

---

* This part appeared in earlier form in JJS 39/1988, pp. 234–50.

[1] A survey of the history of research is to be found in R. leDeaut, *The Current
State of Targum Studies*, Biblical Theological Bulletin IV (1974), *idem, Introduction à
la littérature targumique*. Rome 1966 (unfortunately this is not up-dated and also Jew-
ish, traditional and modern treatments are not taken into account) J. Bowker, *The
Targums and Rabbinic Literature*, Cambridge University Press 1969; P. Schäfer, *Targum*, Theologische Realenzyklopädie VI, Berlin 1977; A. Shinan, *op. cit.*; G.
Vermes, *Scripture and Tradition in Judaism, Haggadic Studies*, Leiden 1961; P. Kahle,
Masoreten des Westens, vol. II 1930. For studies on specific texts or topics, see also:
A. Berliner, *Targum Onkelos*, vol. II 1884; M. Aberbach/B. Grossfeld, *Targum Onke-
los to Genesis: A Critical Analysis together with a translation*, New York 1982; M. McNe-
mara, *The Palestinian Targum to the Pentateuch and the New Testament*, Rome 1966;
S. Gronemann, *Die jonathanische Pentateuchübersetzung in ihrem Verhältnis zur Halakha*,
Leipzig 1879; R. Hayward, *Divine Name and Presence: the Memra*, Totowa N.J. 1981;
R. Syren, *The Blessings in the Targums*, Acta Aboensis 1986; S.D. Luzzato, אוהב גר
Cracovia 1845; B.S. Berkovitz, חליפות שמלות, Wilna 1874; S.B. Shefftel,
ביאורי אונקלום, München 1888.

[2] On the whole, O seems to have reached authoritative status at a relatively early stage. It is frequently quoted by Midrash and Talmud as "our Targum" (bKid
49a etc.). PJ remained open to changes longer and some additions were introduced
as late as the seventh century (PJ on *Num* 24:9 etc.).

[3] Consider the conflicting evidence/reference: m*Meg* 4:4–10; y*Meg* 3a and 4a;
b*Ned* 37b; a*QTrgLev*; a*QTrgJob*; see also *Schürer* I, pp. 99ff; Frankfurt 1892, pp.
655–87.

and Hellenistic writers on the other. While thus extrapolating "Targumic conceptions" underlying these renderings, one has always to bear in mind the nature of this translation literature. It is bound to Scripture in that nothing of the *Vorlage* can be omitted nor the other changed. Moreover, embellishments can be introduced only within certain limits. Each targum's general translation techniques have to be examined and errors or negligence have to be considered as possible explanations for a departure from the text.

Characteristic of all the Palestinian traditions, the Targums take the blessing of Jacob (*Gen* 49) as the starting point for their evaluation of Joseph. They were thus inspired by the late biblical emphasis on Joseph[4] and by the particular contents of the poetry pertaining to him (vss. 22 – 26). The biblical metaphors are particularly rich and somewhat obscured by numerous textual corruptions. Two important features of this inner-biblical Midrash nevertheless emerge: 1) Joseph receives overwhelmingly positive notice. His abundant fruitfulness is extolled and he is portrayed as the victim of his adversaries; 2) Divine providence is invoked. In this way, the originally more secular story acquires a distinctly religious frame.

The Targums render this passage in various forms. Focussing on *Gen* 49:24,[5] O summarizes:

> And his prophecy was fulfilled for he observed the Law in secret and placed his trust in Divine power, then gold was lifted on his arms, he took possession of a kingdom and became strong. This was for him from before God, the Mighty One of Jacob, who with his word sustains fathers and sons, the seed of Israel.

As has been previously recognized[6] the mention of the secret law observance refers to Joseph's impeccable behaviour in the encounter with Potiphar's wife. This and his alleged general trust in God made Joseph worthy of Divine protection which subsequently resulted in his successful career.

Similarly, also N and FT point of Joseph's chastity as his quintessential characteristic (*Gen* 49:22):

---

[4] Judah's predominance seems more natural and appears to have preceded Joseph's eminence which resulted from successive redaction.

[5] "Yet his bow remained unmoved, his arms were made agile, but the hand of the Mighty One of Jacob, by the Name of the Shepherd, the Rock of Israel".

[6] See e.g. M. Aberbach/B. Grossfeld, *Targum Onkelos on Genesis 49*, Missoula 1976, p. 52; Y. Komlosh, המקרא באור התרגום, 1973, p. 191.

> ... and the daughters of the kings and of the rulers said to one another, behold this is Joseph the pious man (נבר חסידא) who has not gone after the appearances of his eyes nor the imagination of his heart. Those are they who destroy the son of man from the world. Because of this there will arise from you two tribes, ...

In connection with Joseph the term נבר חסידא is used. This is not a *terminus technicus* for צדיק[7] but a simple equivalent of the biblical איש חסיד.[8] Nevertheless, parallel to the metaphor of the vine (N *Gen* 49:22), there is a tendency towards categorizing Joseph on account of his chastity.

FT[9] praises him equally:

> Love, favour and grace was bestowed on him from heaven ... because of his Yezer which he controlled.

Finally, PJ paraphrases *Gen* 49:22:

> My son, who has grown, Joseph, my son, who has grown and become strong ... because you have suppressed your Yezer in the business with your mistress and with your brothers, I liken you to a vine planted by the springs of the water, which spreads its roots and breaks the teeth of the stones ...

It emerges that the Targums took the encouter with Potiphar's wife as the most significant event in Joseph's life. According to them, his behaviour at this point qualified him as an ethical-religious prototype of considerable import. Other episodes tended to be considered in the light of this paradigmatic conduct. It is conceivable that this evaluation of Joseph was furthermore evoked by the sequence of the biblical chapters. The flow of the narrative is interrupted in *Gen* 38, where the story of Judah's incest is interposed. Thus, the ambiguous image of the young Joseph is set apart and his laudable comportment accentuated by contradistinction to Judah.

This view of Joseph is shared by numerous other Palestinian traditions, most conspicuously by the *Testament of Joseph* 2–16. Talmudic passages[10] also conclude: ''They said about Joseph the Righteous: every day Potiphar's wife was talking to him persuasively ... Joseph obliges all the wicked''.

---

[7] This would be translated as צדיק or זכי.

[8] This is a hapax *legomenon* in the Pentateuch, *Dtn* 33:8 in connection with Aaron.

[9] Machsor Vitry, ed. Hurwitz, p. 342.

[10] E.g.: b*Yoma* 35b; see also b*Sotah* 36b.

Having established the case with Potiphar's wife as the focal point of the Targums, we shall now look in more detail at *Gen* 39. In contrast to the Hellenistic writers,[11] the Targums show no particular interest in the nature of the transgression which Joseph avoided. Thus, it is not indicated whether he would primarily have violated the confidential relationship to his benefactor or sinned because of his intercourse with a married woman. Instead, it is assumed that the audience will grasp the point intuitively. The Targums' real concern is to highlight the religious and didactic value of Joseph's behaviour.

In this vein, *Gen* 39:10[12] was modified. One O tradition, Ixar 1490, and N embellish "... but Joseph did not agree to sleep with her *in this world in order not to be with her in the world to come*". This is almost verbatim paralleled in FT/Machsor Vitry,[13] which however leaves out the first insertion "in this world". Possibly the contrast was self-evident. FT Paris 110 paraphrases: "*to sleep with her in this world in order not to be with her in Gehinom in the world to come*". These expansions respond to an exegetical impetus, i.e. the notion that each biblical phrase has an independent meaning.[14] This interpretative tradition enjoyed wide circulation. It was not only a firm part of N and marginal to O and FT, but also present in the midrash. In *GR* it is quoted anonymously as an apparently well-established tradition, and in talmudic passages it frequently occurs, almost as though it was part of the biblical text. PJ, on the other hand, inserts the expression: "*in order not to be with her on the day of the great judgement in the world to come*". Here, the עוה"ז is neither mentioned nor contrasted to the עוה"ב. More importantly, PJ introduces the notion of the day of judgement, which links this tradition to earlier apocalyptic interpretations. The *Book of Jubilees* 39:6 – 7 mentions that for fornication "a judgment of death has been ordained in the heavens above before the Lord the Most High and the sin will be recorded against him in the eternal books for ever before the Lord. And Joseph remembered these words and did not

---

[11] Philo, *Jos* 42 – 47; Josephus *JA* I: 49 – 53; for details, see above.

[12] "And it came to pass that she talked to him day after day but Joseph did not agree to sleep with her or to be with her".

[13] ed. Hurwitz, p. 342.

[14] Cf. *GR* 1070. One of the quoted sayings does not offer the same explanation. Nevertheless, it also attributes two distinct meanings to the apparently synonymous biblical verbs.

want to lie with her''. PJ's different mode of expression is not directly prompted by the biblical text but rather by earlier, reshaped
material. It has a more dramatic connotation, which conforms to his
generally imaginative tendency,[15] but is not paralleled in the
midrashic corpus. The effects of all these insertions is that Joseph's
perseverance is given a religious dimension and the protagonist becomes somewhat of a folk-hero.

Also *Gen* 39:11[16] receives considerable treatment by the Targums.
O, N and PJ concentrate on the ambiguous term לעשות מלאכתו
clarifying the nature of that work and, by implication, also Joseph's
motivation to return to his master's house. Thus, מלאכה normally
rendered as עבידה, is here paraphrased as: (he came up to the
house) "*to check the accounts*". Parallel to LXX, the two FT traditions
do not particularly relate to this issue. They might originate from a
time when this expression had not yet become problematic. S.D.
Luzzatto (*ad.loc.*) suggests that Joseph's work was more clearly
defined so as to indicate that he was not a slave nor a servant. According to him, the Targums' objective was the patriarch's social
standing. But in view of the previous verse, it is manifest that they
were primarily concerned with the moral aspects of the story. It was
important for them to present Joseph as entirely innocent and as the
victim of the woman's intrigue. This emphasis might have responded to an increasingly critical exegesis on this point.

PJ preserves some of this material in connection with *Gen* 49:24:

> And his erect organ returned to its previous condition so as not to have
> intercourse with his mistress and his hands were withheld from volup-
> tuous thoughts and he suppressed his Yezer thanks to the strict in-
> struction he received from Jacob.

These two different versions of PJ are also reflected in midrashic
literature. The prevalent, brief interpretation is generally attributed
to the Tanna R. Judah, whereas the expanded version is transmitted
in the names of the Amoraim R. Samuel b. Nahman, R. Abin and
R. Huna. Significantly, many passages (e.g. *GR ad.loc.*, b*Sotah* 36b)
contain a discussion between Rab and Samuel, of the transitional
period, in which each defends one version respectively. Rashi[17] saw

---

[15] See also A. Shinan, *op. cit.*, p. 244.
[16] "But one day, when he went to the house to do his work (לעשות מלאכתו) and
none of the men of the house were in the house, she caught him by the garnment,
saying: lie with me!"
[17] On b*Shab* 49b.

these two positions as opposites. He held that the one affirms
Joseph's integrity whereas the other exposes his temporary weakness. Rashi is correct in that these two types of interpretation are
stylistically too different or have originated from the same background. But the question must be raised whether, on a spiritual level, they had essentially different implications. Primarily, one should
consider that also in PJ's extended version the expression כבש יצריה
is used. Morally responsible behaviour is thus attributed to Joseph.
Furthermore, a look at PRE will elucidate the underlying meaning.
The passage (p. 305) reads:

> And when he wished to accustom himself to sin, he saw the image of
> his father and controlled his passion.

This is mentioned as one example to testify that "the Holy Spirit
rested on Joseph from his youth".

The tradition of God's providence in this incident is already attested in the *Testament of Joseph* 2:2[18] PJ's extended interpretation
thus belongs to a continuous exegetical tradition (which comple-
ments his and other Targums' shorter versions). In terms of the
wording and the imagery, he clearly resembles the Amoraic versions, to which he might also be closer chronologically. It is
moreover likely, that this particular interpretation does not (any
more) belong to the strata which might have been used liturgically.

In sum, the targums agree on the centrality of *Gen* 39 for the
evaluation of Joseph's character. His behaviour is depicted as innocent and worthy of imitation. N shows Joseph most clearly as a model of righteousness. In addition to this particular case, he highlights
his generally "good deeds" (39:2) and his "beneficence" to society
(39:5), two traditional attributes of the Zaddik.[19] In this way,
didactical needs in the synagogue might have been answered. On
the other hand, PJ emerges as the most heterogeneous of the Targums. While he shares their positive evaluation of Joseph, he also
preserves more narrative material which he shares with the Midrash
and, more loosely, with intertestamental sources.

The next unit of material which we shall examine is the targumic

---

[18] "I struggled with a shameless woman who kept prodding me to transgress
with her, but the God of my fathers rescued me from her burning fire".

[19] See also E.E. Urbach, *op. cit.*, pp. 428–54, R. Mach, *op. cit.*, pp. 14–19, pp.
117–24.

version of *Gen* 37. This chapter precedes Joseph's encounter with Potiphar's wife and relates the events leading up to it. The biblical text focuses on the family situation and in particular on Joseph's position among his brothers. His father's favoritism and the son's reaction to it will determine subsequent developments. The individual interest of the Targums in this section differ to the extent that we shall deal with each separately so as to uncover the individual character of every one.

O introduces a number of significant changes in chapter 37. The first occurs in 37:2,[20] on which O preserves two different traditions. Eight MSS render the expression דיבתם רעה literally, indicating that the report (though correct) was defamatory. On the other hand, two good manuscripts smoothen it to "he revealed their bad character", thus blaming mainly the brothers. This exegetical vacillation within the O tradition reflects a changing awareness of more austere interpretations such as that in the *Testament of Zebulon* 3:2 and midrashic literature. Yet for O the issue is too marginal to have prompted a firmer response.

O also reshapes *Gen* 37:3.[21] All the MSS replace בן זקינים by בר חכים, "the wise son". Two considerations evoked this alteration. 1) The biblical term primarily refers to Benjamin (*Gen* 44:20). The need to substitute it with regard to Joseph might have given rise to the common association of זקן with זה שקנה חכמה.[22] 2) Conforming to a general tendency, O wished to protect the patriarch Jacob: his emphasis on Joseph's talent makes the father's favouratism more natural.[23]

At first sight, O's brief interpretation seems to be paralleled by Hellenistic writers, such as Philo (*Jos* 1:4–5) and Josephus (*JA*

---

[20] "This is the history of the family of Jacob. When Joseph was seventeen years old, he shepherded the flock with his brothers, he was a lad with the sons of Bilhah and Zilpah his fathers' wives. And Joseph brought ill report about them to their father".

[21] "And Israel loved Joseph above all his sons because he was the son of his old age (בן זקונים) and he made him a long-sleeved coat".

[22] See e.g. b*Kid* 32a. Note also that O remains literal on *Gen* 21:2 and that PRE explicitly mentions this exegetical impetus *ad. loc.*. D. Kimhi, Commentary on Psalms 78, also preserves this tradition: חכם בכל דבריו כמו אם היח זקן see also J. Bowker, *op. cit.*, p. 241.

[23] The change of subject ("old age" describes Jacob, whereas "wise" refers to Joseph) also emphasized that the cause of Jacob's preference is not his emotion but Joseph himself.

2:9 – 10). However, Philo in particular presents Joseph's φρόνημα in the context of his general view of the talented individual who is envied by inferior persons. His presentation touches a dimension far beyond O's paraphrase.

Finally, O mitigates the brothers' murderous sentiments (*Gen* 37: 18).[24] All O traditions replace ויתנכלו by וחשיבו, "they thought". O reveals his sympathy for his brothers also in *Gen* 49:23,[25] which he renders:

> And the mighty men and men of dissension were embittered against him and took revenge on him and distressed him.

On the basis of *Gen* 49:5,[26] O identifies the archers with the brothers and consequently softens the tone of the biblical verse. This is the only occurrence (cf. *Gen* 27:41 and 50:15) where O renders שטם as עוק rather than נטר דבב. And this is also the only case where O translates ריב as נקם rather than נצי, thereby suggesting that the brothers executed (justified?) retribution.

In sum, O's description of the original family setting is primarily motivated by an apologetic concern for all of Israel's ancestors. Joseph is depicted as wise, but sympathy is also shown for his brothers. In this overall attitude O remains quite unparalleled in the interpretative traditions.

Targum N on *Gen* 37 remains almost as literal as LXX. In accordance with its habitual disposition, N emphasizes some religious and ethical aspects of the story. The "man' (איש, *Gen* 37:15) who met Joseph on the way to Shekhem is transformed into an "angel in image of a man". Throughout the Pentateuch, N is inclined to recognize in anonymous figures signs of Divine providence (e.g. *Gen* 18:2 and 32:25), thus conforming to a broader tendency to embellish biblical stories with angels.[27] This exegesis is paralleled in *GR* 1017

---

[24] "And they saw him from afar and before he came near to them, they conspired (ויתנכלו) against him to kill him".

[25] "And they fiercely attacked him and fought him and the archers harrassed him".

[26] Here Levi and Simon are described as the brothers whose "weapons of violence are their swords" F. Delitzsch, *A New Commentary on Genesis*, Edinburgh 1889, vol. II, p. 394, conjectures that this association rests on *Ps* 120:3 – 4. This is not convincing since nothing in the psalm refers to the brothers.

[27] See also E.E. Urbach, *op. cit.*, p. 115, E. Kautzsch, *Biblische Theologie des Alten Testamentes*, Tübingen 1911, p. 84; P. Schäfer, *Die Rivalität zwischen Engeln und Menschen*, Berlin 1985, pp. 43 – 56.

and more indirectly in *Tanh Vayasheb* 7.

Also in Reuben's speech (*Gen* 37:22) the criminal nature of the brothers' intentions is made explicit:

> And Reuben said to them: do not shed *innocent* blood. Cast him into the pit in the wilderness and do not lay the hands *of murderers* on him. This was in order to save him from them and to return him to his father.

N always qualifies blood as "innocent" in the case of unjustified homicide and thus alludes to divine retribution (cf. e.g. *Dtn* 19:10). N's specification "murderers" emphasizes the moral dimension of the story as well. The *Testament of Zebulon* 2:2 contains a similar interpretation. On the verge of being killed, Joseph addresses his brothers: "do not lay your hands on me to shed innocent blood for I have not sinned against you". The same concept is here invoked, αἷμα ἀθῷον being equivalent to αἷμα ἀναίτιον (*Dtn* 19:10).[28] Another parallel is to be found in Reuben's speech according to Josephus (*JA* 2:20ff). The latter invokes God's omniscience and ultimate justice, thereby stressing the enormity of the crime.

Clearly, these three traditions share the same spiritual background. But it is not necessary to assume mutual dependence since each projects its own scene and different language is used. It emerges that N (FT) took no particular interest in this phase of the Joseph story. He only transforms a few phrases in light of his faith.

Let us consider PJ's presentation. On *Gen* 37:2 he expands in the following way:

> Joseph was seventeen years old *when he left the Beit Midrash.* He was guarding the flock with his brothers, and as a youth, he grew up[29] with the sons of Bilhah and Zilpah, his father's wives. And Joseph brought ill report of them *for he saw them eating meat, and the ears and the tail, torn from a living animal.* And he came and told his father.

In this version, the biblical Joseph acquires new features. Firstly, he is reputed to have studied in the Beit Midrash. In no other source is such a tradition inserted into the biblical text at precisely this point. However, *GR* 1010 relates in the name of Nehemia that Israel

---

[28] In LXX it is used to render דם נקי in the sense discussed above.

[29] With this slightly longer translation PJ improves the awkward Hebrew original נער את.

loved Joseph because "all the Halakhot which Shem and Ever had passed to him (Jacob), he transmitted to him (Joseph)". In both cases early rabbinic training is attributed to Joseph. This is patently anachronistic in its emphasis on rabbinic education.

Secondly, according to PJ, Joseph accuses his brothers of violating even the basic Noachic laws.[30] S. Gronemann holds[31] that this insertion simply conforms to PJ's tendency to offer concrete elucidations for Halakhic precepts. However, this issue seems to be more complicated. Although the interest in details is unique in targumic literature, similar versions are extant in other sources and intricate questions as to their character in relation to PJ arise.

> The earliest attestation is in the *Testament of Gad* 1:4–9:
> And Joseph said to his father, the sons of Zilpah and Bilhah are killing the best animals and eat them against the advice of Judah and Reuben. He saw that I had set free a lamb from the mouth of a bear which I then killed, but I had killed the lamb when I was saddened seeing that it was too weak to live and we ate it. This he told his father.

The general tone resembles PJ. Yet it contains numerous specifications which are lacking in PJ and, conversely, misses others which PJ contains. Both interpretations, however, enhance the negative notice which Joseph receives in the bible. This exegesis recurs in *GR* 1009, 1062 and *Tanh Vayasheb* 7, where it forms part of a trilogy of Joseph's defamations, which God retributes in equal measure. PRE (p. 291) contains a simpler version:

> And *he saw* the sons of his father's concubines eating flesh of the roes and the flesh of the sheep whilst they were alive and he brought a reproach against them before Jacob.

Again, we find that PJ is most paralleled by PRE. Since the main point of this tradition is attested much earlier, we may assume that both PJ and PRE belonged to an environment in which material of old was reshaped.

Furthermore, PJ explains Jacob's love for Joseph thus: "because the features of Joseph were similar to his own". This expansion was not evoked by an exegetical difficulty. It is a free embellishment, which is attested in its crude form already in the *Testament of Joseph*

---

[30] Cf. PJ on *Gen* 9:14, b*San* 59a; see also G. Friedländer, *op. cit.*, p. 241, n7; J. Bowkwer, *op. cit.*, p. 241.
[31] *Op.cit.*, p. 97.

18:4: "in every way was I like Jacob . . .''. It has its almost precise analogy in *GR*, in the saying of R. Judah: "the splendor of his features was similar to his". It is, however, not to be found in PRE. Thus, *GR* and *PJ* on this point drew from similar traditions which in turn were based on earlier material.

In *Gen* 37:14 PJ adds a new dimension to the biblical verse. He paraphrases:

> And he (Jacob) said to him (Joseph): Go now, look after the welfare of your brothers and the flock and report back to me. *And he sent him on account of the profound counsel (עיטא עמיקתא) which had been given to Abraham in Hebron. And on that day began the Galut of Egypt and Joseph stood up* and went to Shekehm.

This complex expansion on "he sent him from the valley of Hebron" was inspired by *Num* 13:22[32] and *Gen* 15:13.[33] PJ is the only one of the Targums which exhibits a "historical" awareness at this point of the Joseph story. Midrashic interpreters (*Tanh Vayasheb* 8, *GR* 1051 etc.), on the other hand, showed a keen interest in the effect of the sale for the fate of Israel.

In *Gen* 37:15 PJ identifies the איש with "Gabriel in the image of man". Like N, PJ is fond of angeology. But usually he inserts unspecified angels (e.g. on *Gen* 18:2 and 32:25). It has been rightly suggested that PJ derived the figure of Gabriel from *Dan* 9:21.[34] PRE inserts the same imagery and *Dan* 9:21 is quoted as a scriptural prooftext. Thus, PJ enriches the *Vorlage* by affirming God's particular protection of Joseph. His intention parallels N, but the form of execution resembles that of PRE.

Finally, PJ reshapes *Gen* 37:28.[35] He points out that for twenty silver coins received for their brother "they bought from them (i.e. the merchants) sandals". This insertion associates Joseph with the innocent just man mentioned in *Amos* 2:6 and adds to the crime.

---

[32] They *went up* to Hebron. This expression obviously contradicts the assumption of the city's location in a valley. See also G. Vermes, Bible and Midrash, Early Old Testament Exegesis, *Cambridge History of the Bible*, Cambridge 1970, p. 209; J. Bowker, *op. cit.*, p. 241.

[33] God said to Abraham: "Know that your descendents will be strangers in a land that is not theirs".

[34] E.g. J. Bowker, *op. cit.*, p. 242.

[35] "Then the Midrashic traders passed by. And they drew Joseph up and lifted him from the pit and sold him to the Ishmaelites for twenty shekel of silver and they took Joseph to Egypt".

Possibly, this association of *Gen* 37:28 with Amos was inspired by the synagogue reading: the Haftorah for this precisely *Amos* 2:6.

This tradition is first attested in the *Testament of Zebulon* 3:2:

> But Simon and Gad and our brothers accepted the money and bought shoes for themselves, their wives and children.

The same version is later also transmitted in PRE (p. 293) and MHG (*ad. loc.*): "and each of them took two pieces of silver to purchase shoes for their feet".

In sum, the Targums exhibit highly disparate interests concerning *Gen* 37. N does not react specifically to the figure of Joseph and finds but little stimulus for general theological insertions. O ameliorates the reputation of all the parties concerned: Jacob's favouritism is explained, Joseph's complacence softened or overlooked and the brothers' aggression is played down. For O the apologetic objective had priority over specific ethical concerns. In this capter, PJ's more narrative character comes most into play and we receive the fullest picture of the young Joseph in this document. In addition to the difference in length, PJ also takes an interest in other biblical items. His critical awareness of Joseph's complacency and his consciousness of the historical consequences of the sale are anticipated in intertestamental literature, especially the *Testament of the Twelve Patriarchs*, and paralleled in Midrash, particularly PRE. Presumably, there existed a "channel" through which early material reached midrashic interpreters who subsequently reshaped it, without, however, changing the general intention. A source of the same tradition as PRE seems to have provided a considerable part of PJ's material in this section.

In this last section we shall examine the targumic renderings of Joseph in Egypt. Given the large amount of biblical material, we shall take a condensed look, focussing strictly on the protagonist. This paragraph naturally falls into three parts: Joseph in prison and Joseph's first and second encounter with his brothers. The first two points receive only brief notice in the Targums. The third, and in particularly Judah's speech to Joseph (*Gen* 44:18), is substantially expanded in the Palestinian Targums and becomes there a second focus of the story.

Gen 40 relates how Joseph interpreted the dreams of his fellow-prisoners[36] and how he was proved right by their immediate fulfilment on Pharaoh's birthday. The chapter closes by stressing that the chief butler, whom Joseph had asked to assist his own promotion, "did not remember Joseph but forgot him" (*Gen* 40:23). The Palestinian Targums respond to this issue. PJ paraphrases:

> And because Joseph abandoned the favour from above and put his trust in the chief butler, a mortal,[37] therefore the chief butler did not remember Joseph and forgot him until the appointed time before the Lord came for Joseph to be released.

N contains an expanded version, inserting a reference to *Jer* 17:5, "cursed be the son of man who trusts in flesh and who places his trust in flesh". On the basis of *Jer* 17:7, FT further adds a blessing of "the man who trusts in the name of the Memra of the Lord and who makes the Memra of the Lord his trust". These embellishments may have been inspired by the apparent redundancy of the biblical text. Their length and tone are remarkable. The issue of Joseph's trust in God during his imprisonment had already captured the imagination of the earliest interpreters. But in such passages as the *Testament of Joseph* 1:5–7, the subject is mentioned in favour of Joseph. Looking back on his life he is reputed to remember God's providence and to express his gratefulness. Midrashic interpreters (e.g. *GR* 1085) were more aware of Joseph's shortcomings but they allude to them cautiously by pointing to other examples of God's enduring support. Philo (*Jos* 99) is equally careful in his remark. It is in our targumic versions that Joseph receives the most severe criticism. This is particularly noteworthy in view of the Targums' otherwise notably lenient interpretation of Joseph. J. Bowker suggested that this insertion served both as a warning and as an encouragement for Jews in situations of danger and persecution.[38] It is possible that this objective was at the heart of the *Testaments of the Twelve Patriarchs*, but perhaps also of the rabbis. The different mode and tone of expression in the Targums may reflect their didactical inclinations.

---

[36] In accordance with midrashic interpretation, N and PJ give them an allegorical meaning, referring to the ensuing slavery of Israel in Egypt.

[37] Literally: "flesh which passes". J. Bowker, *op. cit.*, p. 250, translates עביר as "he transgressed". But this translation disregards the syntax of the sentence. N's version of this verse corroborates our point.

[38] *Op.cit.*, p. 251.

In chapter 42 the first meeting between the brothers is narrated. In the interval, their respective ranks have changed considerably. While the brothers suffer from economic depression, Joseph has risen to the second most powerful position in Egypt. It is almost impossible that they should recognize the high-ranking officer upon their arrival. Having also the advantage of knowledge over them, Joseph is able to test the genuineness of their attitudes and to see his childhood dreams fulfilled. The very moment of their encounter at the grain market (*Gen* 42:6 – 7)[39] had been the object of interest from early on.

O paraphrases vs 7 thus:

> And he recognized them and considered what he should say (חשיב מא דימליל). And he spoke harshly.

This rendering has long been recognized as an alteration in favour of Joseph.[40] The ambiguous term ויתנכר is replaced by an acceptable act of contemplation, thus emphasizing that Joseph was motivated by sympathy for his brothers, not by revenge. By contrast, N accuminates the wording of *Gen* 42:7, rendering it: "he showed himself hostile".

PJ reshapes the recognition scene more substantially. *Gen* 42:6 is rendered with astonishing freedom:

> Now Joseph was the governor over the land *and as he knew that his brothers were coming to purchase, he appointed guards at the gates of the city so as to register everybody who entered on that day, namely the name and his father's name.* And it was he who sold grain to all the people of the land. And the brothers came *and they searched in the streets and in the open places and in the taverns, but they did not find him.* And they entered the house and bowed themselves down with their faces to the ground.

PJ changed this verse with a view to enhance the anticipation of the meeting on both sides. We shall concentrate on the aspects pertain-

---

[39] "Now Joseph was the governor (שליט) over the land. And it was he who sold to all the people of the land. And Joseph's brothers came and bowed themselves down before him with their faces to the ground. And Joseph saw his brothers and recognized them (ויכרם) and he made himself a stranger (ויתנכר) and he spoke harsh words to them: from whence do come? he said. They said: from the land of Canaan to buy food".

[40] S.D. Luzzatto's comment, *ad. loc.*, followed by B.Z. Berkovitz, *ad. loc.*, is valid until today: "Onkelos improved the language by way of honouring Joseph, because all his estrangement to them was nothing but that he considered what to say to their ears".

ing to Joseph. The insertion of the guards and their activities appears to have been prompted by an exegetical impetus: the same biblical verse relates that Joseph was the governor, yet he himself did the selling. These two were considered incompatible.[41] This tradition enjoyed wide circulation in midrashic literature (e.g. *GR* 1122 – 26, *TanhMiketz* 10). In these fuller versions, Joseph's measure becomes more transparent: he is reputed to have asked every day for the registration accounts until he recognized the brothers' names. It was in this way that he allegedly learnt when they arrived. PJ's rendering presupposes this information and offers an abbreviated form which conveniently fits into the flow of the biblical verse.

In *Gen* 42:7, PJ clarifies the sense of ויתנכר by adding: "to their eyes" did he make himself a stranger. This is a merely explanatory addition which lacks the apologetic tone of O and the critical connotation of N. Whereas O's and N's interpretations are quite unique, PJ's has a clloe parallel in *GR* 1127, where the Tanna R. Nehemia, R. Akiba's student, is reputed to have said: "he made himself like a stranger to them". The lack of controversy shows that this interpretation was well accepted. The biblical expression was (no longer?) problematic and PJ reflects this nonchalance. Instead, he is interested in those parts of the story which lend themselves to imaginative edification.[42]

Our final point of discussion will be *Gen* 44:18ff. This altercation between Judah and Joseph just before the latter discloses his identity constitutes in a way the climax of the whole Joseph story. For targumic and midrashic interpreters this passage was significant and numerous versions of it exist. Based on the expression "you are like Pharaoh", they add a highly aggressive tone of the biblical speech of Judah.[43] Most of these interpretations focus on Judah and his threats to destroy Egypt and its population, including Joseph and Pharaoh. Select passages in the main Targum traditions and two *Tosefta Targums* disclose, however, interesting insights into the figure

---

[41] See also Ramban, *ad.loc.*: "I do not see how the governor over the land, the second of the king of Egypt, would sell to everybody".

[42] In the same vein, PJ adds to *Gen* 42:8: "And Joseph recognized his brothers, *for when he was separated from them they had already the mark of a beard*, but they did not recognize him, *for he had not yet the mark of a beard, but that hour he had*".

[43] See G. Vermes, *Scripture*, op. cit., p. 20; M. Bernstein, A New Manuscript of Tosefta Targum, *Ninth World Congress of Jewish Studies*, Jerusalem 1986, p. 153; N. Leibovitch, *op. cit.*, pp. 344 – 9.

of Joseph. In this essay we shall limit ourselves to these latter aspects.

FT renders *Gen* 44:19 thus:

> When Joseph saw that Judah's anger was aroused and that the hairs came forth from his chest, he rent his garments and signalled to Manasseh and stamped his foot in the palace and they all trembled and Judah thought to himself and said: such strength must come from the house of my father and he therefore softened his words . . .

Characteristic of N's compilatory composition here, he offers a more extended version which connects incompatible elements: "And when the beloved and noble Joseph saw that the haughtiness of his brother Judah had gone, Joseph was agitated and trembled before Judah . . .". Finally, in the Tosefta version, Joseph himself "struck the pillar". In these folkloristic accounts the verbal confrontation almost culminates in a physically violent encounter. At the last moment Joseph allegedly resorted to a demonstration of almost magic power. This makes Judah recognize him and provides the turning point of the narrative after which the Targums revert to the biblical text.

Two *Tosefta Targums* contain a dialogue between the protagonists which concentrate equally on Judah and Joseph. The longer version is a poetic double accrostic recently found in a MS of Columbia University and first published by M. Bernstein.[44] In its present form it appears to have been attached to *Gen* 45:4,[45] but must originally have belonged to an earlier part of the narrative (*Gen* 44:18?). It reads as follows:

1 Come so that we may argue about the charge, oh Egyptian, said Judah
2 A king spoke and ordered your judgement, said Joseph to them
3 According to what sentence did you judge us, oh Egyptian, said Judah
4 According to the sentence with which you judged your brother Joseph in Dotan, said Joseph
5 We have stolen your cup, here we pay, oh Egyptian, said Judah
6 Thieves you have always been, said Joseph
7 Here we pay you the price of your cup, oh Egyptian, said Judah
8 The reward for your brother on whom you trampled with your feet, said Joseph

---

[44] *Op.cit.*, p. 157, my translation is based on it.
[45] The "linking formula" corresponds verbatim to O*Gen* 45:4, except the first word of 45:5 where the Tosefta uses עתה instead of O's כען.

9 Behold the money which we found at the opening of our bags I am returning to you from the land of Canaan, oh Egyptian, said Judah

10 It is yours not mine, said Joseph

11 Secret and open things are revealed before you, oh Egyptian, said Judah

12 For about everything you do my cup informs me, said Joseph

13 And you threw at me words like sharp arrows, oh Egyptian, said Judah

14 Throwers you have always been, said Joseph

15 We have seen kings and rulers but a king like you we have not seen, oh Egyptian, said Judah

16 You have seen when you were weighing the reward for your brother on the scales, said Joseph

17 I am superior to you and my father is superior to Pharaoh, oh Egyptian, said Judah

18 The nails of my father are superior to you and me and all the Egyptians, said Joseph

19 Rightly we spoke when we said that we were evelen brothers, oh Egyptian, said Judah

20 Rightly you spoke when you said twelve brothers, said Joseph

21 We are all the sons of one man, oh Egyptian, said Judah

22 You all joined together regarding your brother and did not put him on a camel, said Joseph

23 Oh, that no grain is sold in Egypt, oh Egyptian, said Judah

24 Woe, because you did not take your brother and did not put him on a camel

25 How shall we go and what shall we say to our elderly father, oh Egyptian, said Judah

26 Go and tell that Benjamin went after Joseph his brother, said Joseph

27 The fire of Shekhem is kindled in my heart, oh Egyptian, said Judah

28 The tears of your elderly father extinguish it, said Joseph

29 Our father is elderly and you have distressed him, oh Egyptian, said Judah

30 Your father is elderly and you have distressed him by the selling of Joseph your brother, said Joseph

31 The eyes of my father (are upon) us on the journey, oh Egyptian, said Judah

32 The eyes of your father are raised to the heavens upon high to hear from the fame of Joseph, said Joseph

33 We will open our mouth and swallow you, oh Egyptian, said Judah

34 (if you) open your mouth (. . .) I will fill your mouth with stones, said Joseph

35 We will dye Egypt with blood, oh Egyptian, said Judah

36 Dyers you have always been, when you dyed the garnment of

Joseph with blood and said that a wild animal devoured him, said
Joseph

37 I call my brother Simon to destroy Egypt before you, oh Egyptian,
said Judah

38 Shouters you have always been when one man called the other and
you said: this is the dreamer who comes, said Joseph

39 We are angry about you with great wrath and there is nothing
which can save you from my hands, oh Egyptian, said Judah

40 Your anger is more gentle than mine, said Joseph

41 Peace be upon me and peace be upon you, oh Egyptian, said
Judah

42 Peace be upon me and you and all Egypt/Israel, said Joseph

43 May my soul be at ease and may your soul be at ease, oh Egyptian,
said Judah

44 May my soul be at ease and your soul and the soul of all the children of Israel, said Joseph.

The form of this accrostic is rather crude in that the length of the
lines and the rhyme vary. Also, the alphabetic order is not consis-
tently maintained in the follow-up lines to Joseph. Without quotation of a biblical verse, this altercation starts abruptly. The exchange
of words is based on a series of reproaches and threats, each of which
is answered by a measure-for-measure argument. The phrases are
partly derived from various passages of the Joseph story, without,
however, corresponding to one particular Aramaic rendering, and
certainly not to O.[46]

Some of Judah's words are reminiscent of other targumic
paraphrases of the speech, but again the connection is loose. The
shorter version of this dialogue in the prose *Tosefta Targum* is, with
the exception of one expression, paralleled here in vs. 28, 34–37a.
However, the sequence of the paralleled verse is inversed and Joseph's response to the "fire of Shekhem" is different (vs. 28 in the
poem Tosefta appears to have no analogy).

In both versions of this alceration Joseph's position is enhanced
vis-à-vis Judah. He emerges as the effortless superior. It is possible
that this "rehabilitation" responded to the widely circulating other
versions in which Judah reduces Joseph to a frightened person.

Does a "targumic Joseph" emerge from this analysis? In continu-
ating of late biblical developments, the Targums unanimously give
the Joseph story religious significance. Focusing on *Gen* 39 and 49,

---

[46] Cf. e.g. vs. 14 זרק to O *Gen* 37:22 רום, N טלק, PJ טלק, vs. 35 צבע to O *Gen*
37:31 טבל; N צבע, PJ טבל.

they transform him into a paradigmatic righteous man who controlled his evil inclination.

The remaining aspects of his life receive rather more diverse treatment. Motivated by didactical objectives, O takes a generally defensive line. Thus, Joseph's more unpleasant characteristics of his youth and his stern behaviour towards his brothers in Egypt are softened. This homogeneous line of interpretation is not paralleled elsewhere.

N (FT) exhibits more detailed interest. While Joseph's youth is commented on only in general theological terms, his sojourn in Egypt receives notable attention. N criticizes Joseph's lack of trust in God and brings out the austerity of his treatment of the brothers. With regard to *Gen* 44:18, N focuses strongly on Judah, but depicts Joseph with sympathy as well. In his presentation of the Joseph story, N appears to be mostly motivated by general ethical considerations which might serve educational purposes.

PJ shares his interest in particular biblical items and his mode of interpretation with the midrash, on the one hand, and intertestamental exegesis on the other. Often but not exclusively he coincides with the *Testament of the Twelve Patriarchs* and PRE. An interpretative continuity clearly existed, but defies closer definition. PJ's access to these additional sources provided him with a more complete and diverse picture of Joseph. Most characteristic of his rendering are the numerous more lighthearted embellishments which turn Joseph into a kind of folk hero.

The targumic focus on *Gen* 39 and the positive evaluation after this event are echoed in Palestinian literature and in particular in midrash. Contrary to this religious portrait, Hellenistic writers highlight completely different aspects of Joseph.

SELECT BIBLIOGRAPHY

M. Aberbach/B. Grossfeld, *Targum Onkelos to Genesis: A Critical Analysis together with a translation*, New York 1982.

——, *Targum Onkelos on Genesis 49*, Missoula 1976.

J.S. Ackerman, *Joseph, Juda and Jacob*, in Literary Interpretations of Biblical Narratives, ed. J.S. Ackerman, Abingdon 1982.

Ch. Albeck, *Das Buch der Jubiläen und die Halacha*, 47er Jahresbericht für die Wissenschaft des Judentums, Berlin 1930.

W.F. Albright, *History and Mythical Elements in the Story of Joseph*, JBL 37/1918.

R. Alter, *The Art of Biblical Narrative*, London 1981.

Y. Amir, *Die Hellenistische Gestalt des Judentums bei Philo von Alexandria*, Neukirchen 1983.

——, *Philo and the Bible*, Studia Philonica 2/1973.

——, *Authority and Interpretation of Scripture in the Writings of Philo*, Mikra, ed. J. Mulder, Assen/Philadelphia 1988.

A.W. Argyle, *Joseph the Patriarch in Patristic Teaching*, The Expository Times 67/1955–56.

H. v. Arnim, *Quellenstudien zu Philo von Alexandria*, Berlin 1888.

J.W. Atkins, *Literary Criticism in Antiquity*, London 1952.

H.W. Attridge, *The Interpretation of Biblical History in the Antiquitates Judaicae of Flavius Josephus*, Scholars Press 1976.

——, *Josephus and His Works*, in: Jewish Writings of the Second Temple Period, ed. M. Stone, Assen/Philadelphia 1984.

E. Auerbach, *Mimesis*, Princeton 1953 (1st ed. 1946).

M. Avi-Yona, *Hellenism and the East*, Jerusalem 1978.

S. Bar-Efrat, *Some Observations on the Analysis of Structure in Biblical Narrative*, VT 30/1980.

J. Barr, *The Semantics of Biblical Language*, Oxford 1961.

——, *Reading the Bible as Literature*, Bulletin of the John Rylands University Library of Manchester 56/1973.

R. Barraclough, *Philo's Politics, Roman Rule and Hellenistic Judaism*, ANRW vol. II, 21.1.

J. Barton, *Reading the Old Testament. Method in Biblical Study*. London 1984.

——, *Oracles of God*, London 1986.

B. Beer, *Das Buch der Jubiläen und sein Verhältnis zu den Midraschim*, Leipzig 1856.

A. Berlin, *Poetics and Interpretation of the Bible*, Sheffield 1983.

M. Bernstein, *A New Manuscript of Tosefta Targum*, in: Proceedings of the Ninth World Congress of Jewish Studies, Jerusalem 1986.

P. Bilde, *Flavius Josephus between Jerusalem and Rome*, 1988.

R. Bloch, *A Methodological Note for the Study of Rabbinic Literature*, in: Approaches to Ancient Judaism: Theory and Practice, ed. W.S. Green, Montana 1978.

W. Booth, *The Rhetoric of Fiction*, Chicago 1961.

J. Bowker, *The Targums and Rabbinic Literature*, Cambridge 1969.

——, *The Haggadah in the Targum Onkelos*, JJS 12/1971.

D. Boyarin, *Old Wine in New Bottles: Interpretation and Midrash*, PT 8/1987.

——, *Intertextuality and the Reading of Midrash*, Indiana University Press 1990.

M. Braun, *Griechischer Roman und Hellenistische Geschichtsschreibung*. Frankfurt 1934.

——, *History and Romance in Greco-Oriental Literature*. Oxford 1938.

E. Brehier, *Les Idées Philosophiques et Religieuses de Philon d'Alexandrie*. Paris 1907.

——, *The Hellenistic and Roman Age*. Chicago 1965.

A. Büchler, *Traces des Idées et des Coutumes Hellenistiques dans le Livre des Jubilées*. REJ 82/1930.

——, *Studies in Sin and Atonement*, New York 1961.

F. Buffière, *Les Mythes d'Homère et la Pensée Grecque*, Paris 1956.

Ch. Burchard, *The Present State of Research on Joseph and Asenath*, in: Perspectives on Ancient Judaism, ed. J. Neusner a.o., University of America 1987.

H. Chadwick, *Philo*, in: The Cambridge History of Later Greek and Early Medieval Philosophy, Cambridge 1967.

R.H. Charles, *The Book of Jubilees*. London 1902.

——, *The Apocrypha and Pseudepigrapha*, Oxford 1913.

S. Chatman, *Story and Discourse*. New York 1978.

——, *Characters and Narrators. Filter, Center, Slant and Interest Forms*. PT 7/1986.

I. Christiansen, *Die Technik der Allegorischen Auslegung bei Philon von Alexandrien*. Tübingen 1969.

G.W. Coats, *The Joseph Story and Ancient Wisdom*. CBQ 35/1973.

S. Cohen, *Josephus in Galilee and Rome*. Leiden 1979.

D. Cohn, *Transparent Minds. Narrative Modes for Presenting Consciousness in Fiction*. Princeton 1978.

L. Cohn, *Einleitung und Chronologie der Schriften Philos*. Philologus, Sup. Bd. 7/1899.

——, *An Apocryphal Work Ascribed to Philo of Alexandria*. JQR 10/1989.

D. Daube, *Typology in Josephus*. JJS 31/1980.

R. le Déaut, *Introduction à la Littérature Targumique*. Rome 1966.

G. Delling, *Perspektiven der Erforschung des Hellenistischen Judentums*. HUCA 45/1974.

A. Dillmann, *Das Buch der Jubiläen*. Jahrbücher der Biblishen Wissenschaft, Göttingen 3/1951.

J. Dillon, *The Middle Platonists*. London 1977.

E.R. Dodds, *The Greeks and The Irrational*. United California Press 1951.

H. Drexler, *Die Entdeckung des Individuums*. Salzburg 1966.

J. Duchemin, *Aspects Pastoraux de la Poésie Homérique*. Revue des Études Grecques 73/ 1960.

A.B. Ehrlich, *Randglossen zur Hebräischen Bibel*. Hildesheim 1968.

E.L. Ehrlich, *Die Träume im Alten Testament*. BZAW 73/1953.

O. Eissfeldt, *Zur Kompositionstechnik des Pseudo-Philonischen Liber Antiquitatum Biblicarum*. NTT 56/1955.

H. Erbse, *Die Bedeutung der Synkrisis in den Parallelbiographien Plutarchs*. Hermes 84/1956.

L.H. Feldman, *Use, Authority and Exegesis of Mikra in the Writings of Josephus*. in: Mikra, ed. J. Mulder, Assen/Philadelphia 1988.

——, *Flavius Josephus Revisited: the Man, his Writings and his Significance*. ANRW vol. II, 21.2.

——, *Hellenisation in Josephus' Antiquities. The Portrait of Abraham*. in: Josephus, Judaism and Christianity, ed. L.H. Feldman, Detroit 1987.

——, *How much Hellenism in Jewish Palestine?* HUCA 57/1986.

——, *Josephus and Modern Scholarship 1937–80*. New York/Berlin 1984.

L. Finkelstein, *The Book of Jubilees and Rabbinic Halakha*. HTR 16/1923.

——, *Akiba, Scholar, Saint and Martyr*. New York 1970.

H.A. Fischel, *Essays in Greco-Roman and Related Talmudic Literature*. New York 1977.

G. Foot-Moore, *Judaism in the First Centuries of the Christian Era*. New York 1958.

——, *Fate and Free Will in the Jewish Philosophies to Josephus*. HTR 22/1929.

——, *Simon the Righteous*. in: Jewish Studies in Memory of Israel Abrahams, New York 1927.

E.M. Forster, *Aspects of the Novel*. Harmondsworth 1963.

Z. Frankel, *Über den Einfluß der palestinischen Exegese auf die alexandrinische Hermeneutik.* Leipzig 1851.

Th.W. Franxman, *Genesis and the Jewish Antiquities of Flavius Josephus.* Rome 1979.

P.M. Fraser, *Ptolemaic Alexandria.* Oxford 1962.

M. Fuhrman, *Einführung in die antike Dichtungstheorie.* Darmstadt 1973.

H.G. Gadamer, *Wahrheit und Methode. Grundzüge einer philosophischen Hermeneutik.* Tübingen 1960.

J. Garvey, *Characterization in Narrative.* PT 2/1978.

Ch. Gill, *The Question of Character and Personality in Greek Tragedy.* PT 7/1986.

——, *The Ethos/Pathos Distinction in Rhetorical and Literary Criticism.* CQ 34/1984.

J. Goldstein, *Jewish Acceptance and Rejection of Hellenism.* in: Jewish and Christian Self-Definitions. ed. E.P. Sanders, Philadelphia 1981.

——, *I Maccabees. A New Translation with Introduction and Commentary.* New York 1976.

E.R. Goodenough, *The Politics of Philo Judaeus. Theory and Practice.* New Haven 1938.

——, *An Introduction to Philo Judaeus.* Yale 1940.

——, *The Jurisprudence of the Jewish Courts in Egypt.* Yale 1929.

——, *Wolfson's Philo.* JBL 67/1948.

C.L. Grimm, *Das Buch der Weisheit.* Leipzig 1860.

S. Gronemann, *Die Jonathanische Pentateuchübersetzung in ihrem Verhältnis zur Halacha.* Leipzig 1879.

G.M.A. Grube, *The Greek and Roman Critics.* London 1965.

H. Gunkel, *Die Komposition der Josephsgeschichten.* ZDMG 76/1922.

W.K.C. Guthrie, *A History of Greek Philosophy.* Cambridge 1978.

M. Hadas, *Hellenistic Culture, Fusion and Diffusion.* New York 1959.

S. Halliwell, *Aristotle's Poetics.* London 1986.

R.G. Hamerton-Kelly, *Sources and Traditions in Philo Judaus. Prolegomena to an Analysis of his Writings.* SP 1/1972.

D.J. Harrington, *The Original Language of Pseudo-Philo's Liber Antiquitatum Biblicarum.* HTR 63/1970.

——, *The Biblical Text of Pseudo-Philo's Liber Antiquitatum Biblicarum.* CBQ 33/1971.

G.H. Hartman/S. Budick, *Midrash and Literature.* Yale 1986.

J. Haspecker, *Gottesfurcht bei Jesus Sirach.* Rome 1967.

I. Heinemann, *Philon's griechische und jüdische Bildung.* Breslau 1929.

——, *Die Altjüdische Allegoristik.* Breslau 1936.

——, *Die wissenschaftliche Allegoristik.* Mnemosyne Serie 4,2 1948.

R. Helm, *Der Antike Roman.* Göttingen 1956.

M. Hengel, *Judaism and Hellenism.* London 1974 (based on the 2nd enlarged German ed.).

E. Hilgert, *The Dual Image of Joseph in Hebrew and Early Jewish Literature.* Biblical Research 30/1985.

E. Hirsch, *Validity in Interpretation.* Yale 1967.

——, *The Aims of Interpretation.* Chicago 1976.

R. Hirzel, *Die Person. Begriff und Name derselben im Altertum.* Sitzungsberichte der Bayrischen Akademie 1914.

B. Hochman, *Character in Literature.* Cornell University Press 1985.

H.W. Hollander, *Joseph as the Ethical Model in the Testaments of the Twelve Patriarchs.* Leiden 1981.

——/M. de Jonge, *The Testaments of the Twelve Patriarchs.* Leiden 1985.

R.C. Holub, *Reception Theory.* Methuen 1984.

S. Horovitz, *Die Josephserzählung.* Frankfurt 1921.

H. House, *Aristotle's Poetics.* London 1958.

W. Iser, *Der Akt des Lesens.* München 1984.

——, *Der implizite Leser*. München 1979.
B. Jacobs, *Genesis. Das Erste Buch der Tora*. Schocken Verlag 1934.
M.R. James, *Notes on Apocrypha*. JThSt 16/1915.
H.R. Jauss, *Levels of Identification of Hero and Audience*. New Literary History, 2/1974.
M. de Jonge, *The Main Issues in the Study of the Testaments of the Twelve Patriarchs*. NTST 26/1980.
W. McKane, *Studies in the Patriarchal Narratives*. Edinburgh 1979.
——, *Prophets and Wise Men*. Studies in Biblical Theology, 44/1965.
K. Kerenyi, *Die griechisch-orientalische Romanliteratur*. Tübingen 1927.
F. Kermode, *The Classic*. Cambridge Harvard University Press 1983.
——, *The Sense of Ending. Studies in the Theory of Fiction*. Oxford 1967.
——, *The Genesis of Secrecy*. Cambridge Harvard University Press 1979.
——, *Essays on Fiction*. London 1983.
G. Kisch, *Pseudo-Philo's Liber Antiquitatum Biblicarum*. Postlegomena to the New Edition. HUCA 23/1950.
K. Koch, *Is Daniel among the Prophets?* in: Interpreting the Prophets, ed. J.C. Mays/J. Achtemeier, Philadelphia 1987.
A. Kuenen, *An Historico-Critical Inquiry into the Origin and Composition of the Hexateuch*, London 1886.
J. Kugel, *Early Bible Interpretation*. Philadelphia 1986.
——, *In Potiphar's House*. Harper Collins 1990.
A. Kurrein, *Traum und Wahrheit. Das Lebensbild Josephs nach der Aggada*. Regensburg 1887.
E. Lämmert, *Bauformen des Erzählens*. Stuttgart 1988 (1st published 1955).
R. Lane Fox, *Alexander The Great*. London 1973.
S.Z. Leiman, *The Canonization of Hebrew Scripture. The Talmudic and Midrashic Evidence*. 1976.
F. Leo, *Die griechisch-römische Biographie nach ihrer literarischen Form*. Leipzig 1901.
J. Licht, *Story Telling in the Bible*. Jerusalem 1978.
S. Lieberman, *Hellenism in Jewish Palestine*. New York 1950.
——, *Greek in Jewish Palestine*. New York 1965.
R. Löwe, *"Plain" Meaning in Scripture in Early Jewish Exegesis*. in: Papers of the Institute of Jewish Studies London, ed. J.G. Weiss, Jerusalem 1964.
A.A. Long, *Hellenistic Philosophy*. London 1974.
P. Lubbock, *The Craft of Fiction*. London 1921.
R. Mach, *Der Zaddik in Talmud und Midrasch*. Leiden 1957.
B.L. Mack, *Philo Judaeus and the Exegetical Traditions in Alexandria*. ANRW vol. II, 2.1.
A. Marmorstein, *The Doctrine of Merits in Rabbinic Theology*. London 1914.
L. Massebieau/E. Brehier, *Essai sur la Chronologie de la Vie et des Oeuvres de Philon*. RHR 53/1906.
M.G. May, *The Evolution of the Joseph Story*. AJSLL 47/1931.
A. Mendelson, *Secular Education in Philo of Alexandria*. Cincinnati 1982.
R. Merkelbach, *Roman und Mysterium in der Antike*. Beck 1982.
B.J. van der Merve, *Joseph as Successor of Jacob*. in: Studia Biblica and Semitica, Festschrift Th.C. Vriezen, Wageningen 1966.
R. Meyer, *Hellenistisches in der Rabbinischen Anthropologie*. Stuttgart 1937.
O. Michel, *Die Rettung Israels und die Rolle Roms nach den Reden des Bellum Judaicum*. ANRW vol. II 2.2.
T. Middendorp, *Die Stellung des Jesu ben Siras zwischen Judentum und Hellenismus*. Leiden 1973.
E. Milobenski, *Der Neid in der griechischen Philosophie*. Wiesbaden 1964.

J. Milgrom, *The Origin of Philo's Doctrine of Conscience*. Studia Philonica 3/1974–75.
D. Miscall, *The Jacob and Joseph Stories as Analogies*. JSOT 6/1978.
G. Misch, *Geschichte der Autobiographie*. Berlin 1949.
W.J.T. Mitchell (ed.), *On Narrative*. University of Chicago Press 1980.
A. Momigliano, *The Development of Greek Biography*. Harvard University Press 1971.
——, *A. Mauss and the Quest for the Person in Greek Biography and Autobiography*. in: The Category of the Person, ed. M. Carrithers, Cambridge 1985.
R. Morgan with Barton, *Biblical Interpretation*. Oxford 1988.
M.J. Mulder (ed.), *Mikra*, Assen/Philadelphia 1988.
K. Müller-Vollmer (ed.), *The Hermeneutic Reader*. Oxford 1985.
J. Neusner, *Development of a Legend. Studies in the Tradition concerning Johanan ben Zakkai*. Leiden 1970.
——, *Midrash in Context. Exegesis in Formative Judaism*. Philadelphia 1983.
——, *Judaism and Scripture*. Chicago 1986.
V. Nikiprowetzky, *Le Commentaire de l'Écriture chez Philon d'Alexandrie*. Leiden 1977.
S. Niditch/R. Doran, *The Success Story of the Wise Courtier. A Formal Approach*. JBL 96/1977.
D. Patte, *Early Jewish Hermeneutic in Palestine*. Scholars Press 1975.
J. Pepin, *Remarques sur la Theorie de l'Exégèse Allegorique chez Philon*. in: Philon d'Alexandrie, Colloques Nationaux du Centre National de la Recherche Scientifique. Paris 1969.
——, *Mythe et Allegorie*. Aubier 1958.
B.E. Perry, *The Ancient Romances*. University of California Press 1967.
J. Podlecki, *The Peripatetics as Literary Critics*. Poenix 23/1969.
M. Pohlenz, *Die Stoa. Geschichte einer geistigen Bewegung*. Göttingen 1964.
——, *Antikes Führertum*. Leipzig/Berlin 1934.
——, *Kleine Schriften*. Hildesheim 1965.
B. Porten, *The Jews in Egypt*. in: The Cambridge History of Judaism. Cambridge 1984.
G.G. Porton, *Understanding Rabbinic Midrash*. Hoboken 1985.
A. Priessning, *Die literarische Form der Patriarchenbiographien des Philon von Alexandria*. MGWJ N.F. 37/1929.
J. Rabinowits, *"Pesher/Pittaron". Its Biblical Meaning and its significance in the Qumran Literature*. RQ 8/1973.
G. v. Rad, *Die Josephsgeschichte und die ältere Chokma*. SVT 1/1953.
T. Rajak, *Josephus: The Historian and his Society*. London 1983.
S. Rappaport, *Agada und Exegese bei Flavius Josephus*. Frankfurt 1930.
D.B. Redfort, *A Study of the Biblical Story of Joseph*. Leiden SVT 20/1970.
W. Richter, *Exegese als Literaturwissenschaft*. Göttingen 1971.
S. Rimmon-Kenan, *Narrative Fiction. Contemporary Poetics*. Methuen New York 1983.
D. Robertson, *The Old Testament and the Literary Critic*. Philadelphia 1977.
M. Rostovzeff, *Greece*. Oxford 1963.
S. Rubin, *Die Josephsgeschichte in neuer Beleuchtung*. Biblische Probleme. Wien 1931.
L. Ruppert, *Die Josephserzählung der Genesis*. München 1965.
D.A. Russel, *Plutarch*. London 1973.
——, *Theories of Literature and Taste*. in: The Classical World, ed. D. Daiches, London 1972.
——/M. Winterbottom, *Ancient Literary Criticism. Principal Texts in New Translations*. Oxford 1972.
S. Sandmel, *Philo's Environment and Philo's Exegesis*. Journal of Bible and Religion 22/1954.
——, *Philo's Place in Judaism*. Cincinnati 1956.

——, *Philo of Alexandria. An Introduction*. Oxford 1979.
——, *Parallelomania*, JBL 81/1962.
R.S. Sarasson, *The Study of Rabbinic Literature*. in: Studies in Aggadah, Targum and Jewish Liturgy in Memory of Joseph Heinemann. Jerusalem 1981.
M. Savage, *Literary Criticism and Biblical Studies. A Rhetorical Analysis of the Joseph Narrative*. in: Scripture in Context, ed. C.D. Evans a.o., Pittsburgh 1980.
P. Schäfer, *Studien zur Geschichte und Theologie des Rabbinischen Judentums*. Leiden 1978.
S. Schechter, *Aspects of Rabbinic Judaism*. New York 1961.
A. Schmitt, *Interpretation der Genesis aus hellenistischer Sicht*. ZAW 86/1974.
W. Schmitt, *Die Hintergründe der neuesten Pentateuchforschung und der literarische Befund der Josephsgeschichte in Genesis 37–50*. ZAW 97/1985.
C. Schneider, *Kulturgeschichte des Hellenismus*. München 1967.
R. Scholes/R. Kellog, *The Nature of Narrative*. Oxford 1966.
I.L. Seeligmann, *Menschliches Heldentum und göttliche Hilfe*. Theologische Zeitschrift 10/1963.
D. Shepherd, *The Authority of Meaning and the Meaning of Authority. Some Problems in the Theory of Reading*. PT 7/1986.
A. Shinan, *The Aggadah in the Aramaic Palestinian Targums to the Torah*. Jerusalem 1979.
C. Siefried, *Philo von Alexandria als Ausleger des alten Testaments*. Jena 1875.
M. Simon, *Verus Israel*. Paris 1948.
H.D. Slingerland, *The Testaments of the Twelve Patriarchs. A Critical History of Research*. Montana 1977.
M. Smallwood, *Philonis Alexandri Legatio ad Gaium*. 1961.
R. Smend, *Die Weisheit des Jesus Sirach*. Berlin 1906.
E.W. Smith, *Joseph Material in Joseph and Asenath and Josephus' Relation to the Testament of Joseph*. in: Studies in the Testament of Joseph, ed. G. Nickelburg, Montana 1975.
A. Sommer, *Der Begriff der Versuchung im Alten Testament und Judentum*. Breslau 1935.
D.P. Spence, *Narrative Truth and Historical Truth. Meaning and Interpretation in Psychoanalysis*. New York 1982.
E.A. Speiser, *Genesis. The Anchor Bible*. New York 1964.
H. Sproedowsky, *Die Hellenisierung der Geschichte von Joseph in Ägypten bei Josephus Flavius*. Greifswald 1937.
F.K. Stanzel, *Theorie des Erzählens*. Göttingen 1979.
M. Steif, *Zur Bedeutung von* נער *in der Bibel*. MGWJ N.F. 37/1929.
E. Stein, *Die Allegorische Exegese des Philon aus Alexandria*. Giessen 1929.
M. Sternberg, *The Poetics of Biblical Narrative*. Indiana University Press 1985.
T.C.W. Stinton, *Hamartia in Aristotle and Greek Tragedy*. CQ 25/1975.
L. Strack/G. Stemberger, *Einleitung in Talmud und Midrasch*. München 1982.
D.R. Stuart, *Epochs of Greek and Roman Biography*. Berkeley 1928.
S.R. Suleiman/I. Crosman (ed.), *The Reader in the Text*. Princeton 1980.
R. Syren, *The Blessings in the Targums*. Acta Aboensis 1986.
G. Tachauer, *Das Verhältnis von Flavius Josephus zur Bibel und Tradition*. Erlangen 1871.
S. Talmon, *The Presentation of Synchroneity and Simultaneity in Biblical Narratives*. Scripta Hierosolymitana 27/1978.
J. Tate, *The Beginnings of Greek Allegory*. Classical Review 41/1927.
——, *On this History of Allegorism*. CQ 28/1934.
——, *Plato and Allegorical Interpretation*. CQ 23/1929.
E. Tov, *The Septuagint*. in: Mikra, ed. M.J. Mulder, Assen/Philadelphia 1988.
J.M. Toynbee, *Dictators and Philosophers in the First Century AD*. Greece and Rome 13/1944.

J. Trachtenberg, *Jewish Magic and Superstition*. New York 1987.
R. Travers Herford, *Talmud and Apocrypha*. London 1933.
L. Treitel, *Philonische Studien*. Breslau 1915.
——, *Ursprung, Begriff und Umfang der Allegorischen Schriftenerklärung*. MGWJ 55/1911.
E. Yassif, *Traces of Folk Traditions in the Second Temple Period in Rabbinic Literature*. JJC 39/1988.
J.C. VanderKam, *Textual and Historical Studies in the Book of Jubilees*. Scholars Press 1977.
C. Vatin, *Recherches sur le Mariage et la Condition de la Femme Mariée à l'Époque Hellenistique*, Paris 1970.
J. Vergote, *Joseph en Egypte*. Louvain 1959.
G. Vermes, *Bible and Midrash. Early Old Testament Exegesis*. Cambridge History of the Bible, Cambridge 1970.
——, *Scripture and Tradition in Judaism. Haggadic Studies*. Leiden 1961.
——, *The Haggadah in the Onkelos Targum*. JSS 8/1963.
A. Wardman, *Plutarch's Lives*. London 1974.
R.T. Wallis, *The Idea of Conscience in Philo of Alexandria*. Studia Philonica 3/1974–75.
T.B.L. Webster, *Some Psychological Terms in Greek Tragedy*. Journal of Hellenic Studies 77/1957.
F. Wehrli, *Zur Geschichte der Allegorischen Deutung Homers*. Dissertation Borna-Leipzig 1928.
——, *Theoria und Humanismus*. Artemis Verlag 1972.
K.J. Weintraub, *The Value of the Individual*. Chicago 1978.
M. Weiss, *Einiges über die Bauformen des Erzählens in der Bibel*. VT 13/1963.
——, *Weiteres über die Bauformen des Erzählens in der Bibel*. Biblica 46/1965.
——, *Die Methode der "Total-Interpretation"*, SVT 22/1972.
A.C. Welch, *The Story of Joseph*. Edinburgh 1913.
J. Welthausen, *Die Komposition des Hexateuchs und der historischen Bücher des Alten Testaments*. Berlin 1899.
P. Wendland, *Philo und die kynisch-stoische Diatribe*. Berlin 1895.
——, *Die hellenistisch-römische Kultur in ihren Beziehungen zu Judentum und Christentum*. Tübingen 1912.
S. West, *Joseph and Asenath. A Neglected Greek Romance*. CQ 24/1974.
C. Westermann, *Genesis 37–50*. Neukirchen 1982.
——, *Studien zur Vatergeschichte. Verheißungen der Väter*. Göttingen 1976.
H. White, *The Rhetoric of Interpretation*. PT 9/1988.
——, *The Value of Narrativity in the Representation of Reality*. in: On Narrative, ed. W.J.T. Mitchell. Chicago 1980.
U. v. Wilamowitz-Möllendorff, *Der Glaube der Hellenen*. Darmstadt 1959.
R. Wilson, *The Bright Chimera. Character as a Literary Term*. Critical Inquiry 5/1979.
H.A. Wolfson, *Philo: Foundations in Religious Philosophy in Judaism. Christianity and Islam*. Harvard 1949.
A.G. Wright, *The Literary Genre Midrash*. New York 1967.
S. Zeitlin, *The Legend of the Ten Martyrs and its Apocalyptic Origins*. JQR 36/1945–46.
——, *The Book of Jubilees and the Pentateuch*. JQR 48/1957–58.
E. Zeller, *Die Philosophie der Griechen*. Hildesheim 1963.
L. Zunz, *Die gottesdienstlichen Vorträge der Juden*. Frankfurt 1892.

יאבן, הדמות בסיפורת, תל אביב 1986.
—, התיאוריה של הדמות בסיפורת: מעמדה, תפקידה ביצירה ודרכי תבניתה בסיפורת, הספרות 1971/1.
—, הדיבור הסמוי, הספרות 1968-9/1.
א.א.אורבך, חז״ג. פרקי אמונות ודעות, ירושלים 1969.
—, אסכזיס ויסורין בספרות חז״ל, ספר יובל ליצחק בער, ירושלים תשכ״א.
ו.איזר, אי-מגברות ותנובתא של הקורא: למבנה המשיכה של הטקסט הספרותי, הספרות 1975/21.
ג.אלון, תולדות היהודים בארץ ישראל בתקופת המשנה והתלמוד, תל אביב 1977.
ר.אלטר, סצנות-דפוס במקרא וחשיבותא של הקונוונציה, הספרות 1978/27.
א.באומגרטן, הלוח של ספר היובלים והמקרא, תרביץ 63/32 – 1962.
ש.בר-אפרת, העיצוב האמנותי של הסיפור במקרא, ירושלים 1984.
ב.ש.ברקוביץ, חליפות שמלות, וילנה 1874.
מ,דבשני, החלומות בסיפור יוסף, בית מקרא 1964/21.
א.א.הלוי, ערכי האגדה וההלכה לאור מקורות יווניים ולטיניים, תל אביב 82 – 1979.
—, פרשיות באגדה לאור מקורות יווניים, תל אביב 1973.
—, שערי האגדה, תל אביב 1982.
א.הולץ, בעולם המחשבה של חז״ל, תל אביב 1978.
י.היינמן, אגדות ותולדותיהן, ירושלים 1974.
י.היימנן, דרכי האגדה, ירושלים תשי״ד.
—, להתפתחות המונחים המקצועיים לפירוש המקרא, לשוננו יד /תש״ד.
א.השל, תורה מן השמיים באספקלריה הדורות, לונדון תשכ״ב-תשכ״ה.
מ.וייס, המקרא כדמותו, ירושלים 1967.
ד.וונסטון, החכם בתורתו של פילון, דעת11 /תשמ״ג.
י.זקוביץ, סיפור בבואה, מימד נוסף להערכת הדמויות בסיפור המקראי, תרביץ 1985/54.
נ.טוקר, אומנות הגילוי והכיסוי בסיפור יוסף ואחיו, בית מקרא 1965/24.
נ.כהן, ״אגרפוס נומוס״ בכתבי פילון: בדיקה מחודשת, דעת טו /תשמ״ה.
י.כהן-ישר, מקומו של פילון במחשבת ישראל, סיני 1974/84.
—, האם ידע פילון האלקסנדרוני עברית?, תרביץ 1965/34.
י.לוי, עולמות נפגשים, ירושלים 1969.
ז.לוי, הרמניטיקה, תל אביב 1986.
ש.א.לוונשטם, מסורת יציאת מצרים והשתלשלוחה, תל אביב 1965.
ש.ד.לוצטו, אוהב גר, קרקוביה 1845.
נ.ליבוביץ, עיונים בבראשית, ירושלים תשכ״ו.
י.ליכט, הנסיון במקרא וביהדות של הבית השני, ירושלים 1973.
ע.מאיר, הדמויות הפעולות בסיפורי התלמוד והמדרש, חיבור לשם קבלת התואר דוקטור לפילוסופיה של האוניברסיטה העברית בירושלים 1986.
—, הסיפור הדרשני, תל אביב 1987.
—, סיפור מחלת חזקיהו באגדת חז״ל, הספרות 31 – 1981/30.
ע.מ.מלמד, מפרשי המקרא, ירושלים תשל״ח.
ח.מנטל, האם ידע פילון עברית? תרביץ 1963/32.
מ.צ.סגל, פרשנות המקרא, ירושלים 1980.
מ. עמנואל, לדמותא של יוסף, בית מקרא 1971/47.
מ.פרי /מ.שטרנברג, זהירות ספרות! לבעיות האינטרפרטאציה והפואטיקה של הסיפור המקראי, הספרות 71/2 – 1969.
ד.פלוסר /ש.שפראי, נדב ואביהוא במדרש ובדברי פילון, מלאת תל אביב 1984.
י.פרנקל, שאלות הרמניטיות בחקר סיפור האגדה, תרביץ מז /תשל״ח.
—, עיונים בעולמו הרוחני של סיפור האגדה, תל אביב 1981.
ג.צורן, לקראת תיאוריה של המרחב בסיפור, בספרות 30 – 1981/31.
י.קויפמן, תולדות האמונה הישראלית א-ו, ירושלים 1956.
י.קומלוש, המקרא באור התרגום, 1973.
ש.קמין, רש״י פשוטו של מקרא ומדרשו של מקרא, ירושלים 1986.
פ.קרני, היסודות ההגנותיים של פרשנות פילון האלכסנדרוני, דעת 1985/14.

——, מצרים המקראית בתפישתו של פילון, שנתון למקרא ולחקר המזרח הקדום, ירושלים תל אביב ה־ו 1982.

א.י.רוזנטל, סבלנות דתית בפרשנות המקרא של ימי הביניים, מחקרים ומקורות, ירושלים 1967.

מ.שטרנברג, מבנה החזרה בסיפור המקרא: אסטאטגניות של עודפנות אינפורמאציונית, הספרות 1977/25.

ג.שיינטוך, לקראת ניתוח אלקוציוני של השיחה בסיפור המקרא, הספרות 31–1981/30.

א.שנאן, אגדתם של מתורגמנים, ירושלים 1979

——, עולמה של ספרות האגדה, תל אביב 1987.

ש.ב.שפטל, ביארי אונקולוס, מינכן 1888.

LIST OF ABBREVIATIONS

ANRW	Aufstieg und Niedergang der Römischen Welt, ed. W. Haase, Walter de Gruyter/Berlin, New York
BZAW	Beihefte zur Zeitschrift für Alttestamentliche Wissenschaft
CPJ	Corpus Papyrorum Judaicarum, ed. V.A. Tcherikover/A. Fuks, Harvard University Press/Cambridge
CQ	Classical Quarterly
C-W	Philonis opera quae supersunt I–VI, 1896–1930 (reprinted 1962)
EB	Biblical Encyclopaedia (Hebrew), Bialik/Jerusalem
EJ	Encyclopaedia Judaica, Keter/Jerusalem
ET	Talmudic Encyclopaedia (Hebrew), The Israel Institute for the Complete Talmud
GR	Genesis Rabbah, ed. J. Theodor/Ch. Albeck, Wahrmann/Jerusalem 1965
HTR	Harvard Theological Review
HUCA	Hebrew Union College Annual
IDB	The Interpreter's Dictionary of the Bible, Abindon/Nashville
JA	Jewish Antiquities of Flavius Josephus, ed. with an English Translation by H.St.J. Thackeray, Harvard University Press/Cambridge
JBL	Journal of Biblical Literature
Jos	The Life of Joseph by Philo, ed. L. Cohn/P. Wendland and S. Reiter, 1896–1930 (reprinted 1962)
JJS	Journal of Jewish Studies
JQR	Jewish Quarterly Review
JRST	Journal of Religious Studies
JSOT	Journal for the Study of the Old Testament
JSS	Journal of Semitic Studies
JTHST	Journal of Theological Studies
OCD	Oxford Classical Dictionary, ed. N.G.L. Hammond/H.H. Scullard, Clarendon/Oxford
PT	Poetics Today
RE	Pauly-Wissowa, Realenzyklopädie der classischen Altertumswissenschaft
REJ	Revue des Etudes Juives
Schürer	E. Schürer, The History of the Jews at the Time of Jesus Christ, revised ed. by G. Vermes, F. Millar (M. Goodman)
SVT	Supplements to Vetus Testamentum
ZAW	Zeitschrift für Alttestamentliche Wissenschaft
ZDMG	Zeitschrift der Morgenländischen Gesellschaft
ZGWJ	Zeitschrift für Geschichte und Wissenschaft des Judentum
XII	The Testaments of the Twelve Patriarchs, ed. M. de Jonge, Brill/Leiden 1978
LXX	Septuagint, ed. A. Rahlfs 1935

GENERAL INDEX

INDEX OF REFERENCES TO THE HEBREW BIBLE

1 M. Hengel. *Die Zeloten.* Untersuchungen zur jüdischen Freiheitsbewegung
in der Zeit von Herodes I. bis 70 n. Chr. 2. verbesserte und erweiterte Auflage.
1976. ISBN 9004043276

2 O. Betz. *Der Paraklet.* Fürsprecher im häretischen Spätjudentum, im
Johannes-Evangelium und in neu gefundenen gnostischen Schriften. 1963.
ISBN 9004001093

5 O. Betz. *Abraham unser Vater.* Juden und Christen im Gespräch über die
Bibel. Festschrift für Otto Michel zum 60. Geburtstag. Herausgegeben von
O. Betz, M. Hengel, P. Schmidt. 1963. ISBN 9004001107

6 A. Böhlig. *Mysterion und Wahrheit.* Gesammelte Beiträge zur spätantiken
Religionsgeschichte. 1968. ISBN 9004001115

7 B. J. Malina. *The Palestinian Manna Tradition.* The Manna Tradition in the
Palestinian Targums and its Relationship to the New Testament Writings.
1968. ISBN 9004001123

8 J. Becker. *Untersuchungen zur Entstehungsgeschichte der Testamente der zwölf
Patriarchen.* 1970. ISBN 9004001131

9 E. Bickerman. *Studies in Jewish and Christian History.*
1. 1976. ISBN 9004043969
2. 1980. ISBN 9004060154
3. 1986. ISBN 9004074805

11 Z. W. Falk. *Introduction to Jewish Law of the Second Commonwealth.*
1. 1972. ISBN 9004035370
2. 1978. ISBN 9004052496

12 H. Lindner. *Die Geschichtsauffassung des Flavius Josephus im Bellum Judaicum.*
Gleichzeitig ein Beitrag zur Quellenfrage. 1972. ISBN 9004035028

13 P. Kuhn. *Gottes Trauer und Klage in der rabbinischen Überlieferung.* Talmud und
Midrasch. 1978. ISBN 9004056998

14 I. Gruenwald. *Apocalyptic and Merkavah Mysticism.* 1980. ISBN 9004059598

15 P. Schäfer. *Studien zur Geschichte und Theologie des rabbinischen Judentums.* 1978.
ISBN 9004058389

16 M. Niehoff. *The Figure of Joseph in Post-Biblical Jewish Literature.* 1992.
ISBN 900409556X